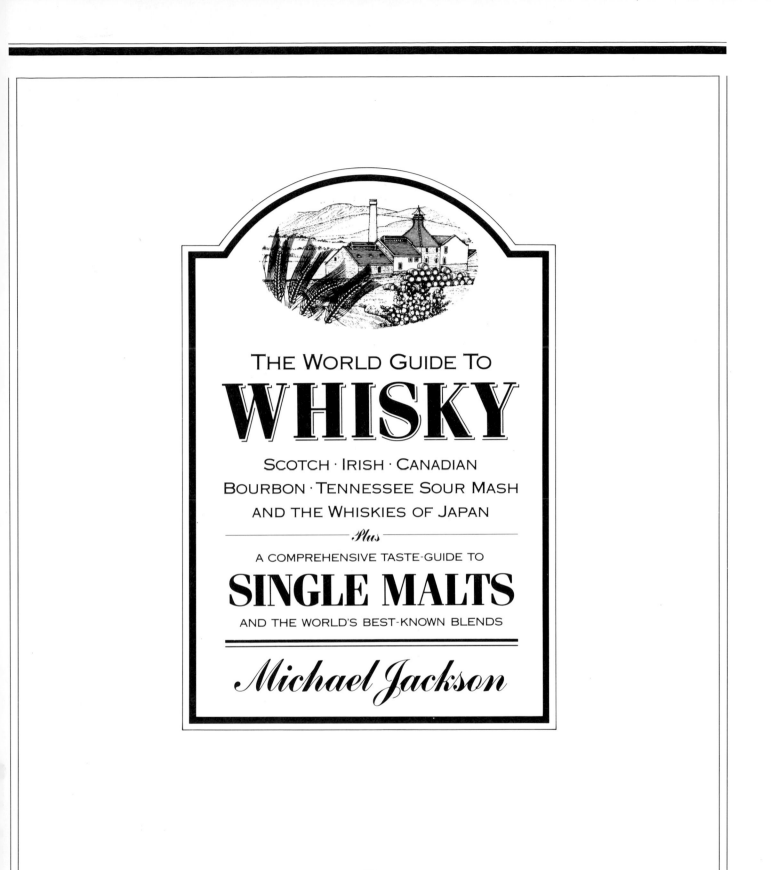

THE WORLD GUIDE TO

WHISKY

SCOTCH · IRISH · CANADIAN
BOURBON · TENNESSEE SOUR MASH
AND THE WHISKIES OF JAPAN

Plus

A COMPREHENSIVE TASTE-GUIDE TO

SINGLE MALTS

AND THE WORLD'S BEST-KNOWN BLENDS

Michael Jackson

SALEM HOUSE PUBLISHERS
TOPSFIELD · MASSACHUSETTS

This book is dedicated
to my mother Margaret,
with good wishes for
her future happiness

First published in the United States by
Salem House Publishers, 1988,
462 Boston Street, Topsfield, MA 01983

First published in Great Britain in 1987 by
Dorling Kindersley Limited, London

Produced by Michael Jackson for Dorling Kindersley

Library of Congress Cataloging-in-Publication Data

Jackson, Michael, *1942-*
   The world guide to whisky.
   Includes index.
   1. Whisky.   I. Title.
   TP605.J33   1987   641.2′52   87-9429

ISBN 0-88162-284-2

Printed and bound in Hong Kong

Contents

"Say WHEN, Man!!"

Whiskey with the Irish spelling is offered by the Isle of Man. This seems appropriate, since the island is said to have been torn by a giant from the fields of Northern Ireland to make way for Lough Neagh. The Czechs are keen on Scottish-style whiskies like Private Club, but also make American-accented ryes. That is, after all, their local grain. Countries as diverse as Jamaica and Germany have the odd Scottish-style whisky. India even has a malt – light and crisp, despite its Irish spelling. Australia is a substantial producer of whiskies in broadly the Scottish style.

THE WATER OF LIFE

Some spirits are timorous, others feel the need for disguise, but whisky is bold and proud. There are spirits of such aimless material origin that they must be distilled to the point of breathlessness: driven to a colourless, tasteless submission that passes in the West for vodka. They are for drinkers who suffer from Fear of Flavour, an affliction of our times. Western vodkas are fit only for drowning in fruit juices. Other spirits are refined into acquiescence then revived by the application of herbs, berries or fruits: they are the aquavits, schnapps and gins of Scandinavia, Germany, The Netherlands and England. Then there are the spirits that speak fearlessly of their origins: the traditional styles of rum and Tequila, the classic brandies of France, the whiskies of Scotland and Ireland, Canada and the United States, and in recent times Japan. These have not been distilled to neutrality, nor in the main have they been flavoured, except by the wood in which they have been matured. More timorous spirits are produced from anything that can be distilled – what does it matter if only neutrality is sought? – but rum and tequila, brandy and whisky, speak of the sugar cane, the mezcal plant, the fruit or the grain.

The noblest of these bold spirits are, by common consent, the Cognac of France and the whisky of Scotland. In this duopoly, the finesse of Cognac has for too long been allowed to upstage the profundity of Scotch. This is the fault of the Scots themselves. Only in the 1980s did they finally come to accept that the rest of the world might be sufficiently discriminating to enjoy their single-malt whiskies, the keys to the appreciation of Scotch. Nor have the Irish, the Canadians or the Kentuckians made a very good job of explaining the character of their whiskies (or whiskeys, depending upon the spelling preferred locally). The Tennesseans have done better.

Meanwhile, Scotches that had barely been outside their home glen have found

The waters of Loch Lomond. Many a loch feeds a distillery, but water is only the beginning . . .

themselves in smart hotels in London and fashionable restaurants in New York, Los Angeles and Tokyo. In 1984, Ireland introduced its first single malt in living memory, and its whiskies began to attack the British market with a vigour not seen for almost a century. Canada's whiskies have enjoyed a long period of growing popularity, but – again around 1984 – the American style of rye found itself in insufficient supply to meet consumer demand. Sightings of straight rye had become rare but, happily, reports of its death had been exaggerated. Nor was it only the Wild Turkey that strutted out of its hollow in Kentucky or Jack Daniel's that proclaimed itself a sippin' whiskey.

In its nobility, its profundity, its bigness, its complexity, whisky of either spelling is a pleasure meant for men and women who enjoy drink, and probably food. It is not suitable for people who are afraid of their own shadow. When the Scots entered the English market in the early part of this century, they produced lighter blends for the Sassenach. At length, the Irish followed by lightening theirs. After the rigours of Prohibition, Canadian and American distillers were anxious to prove that their products were respectable and peaceable. In the 1960s and 1970s, whisky distillers made lighter blends in a vain attempt to compete with vodka and white rum. Appeasement rarely works. Whisky is not for people who think they have discovered delicacy but are really experiencing blandness. The mass market may saturate itself in tastelessness but the discerning drinker increasingly reaches for

something with a palate. Many nations have their own distilling traditions, and more than one refers to its native spirits as "the water of life". This is the meaning of the Scandinavian *aquavit*, the French *eau-de-vie* and the Gaelic *whisky*. Warm countries like France grow grapes to produce a fermented drink, wine, and a distilled one, brandy. Colder climes grow grain; their fermented and distilled drinks are beer and whisky respectively. Barley is the defining raw material of beer and of Scottish and Irish whisky-distilling.

The palate of whisky begins with the water used, which may be soft or hard, peaty or crystal-clean. There may be dryness from the use of peat in malting, sweetness from barley or corn, spiciness from rye, fruitiness from yeast, oakiness from the barrel, and perhaps the kiss of sherry or even of sea air.

In Europe, Scotland and Ireland are the classic whisky-distilling countries, each with its own style. No whisky is distilled in England, though some producers are headquartered there. Within the British Isles, the Welsh and Manx try their hands at making whisky, but their products are curiosities. In the New World, the tradition has been implanted in Canada and the United States, with Australia's whiskies increasingly candidates for respect. Japan already makes whisky to a quality and quantity that renders it an important producing nation. Elsewhere, scores of countries produce whisky but without making a significant contribution to style.

People do not seem so frequently or thoroughly to bother faking other drinks, but whisky is forever the subject of such attentions. In 1984, 22,500 cases of counterfeit Johnnie Walker whisky, betrayed only by the absence of the words "produce of Scotland" (was that carelessness or conscience?) were seized at an Italian port. They had come from Bulgaria, shipped by a state enterprise. In the same year, it was alleged that the C.I.A. had offered bottles of whisky as inducements to senior civil servants in India in exchange for secrets. In the British Parliament the previous year, Lord Booth-by, a distinguished Conservative, attacked his own Government over the high level of taxation on Scotch. When he received what he deemed a "courteous but rather unin-formative reply", he asked "whether Her Majesty's Government realise that in the modern world Scotch whisky is about the only thing left that brings guaranteed and sustained comfort to mankind".

He was supported from the Labour benches by Lord Shinwell. Having failed in an attempt to make whisky available under the National Health Service, Shinwell sug-gested that members of the House of Lords should be allowed to claim it as an expense, "since there is general consumption of this liquid by noble Lords, and since many of them cannot do without it because it is in the nature of a medicine". Lord Shinwell was 99 years old at the time, and went on comfort-ably to achieve his century, so he was well qualified to give testimony on behalf of the "Water of Life".

Although some peat is cut mechanically, this can make for an overly dry and dense fuel. The hand-cutting of peat is part of the year's cycle on some Scottish islands. The lone cutter (above left) pays a nominal fee for the right to take fuel for his own use. He is one of about 300 people on his island who cut peat as a domestic fuel. He cuts about 600 bags a year, though in his adult life this has amounted to less than half an acre. The peat-cutters on the left and above are distillery workers at Laphroaig. The company has its own peat bog, guaranteeing the typical character of its malts. Ideally, a team of three is needed to cut and stack peat, in an operation of almost mechanical efficiency. The narrow spade, with a sharp blade, cuts into the earth like a knife through butter. The broader spade, and fork, are used to lift and stack the peat.

The art and science of whisky-making

Whisky is born out of a sequence of procedures that arouse the senses at every stage. It begins with the water, often issuing from a spring, stream or well near the distillery, and feeding into a dam or pump-house. Water used for distillation generally has little, if any, treatment other than a simple filtration. If a single ingredient determined the siting of most distilleries, it was the availability of clean water, especially in the days when such a resource could not be taken for granted.

The barley, rye or corn can be brought in by sea, road or rail – truckloads of golden grains to be tipped or sucked into the gabled stores or towering silos. The maltster or distiller will occasionally take a handful, whimsically, for the tactile pleasure of the grains running through his fingers. Perhaps he will chew on a grain or two for its fresh, grassy, nutty taste. If the barley has already been malted, it will have a crisp texture and a biscuity taste. In Scotland, it will probably have a smoky tinge, too, imparted by its having been kilned over a peat fire. Not only does the Scottish countryside gather water and grow barley, the earth itself provides peat as fuel for the malting kilns. As for ingredients, all else that is required is yeast, a natural micro-organism. The yeast looks as innocent as it does to the baker, but during fermentation it seethes and bubbles and can fill a room with carbon dioxide. It is as though the fermentation vessels were hungrily consuming the air of the atmosphere.

The senses of touch, taste, sight and smell are aroused constantly. Barley being steeped in the maltings has a grassy bouquet, like a country fair on a spring day. In Scotland, the kilning of malt over peat produces dense smoke, pungent as pine. The infusion of malt in warm water, or the cooking of corn, releases sweet, rich aromas. In fermentation, the air is sharp with fruitiness, like that of apples or strawberries. In distillation, the fruitiness has become more spirity, and that same aroma fills the warehouses where the whisky is aged. In Scotland, there may also be the brininess of the sea, lapping or crashing against the outside walls of the warehouse.

In some distilleries, there is wood everywhere: head-banging beams, catwalks and stairways in the barley stores and malt barns, leading to tun rooms with fermentation vessels made from Oregon pine, larch or cypress. In the United States, stacks of sugar maple wait to be burned into charcoal for filtration. Barrels made of white oak from Georgia are charred on the inside, roaring and screaming in the cooper's shop as they exhale flame and steam. The char on the inside will help the wood yield flavour and colour, first to Bourbon, then to Scotch. Whisky wood is forged in flame, yet fire is the distiller's nightmare – nothing blazes like a careless warehouse full of spirit in those same barrels. There are fires in the history of almost every very old distillery.

The metal of a distillery has its own beauty: muscular, cast-iron mash tuns, often with gleaming, copper domes, hiding rakes that look like oldfangled harvesting machines; copper stills, some shaped like kettles and others columns, both battened with inspection hatches and exhaust valves,

Hand-made whisky? Even in Japan, mechanization has not taken over, as barley is decanted.

polished as proudly as mirrors; and, as the still discharges, gleaming brass-and-glass "safes" or, in the U.S. "try boxes" (sometimes decorated with the American eagle), where the clarity of the liquid reveals whether it can be collected as spirit.

At every stage – in selecting the raw materials and assessing their quality and character, in determining the duration of each procedure and the cycles of temperature to be operated, in knowing the behaviour of his equipment, even the buildings, climate and local conditions – the distiller is confronted with variables. The way in which he arranges and manages those, and the resultant permutation of effects, makes his whisky different from anyone else's. The basics of whisky production are perhaps surprisingly simple, but the distiller is dealing with a complex of variables, and his is still an art as well as being a science, despite the density of learned papers on the subject. The basics are malting, mashing or cooking, fermentation, distillation, maturation and blending:-

MALTING is the treatment of a cereal grain, in Scotland barley, elsewhere on occasion rye or, very rarely, wheat or corn, to render more soluble the starches contained within its seed. These will subsequently be converted into sugars and then alcohol. The malting activates enzyme systems within the grain. The procedure is to steep the grain in water to awaken the embryo within the seed. The dampened grain is then allowed partially to germinate. This is halted by a drying and slight cooking over hot air in a kiln. The kilning also develops the flavour and colour of the malt. In Scotland, kilns were originally stoked with peat, which overlaid a smoky flavour. Although peat is no longer the principal fuel, a proportion is usually burned in the kiln because of its contribution to the traditional Scotch whisky palate. Some Scotch whiskies, one in Ireland and some in Japan are distilled exclusively from malted barley. They are known, logically enough, as malt whiskies. Blended Scotches contain both malt and "grain" whiskies. The latter

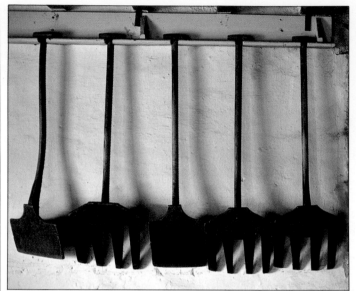

Grains of barley (above left) are steeped in bowl-shaped vessels. The barley is removed from steeping and allowed partially to germinate (above). Now known as "green malt", it must be turned regularly, to keep it cool and separate. Germination is halted by kilning, to produce the finished malt (left).

Malt shovels and forks . . . the traditional means of turning.

Traditional "floor" maltings still operate, though the turning may principally be done with the help of a hand-guided machine.

may be distilled from unmalted barley or, more often, what the Europeans call maize and the Americans corn. To ease the subsequent procedures, both malt and corn are ground in a mill at the distillery. Malt is usually ground in a roller-mill. Corn is often run through a hammer mill. Some distillers feel the gentler roller system provides a better grist.

COOKING is a preparation procedure for unmalted grains, especially corn. It is used in the production of grain whiskies and all the classic North American styles. Cooking breaks down the cellulose walls that separate the starch granules in corn. The starch then absorbs water and gelatinizes. In some distilleries, the corn mash is fed into cooking tubes in a continuous process. In others, a vessel similar to a domestic pressure cooker is used. This system can accommodate temperatures up to 310°F. An alternative

method is to use an open-to-the-atmosphere tub, in which the peak temperature will be lower, typically around 212°F. Cooking may be achieved by heating the vessel itself, or simply by introducing live steam. Some distillers feel that a quick steam-scalding method is less likely to overcook or scorch the grain. This method is slightly less efficient in extracting fermentable sugars, but it may also leave behind some undesirable flavour compounds. Once the corn is cooked, rye may be added, as a seasoning in the production of the various classic American whiskies. Finally, barley malt is always added, for its enzyme action. The temperature of the mash is reduced at each addition. Each cereal has its own preferred mashing temperature.

MASHING completes the conversion of starch into fermentable sugars. Although there is no cooking procedure in the produc-

tion of malt whisky, there is a mashing. The milled malt is mixed with warm water and fed into a vessel in which it is allowed to "rest" while the conversion naturally takes place. The mixing device is known as a mashing machine. The vessel is called a mash-tun. Inside the tun there may be mechanical rakes to homogenize the mash. In the modern, semi-lauter type of tun (taking its name from a German technique used in beer-brewing), rotating knives churn the settled mash. The mash-tun has a slotted false bottom, which is opened to drain off the liquid, now known as wort. The wort is then recycled two or three times. Depending upon the malt and equipment used, some distillers operate a "three-water" mash, others opt for four. Since each water can take an hour to feed into the mash-tun, followed by an hour's rest, then as much as two or three hours to drain, this can be a lengthy procedure.

FERMENTATION converts the sugars into alcohol. Scottish malt distillers generally prefer closed fermentation vessels, in which a rotating "switch-blade" is used to cut the foam if the liquid threatens to "boil over". Grain distillers have both closed and open vessels, though the latter are widely favoured in the United States. The speed and vigour of fermentation can be controlled by having a cooling system. This may be in the vessel itself, or in the hall where the fermentation vessels stand, sometimes known as a tun-room. Wooden fermentation vessels are still widely used, sometimes coexisting with stainless steel in the same tun-room. Types of fermentation differ in that the malt distillers' wort has been filtered through the base of the mash tun; a grain mash may be left turbid, especially in American practice. There are a number of different yeasting techniques. Since the yeast multiplies in fermentation, one method is simply to collect this for re-propagation. Another is to keep a sample of the house yeast in laboratory conditions and propagate from that. A third is to buy-in yeast, usually in a dried form. Yeast may be propagated in

Traditional peat-fired kiln at Laphroaig, Scotland (above). A tracked turning device is used in this maltings in Japan (left), in a variation on the widely employed Saladin system. In these arrangements, cool air may also be blown underneath the green malt.

A shallow copper dome in a distillery is likely to indicate the mash-tun. Designs vary, and some are open, but this is a common style, especially in Scotland. The mechanical rakes shown above are typical in the traditional type of vessel. The filter panels that form the base can be removed for cleaning (far right).

small quantities of malt mash, in jugs, before being pitched into the fermenting vessels. Some distillers use only one yeast; others feel that they require several.

DISTILLATION is the boiling of the fermented wort, known in Scotland as "wash" and in the United States as "beer" (which it almost is). The purpose of this is to leave behind the water and extract the alcohol. Since water does not boil as readily as alcohol, the vapour is splendidly potent. It is collected and condensed back to alcohol. In the production of malt whiskies, the wash is distilled twice, or perhaps three times, and a pot-still is used. This vessel is little more than a heated copper pot. From the pot, a chimney or neck takes the vapour to a worm-shaped tube encased in cold water. As it works its way through tube, the vapour is condensed by the cold. The condenser water becomes warm in the process, and this by-product is used elsewhere in the distillery. It is also exhausted as steam – a familiar sight at distilleries. The pot-still process has changed little since distilling was developed, and it is a most inefficient procedure. However, its very inefficiency produces spirits of a character and individuality that cannot be matched by more modern methods. While the pot-still operates as a batch process, grain whiskies and all of the American classics are produced by a continuous method. The continuous still is shaped like a column. Inside are a series of perforated plates. The beer is introduced near the top of the still, and percolates slowly downward through the plates. Steam is introduced at the bottom, rising through the plates. As the beer proceeds down the column, it is repeatedly boiled by the rising vapour. By the time it

Cleanliness is vital to guard against micro-biological spoilage in fermentation. Closed vessels like these in Canada also help, though some companies prefer open fermenters. Depending upon the type of whisky being made, fermentation can take from 36 hours to five days at the extremes.

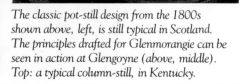

The lock (below) on the aptly-named spirit safe (right) guards the interests of the British exciseman. The inspection hatch (far right) on the still is another classic item of whiskiana.

The classic pot-still design from the 1800s shown above, left, is still typical in Scotland. The principles drafted for Glenmorangie can be seen in action at Glengoyne (above, middle). Top: a typical column-still, in Kentucky.

In whisky-making, the barrel is a container and an instrument of aging. The wood has already been cut into staves when it arrives at this barrel-making plant in Kentucky. The staves are seasoned outdoors for a year, then dried in kilns before being planed and shaped (top right). Barrels are then loosely assembled (middle right), and spend 15 minutes in a steam tunnel to make the wood flexible.

Steamed into shape, the barrels are tightly squeezed in a machine so they can be fitted with hoops. After this torture, they roll into the path of a gas flame that burns their insides for 40 to 55 seconds. A water-bubble system tests the barrels for leaks (not illustrated), and they are hand finished (left). The barrel heads are charred on open hot-plates (far left).

popular age among premium brands. At greater ages, some whiskies become unpleasantly woody, but others go on to achieve a half-century. Because some whiskies "grow up" faster than others, distillers and blenders care more about maturity than age. There is, though, disagreement as to whether it helps to keep warehouses at an even temperature or to use fans to circulate air. Traditionalists feel that the change in temperatures with the seasons of the year helps the whisky to mature. As the barrels contract a little in winter and expand in summer, they inhale and exhale. This breathing may indeed assist in the expulsion of volatile "off" flavours and impart a little Scotch mist or Kentuckian grass to the palate of the whisky. Oxidation of some components of the whisky is one of the phenomena that takes place during aging, extraction of flavours from the wood is another. Research has suggested that vanillin (clearly recognizable in Bourbons) and tannins may come from the oak. It is even possible that hints of pine and mustard-seed might be contributed in this way, though the maturation process is by no means fully understood.

BLENDING probably has its origins in the distant days when distillers could not make a spirit of drinkable purity, and masked their products with herbal flavourings. At that time, there was not a clear distinction between the spirits of different countries. Modern blending began around the turn of the century, when the Scots lightened their malt whiskies with grain spirit and found that the resultant beverage was very saleable in the English market. At about the same time, the Canadians were blending rye whiskies with lighter spirits and enjoying success in the U.S. market. The Scottish model was later followed by Japan and many other nations; the Canadian style was adapted by the Americans for their blended whiskies.

There are dullards who will consort exclusively with one or the other but a palate treated to such monogamy will eventually be driven to drink. The joy is in the encounters and the exploration.

reaches the bottom of the still, it comprises only water and solids; all the alcohol has been boiled off. Column stills are designed in a number of different ways, depending upon the degree of "rectification" (purification) required, and anything from two to five may be ganged together. Distillation can drive off unpleasant flavours while concentrating favourable ones; however, that is a diffficult balance to achieve, and that is the art of the distiller.

MATURATION is the mellowing of whisky by its being stored in oak barrels. Scotch whisky must be matured for three years, and the American classics are usually aged for not less than four years. The optimum period varies according to the whisky, the local conditions, and the palate of the drinker. Many whiskies seem to reach perfection at between ten and 15 years, and that is a

SCOTLAND

To foreigners, including the English, a glass of whisky may suggest a pub but this institution in its pure form belongs farther south. The pub has some difficulty crossing the Cheviot Hills or the Cumbrian Mountains, the river Tweed or the Solway Firth, the Scottish border and the wool country around Hawick, Galashiels and Peebles before arriving, quite flushed and florid, in Edinburgh. In the big cities of Scotland, there are ornate pubs and earthier, more Celtic, bars, and cross-breeds of the two. Elsewhere, it is often a case of drinking in hotels. If there is a dourness to some of these establishments, it may be mitigated by opening hours which, having once been the strictest in Britain, are now the most flexible. Scotland is another country.

The drinker passing through the Borders might call at the Peebles Hydro Hotel, in the town of the same name, to sample from the fine selection of single malt whiskies, even to pause and do some salmon fishing, buy tweeds or knitwear, or explore the country of Sir Walter Scott, before proceeding to the capital.

Still in the Lowlands, between the Pentland Hills and the Firth of Forth, with views of both, Edinburgh is a spectacular and handsome city in which to drink whisky. In the Old Town, dating from the 1400s to the 1600s, there are many pubs of historical interest. The White Horse, in Canongate, gave its name to a whisky (in the same street is a helpful shop specialising in single malts, the Edinburgh outlet for the merchants Cadenheads). The most famous pubs are Deacon Brodie's, a well-liked meeting place, in Lawnmarket, and the touristy Greyfriars Bobby, in Candlemaker Row.

Victorian Edinburgh, with its flourishes and follies, haughtily denies the existence of alcoholic beverages. This hypocrisy might be characterised by the English as being typically Scottish and the other Scots as being classic Edinburgh behaviour. For decades, while there were no pubs or bars on Princes Street, the main thoroughfare, the hidden lane behind it accommodated little else. This lane,

Claret barrels on the back bar, Edinburgh ales and "pressure filtered" whisky in the mirrors, at the Old Toll Bar, a pub of startling grandeur in shipyard country on the river Clyde near Govan.

called Rose Street, is a shadow of its former sins, but still has magnificent Victorian pubs like The Abbotsford, with its carved island bar and a decent selection of single malts. Nearby, in West Register Place, is the Café Royal, with a marble floor, famous tiled murals, and decorative oyster bar.

This is where James Hogg is supposed to have made his pronouncement on whisky: "If a body could just find oot the exac' proper proportion and quantity that ought to be drunk every day, and keep to that, I verily trow that he might leeve for ever, without dying at a', and that doctors and kirkyards would go oot o' fashion".

The quantity is larger in Scotland than in England, though still so mean that anything less than a double might pass unnoticed. The Scottish fifth of a gill equals one ounce; where

that leaves the miserable English sixth, only a mathematician would care. The correct proportion, according to Scottish whisky wags, is "half and half, with lots of water". The implication of that instruction is clearer before you have a few. Less water, but enough to release the aroma, is prescribed by more serious samplers. Whisky merchant Wallace Milroy, a Scot exiled to the fleshpots of Soho, London, puts it romantically: "A drop of water like the dew on a rose". He would agree, no doubt, that a plain spring water, even if it comes to the table in a bottle, is preferable to chlorine cocktail. The water with which the whisky was distilled provides the most compatible companion, but that cannot always be found in faraway places.

Drink and food purists in Edinburgh enjoy a large range of single malts at Henderson's, a bar whose specialities include whisky, sherry, wholefoods and salads. This is on the corner of Thistle and Hanover Streets in the "New Town", the magnificent Georgian quarter of Edinburgh.

In the West End of Edinburgh, next to the King's Theatre and therefore especially busy (even by its own standards) at Festival time, is the richly ornamented Bennet's bar, which serves its own brand of blended whisky from the cask – try the malty "special" rather than the workaday "ordinary" – and has a large selection of singles. There are two pubs with the same family name in Edinburgh; this one is officially called J. B. Bennet, and is in Leven Street, off Lothian Road. It has stained glass doors, engraved mirrors and a lovely fin-de-siècle interior. No lover of either pubs or whisky should miss it.

The revival in the appreciation of whisky, and especially single malts, began to influence the choice at many Edinburgh pubs in the mid 1980s, and Bennet's was a good example. The same was true in many hotels, including the Roxburghe, in Charlotte Square (a part of the New Town designed by Robert Adam); and two modern places, the Ladbroke Dragonara, overlooking the Water of Leith in the West of the city, and the King James, near Leith Walk.

Edinburgh is hardly on a river but it does sit unconcernedly beside a creek, the Water of Leith, which flows into the Firth of Forth. (A firth is a fjord; Scotland is a Norse and Scandinavian country, among its several geographical leanings). Although it has long been subsumed by Edinburgh, the port town of Leith, on the Firth of Forth, remains a famous address in the world of whisky. Leith was the first home of whisky blending and one of the principal ports for the dispatch of the distillate to world markets.

Leith was also once the world's greatest centre for the import of Bordeaux wine. Although this situation had its beginnings in the "Auld Alliance" between France and Scotland against the English, from the 1400s to the 1600s, "claret" was the drink of café society in literary Edinburgh in the 1700s,

and in quality the trade reached a peak in the vintage years leading up to the 1870s. The days have passed when claret was a pub drink in Scotland but the keeping and appreciation of fine wines remains a deeply rooted custom in the great houses of the country. Claret is, after all, the perfect accompaniment to Scottish beef (the tastiest in the world) and might at a pinch be acceptable with grouse; whisky could be the aperitif or the digestif, or both, with a different character of malt for each occasion.

The juxtaposition of these two great drinks in Edinburgh's port was deftly sealed in the early 1980s when the Scotch Malt Whisky Society acquired a wine vault in Leith. The Society then set to work on a salon there for its members, a public house and restaurant, to serve a very wide selection of whiskies, a wine bar, and a museum of whisky. This development, at The Vaults, Leith, promised to offer the visitor just the opportunity to sample whiskies that Edinburgh had for so long neglected to provide.

In whisky, as in most other matters, there has long been a disdainful rivalry between Scotland's two biggest cities. On the Firth of Forth, Edinburgh: patrician, proud to be the capital, albeit of a provincial nation; busy with academe and the professions; with its Festival and tourism and the chance to be a chilly boulevardier, malt whisky in hand. Across the Central Valley, on the Firth of Clyde, Glasgow: the nation's biggest city; still busy with commerce and industry, though not as much as it once was; its splendid Victorian city-centre much restored, amid justifiable pride; its notorious slums long gone, replaced by the new brutalism; instantly friendly (contrary to image) with a wry, Scottish-Irish-Italian-Jewish humour that is its own; culturally and politically a city state. The problem in Glasgow is to drink malt whisky without seeming to be a snob (being a foreigner helps) and to match the locals in thirst.

While deriding such affectations, Glasgow got in first with a specialist whisky pub. This is the Pot Still, in Hope Street, with at least 225

whiskies and often more in characteristically unpretentious surroundings. It's a small, everyday pub, with a mixed clientele, though it has an imposing, carved back bar, brass water-taps on the counter, a brass elbow-rail, pillars to support the anaglypta ceiling, and banquettes.

From its name to its gantry, the Pot Still has set out to specialise in whisky, but there are several Glasgow pubs with good selections. The Outside Inn, at 1260 Argyll Street, near the Art Gallery and Museum, has a large collection. Some unusual whiskies are also available at Dunrobin, at 143 George Street, just to the East of the main square. This is an earthy, characterful pub, small, with booths that have their own doors.

Both cities, but Edinburgh more than Glasgow, have brewing traditions, and Scottish beers are characteristically malty, just as its whiskies are. Edinburgh was once one of Europe's greatest brewing cities, especially noted for its dark ales. It is no longer a great brewing city, but it still serves some excellent dark ales. In both cities, but Edinburgh less than Glasgow, it is not unusual for drinkers to wash the whisky down with a chaser of beer. This combination may be ordered as a "half and half". The Scot, appreciating that reality can be mean, feels that the term "half" fairly describes a full single whisky. Sometimes he may refer to it as a "nip" or a "dram". There is an element of depreciation in this, too, since a dram can in some parts of Scotland be taken to mean a double. The "half" of beer is clear enough, though that is not always the measure preferred. Some drinkers prefer a smaller, rounded glass, without a stem, containing one third of a pint. This is known as a "pony".

The ferocity of premier league drinking in Glasgow is fuelled by the city's explosive blend of ethnicities and faiths. Elsewhere in Scotland, the gloomier aspects of the Celt can cloud with those of the Norseman or Scandinavian to produce prohibitionist and Sabbatarian attitudes. Not only is Scotland another country, it is several. Perhaps all countries are.

The whiskies of Scotland

Scotch is the most complex of whiskies, enigmatic in its interlocking sweetness and dryness. The sweetness is that of malted barley, the ingredient which is uniquely significant in the Scottish tradition. The dryness is a smoky quality imparted by the peat with which the Scots customarily kiln their malts. Within that latter characteristic is a combination of dryness itself, smokiness, peatiness and other tones.

These are given up by the heather of the peat moors; the water that flows over them on its way from the granite spring to the distillery; the clean, mountain air of the Highlands or the sea breezes of the islands, adding a hint of brine to the moorlands and to the atmosphere in the warehouses where the whisky matures; or by the wood used for maturation. A part of the character of Scotch whisky comes from its maturation in sherry butts, while the very occasional port pipe and the frequent Bourbon barrels add their own variations. So do plain and "wine-treated" wood. Whisky that has been matured in a port pipe is not only a gentle sedative but also inspires wonderful dreams.

Each of these elements, and others, contribute to the complexity of Scotch. The importance of water can be over-stressed and romanticised; the idiosyncrasies of the pot still perhaps not sufficiently taken into account, but the peatiness, however subtle, is surely the defining characteristic. In some Scotches, it is intense, in others barely perceptible, but it is always there.

It is strange that there are people who do not like Scotch, but such timid souls do haunt this earth. What they usually dislike is what they describe as a medicinal (or, to be pedantic, phenolic) tang. That is the peat. To complain about it is like dismissing a first growth Cabernet from Bordeaux because it has a hint of cedarwood.

The classic whiskies of Scotland are the straight – or "single" – malts. In most cases, a single malt simply has the same name as the distillery that produced it. In a few instances, the identity is lost to a minor brand-name designed by some heather-brained importer or distributor. The consumer is left to guess the source of the whisky. Any whisky described as a single malt Scotch must come from one (and only one) distillery. This must, of course, be in Scotland. There stand in Scotland almost 120 malt distilleries, though more than a dozen of these are closed and a similar number have not produced for some years. Long after a distillery has ceased production, it may hold stocks of whisky aging in the barrel, and these will gradually find their way into the bottle and on to the market. Just as actors talk about a theatre being "dark", whisky people say that a distillery is "silent", whether for a short season or forever. Many a long-silent distillery survives in spirit, so to speak, its presence delightfully haunting back-bars and liquor stores in faraway places. Among that hundred-odd malt distilleries, only four or five have never seen their whisky available as a single. Some malts have been bottled on only the odd occasion, others are permanently available. Something approaching half the distilleries have, either on an occasional or regular basis, had their whiskies bottled under their own auspices. Most of the rest are marketed, or have been at some time or another, by merchants.

With variations in ages (from the minimum three years to the optimum eight-to-fifteen, and occasionally on to such excesses as 50) and strengths (from the normal 40 per cent in the domestic market and 43 for export, up to specials at 60 per cent), a distiller's product may manifest itself in anything from one to a dozen versions. In some instances, merchants buy new whisky and age it in their own sherry wood to produce a special version. In all of these variations, the malt whiskies of around 100 distilleries are occasionally found in collections of two or three hundred bottlings in specialist shops and pubs. The total number of bottlings in circulation at any one time has in recent years approached 400.

These classic Scotch whiskies are distinc-

In the distance, the mountains whence the water flows. Closer, the hills where peat may be cut. Pagoda-towered, the maltings. The distillery buildings are, on a windy day, lapped by the sea.

"... in a pot still, from pure barley malt." In those days, they knew how to advertise.

The Scotch Malt Whisky Society not only seeks out rare products but also presents them in as natural a form as possible.

A whisky that has been matured at around 60 per cent alcohol is usually diluted by a commercial bottler to a more easily drinkable (and price-able) 40 per cent or so. That degree of dilution makes whisky vulnerable to haze, especially if it is stored cold. To prevent this, it is chill-filtered before being bottled.

The Society buys its whiskies straight from the barrel, at around 60 per cent, and does not chill-filter them. A straight 60 per cent malt might anaesthetise the palate but a dash of water – added by the drinker, who controls the dilution to his own discretion – will still leave a dram of more than 40 per cent. The after-dinner malts better retain their smoothness and fullness if they are not heavily diluted. It is also argued that the absence of chill-filtration preserves taste-notes that would otherwise be lost.

tive, expensive, and not aimed at a mass market, though a number of them increasingly enjoy international reputations. The best known are those produced in the Highlands, not in the most northerly part of the country but in the valleys (or glens) of the river Spey and its tributaries, especially the Livet. The one whisky entitled by law to call itself *The Glenlivet* is historically recognized as the classic of that style but about 20 malt distillers have used the appellation. In recent years, some of these hyphenated whiskies, like Macallan-Glenlivet, have phased out the suffix, to unclutter and emphasise their own proud names. The nearest thing to a household name among single malt Scotches is Glenfiddich, with Glen Grant and Glenmorangie also enjoying increasing popularity.

Glenmorangie is from further north, and there are a number of notable single malts from other areas: Highland Park, from the Orkney islands; Talisker, from Skye; any whisky from Islay; Glen Scotia and Springbank, from Campbeltown; Littlemill, and Rosebank, from the lowlands.

Many of the rarer single malts appear in a list of about 125 bottlings by the merchants Gordon and MacPhail, a label that is internationally renowned among lovers of Scotch whisky but which operates from a friendly little grocer's shop in the small town of Elgin, on the northern edge of Speyside. Gordon and MacPhail gather their rarest whiskies, and most unusual ages, often in short bottling runs, into a speciality range called Connoisseur's Choice. They also have a range of single malts bottled in miniatures (Telephone 0343-45111). A range of about 80 single malts, including some that are also available in distillers' own bottlings, is offered by the merchant William Cadenhead (Telephone 031-556-5864). A portfolio of distinguished "singles", bottled at barrel proof (usually around 60 per cent) and without the loss of flavour entailed in chill filtration, is offered by the Scotch Malt Whisky Society, of Edinburgh (Telephone 031-553-1003).

The *single malt* whiskies of different regions vary in emphasis. Those from the Highlands are by virtue of their numbers the most varied, but they are in general smoky and smooth, sometimes with more than a hint of sherry. Those from the islands are in most cases peatier, and that is especially the case in Islay, which is noted for the "seaweed" tang in its whiskies. The Campbeltown whiskies are almost briny, and those from the Lowlands notably soft.

What the best of them share is individuality, and that is what has prevented them from reaching a wider audience. Each of the great singles combines, unalloyed, the dryness of the peat and the sweetness of the malt and those two elements are the defining characteristics of Scotch whisky. This fullness of flavour is often confused with a big body, but the two are different qualities.

Fearing that the individuality and flavour of the single malts would intimidate the consumer, the Scots have for decades concentrated on blends. The first stage of the traditional blending method is to take a number of single malts and marry them in a vat. This has led to the marketing of several *vatted malts*. These are no longer singles, since they contain several whiskies, but they

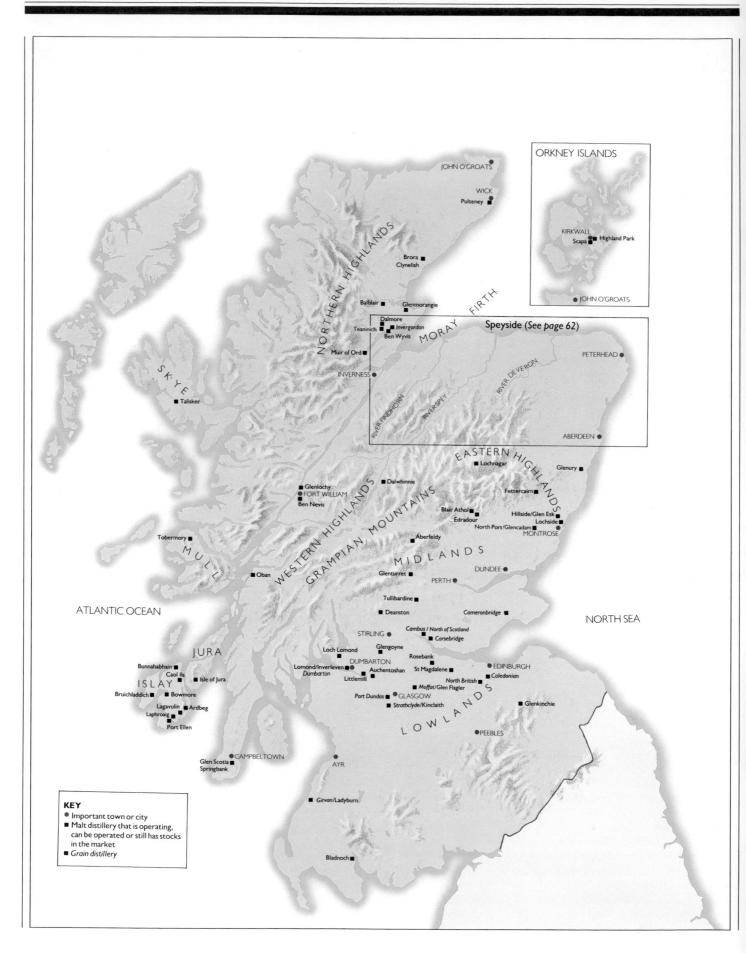

ORKNEY ISLANDS

KIRKWALL
Scapa ■■ Highland Park

JOHN O'GROATS

JOHN O'GROATS

WICK
■ Pulteney

■ Brora
Clynelish

Balblair ■   ■ Glenmorangie
■ Dalmore
Teaninich ■■ *Invergordon*
■ Ben Wyvis

Muir of Ord ■

NORTHERN HIGHLANDS

MORAY FIRTH

Speyside (*See page 62*)

PETERHEAD ■

RIVER DEVERON

RIVER FINDHORN   RIVER SPEY

INVERNESS ●

SKYE

■ Talisker

ABERDEEN ●

■ Lochnagar   ■ Glenury

EASTERN HIGHLANDS

■ Glenlochy   ■ Dalwhinnie
● FORT WILLIAM
■ Ben Nevis

Fettercairn ■

Blair Athol ■   Hillside/Glen Esk ■
Edradour ■   Lochside ■
North Port/Glencadam ■
MONTROSE

WESTERN HIGHLANDS

GRAMPIAN MOUNTAINS

■ Aberfeldy

■ Tobermory

MULL

MIDLANDS

DUNDEE ●

Oban ■   Glenturret ■   PERTH ●

ATLANTIC OCEAN

■ Tullibardine
■ Deanston

NORTH SEA

STIRLING ●   *Cambus / North of Scotland* ■
Carsebridge ■

JURA

Loch Lomond ■   Glengoyne ■
Rosebank ■
DUMBARTON ●
Bunnahabhain ■   *Lomond/Inverleven* ■   Auchentoshan ■   St Magdalene ■   EDINBURGH ●
Caol Ila ■   ■ Isle of Jura   *Dumbarton*   Littlemill ■   *Caledonian* ■
ISLAY   *North British* ■
Bruichladdich ■   ■ Bowmore   *Port Dundas* ■ ● GLASGOW   *Moffat/Glen Flagler* ■
Lagavulin ■ ■ Ardbeg   *Strathclyde/Kinclaith* ■   Glenkinchie ■
Laphroaig ■
■ Port Ellen

LOWLANDS

● PEEBLES

Glen Scotia ■ ● CAMPBELTOWN   AYR ●
Springbank ■

Girvan/Ladyburn ■

KEY
● Important town or city
■ Malt distillery that is operating,
  can be operated or still has stocks
  in the market
■ *Grain distillery*

Bladnoch ■

The whisky regions of Scotland

Scotland has historically been divided into four, universally recognised regions of whisky production. These classic regions are The Lowlands, Campbeltown, Islay and The Highlands. While it is one of the joys of single malt Scotches that they are so diverse in palate, it is also accepted that each region does have some characteristics that are salient among its whiskies.

Several studies of single malt whisky have attempted to group or divide the islands and The Highlands into more manageable sub-regions, without having arrived at a universally agreed categorisation. This book seeks throughout to make the exploration of whisky (and whiskey) easier by grouping distilleries geographically. If the exploration is to be carried out by car, it is helpful to know which distilleries are neighbours. If the exploration is by

shot-glass, a sense of geographical origin helps make sense of the whiskies being tasted. In Scotland, this book defines its sub-regions by dividing The Highlands into West, North, Speyside, East and Midlands, and by grouping the Western Islands (excluding Islay) together.

It further looks at each island and every important valley as a district. When the single malts are looked at in this way, there may in some instances emerge features in common between the whiskies of a particular valley.

Between these districts, there are some affinities of palate. Some, though not all, of the island whiskies share certain characteristics. So do some from the Speyside glens, especially those within watering distance of the Livet. Although these styles are not formally defined, they do have a meaning for malt lovers.

do comprise only malts. Some vatted malts are produced to typify the styles of whisky-producing regions, and have names which reflect that. More often, the aim is the opposite: to provide a balance of the characteristics found in different malts.

Probably the best known vatted malt is Strathconon, one of a range of whiskies produced by Buchanan's. They describe Strathconon as being vatted from four malts, chosen "one for bouquet, another for flavour, a third for body, the last for its ability to blend all four into a balanced, mellow flavour". Another well-known example is Glenleven, by John Haig. Glenleven comprises six malts and has a spicy bouquet, a relatively light body and a long dry finish. A third example is Glencrinan, beautiful, balanced and flavourful, including malts from Glengoyne, Tamdhu and Bunnahabhain among others. Each of these vatted malts is 12 years old.

In the acquisition of a taste for malt whiskies, the vatted products offer a useful intermediate step but that is also their limitation, and perhaps that is why there are few major labels in this market. The various distilling companies have only a dozen or so labels. Vatting does, however, provide a blender or wine merchant with the opportunity to create a high quality house label of whisky. The affirmation "pure malt" may be attached to a single (as it is, for example, in the case of Glenfiddich) but it could equally

be used—and often is—on vatted products. A "Highland malt" might be a single from an unidentified distillery, but could equally be vatted. A number of similar designations are used to tell the drinker that the dram is all-malt, but sometimes without making clear whether it is single or vatted, or specifying the source. In some instances, the distiller of the original whisky may have, for his own commercial reasons, insisted that it should not be identified.

The object of blending is to iron out the rough edges of individual whiskies and produce something that will appeal to (or be acceptable to) a broader taste. All of the biggest-selling Scotches are blended not only from malts but also from the lighter and more neutral-tasting grain whiskies, made from unmalted barley or, more often, corn. While the 100 or so malts are extremely diverse in palate, grain whiskies are by nature less idiosyncratic. They do, nonetheless, have their differences, and there are variations in the whiskies produced by the dozen or so grain distilleries. These are much larger distilleries, in general less picturesque, and a higher proportion of them is in the Lowlands, sometimes in urban locations. Only one grain whisky, from Cameronbridge, in Fife, is regularly made available as a "single". It is marketed as Old Cameron Brig, and is to some degree sold for its curiosity value; Cameronbridge was the first distillery in the world to make grain whisky.

While grain whisky is by nature light-bodied, Cameronbridge is one of the fuller examples, and it is smoother and more characterful than might be expected.

The blender has at his disposal the smooth, smoky Highland malts; the dry, peaty products of the islands; the salty, tangy Campbeltown whiskies; and the soft, sweet Lowlands distillates. From these different regions, he will select ten or a dozen whiskies that will shape the palate of his blend. Several of these will come from the Highlands, since that region offers the variety of complex, elegant whiskies with which he can achieve a sense of light and shade. The islands offer much more pungent whiskies, and these will be used in a tiny proportion; a little of them goes a long way. With only two distilleries, Campbeltown is these days not always included, but it may be, for its own particular character. The Lowlands whiskies soften and smoothen the blend but, being less assertive, may also provide some "filling".

In choosing his malts, the blender will have in mind also the contribution to palate made by different periods of aging, and of the wood used. Young whiskies contribute brashness and vigour, older ones are mature and mellow. If the final blend is to bear no age statement, its youngest whiskies may be three years old. Otherwise, the age on the label is that of the youngest whiskies. New casks will contribute more flavour than old wood; sherry butts a character different from Bourbon barrels.

For every one of his first-choice malts, the blender will also include one, or even two, similar supporting whiskies. Even in the matter of the blander grain whiskies, a well-made blend will include two, and more often three, distillates, each slightly different in its emphasis. If a first-choice list of ten or a dozen malts is each backed by one or two supporting whiskies, and two or three grains are employed, it is easy to see how the numbers mount. A well-made blend will never comprise fewer than a couple of dozen whiskies, and 30 is about average. It is not unusual for the number to exceed 40.

One reason for the supporting whiskies is the wish to smoothen out even the hint of a rough edge imparted by any of the first choices. Another reason is insurance: if there are in future any problems in the consistency or supply of any of the first choices, there is always an understudy practised in the part. Most *blended Scotch whiskies* have been around a long time. The blender's prime concern is to maintain consistency in his product, so that its loyal buyers will not be disappointed or surprised by it. If he is required to create a new blend, he will not start from scratch, but will use existent products as guidelines around which to work.

The highest proportions of malt whisky in a blend tend to be found in a few very small brands. Some English brewers buy Scotch whiskies to blend as own-brands for their "tied" pubs. A small brewer that years ago stocked up with single malts at the prices of the period may today use them more lavishly than is the custom in the faster world of major brands. The independent brewery of Holts, in Manchester, has an outstandingly malty blend, though such "finds" are, of course, rare. Among major labels, Teacher's set a precedent by launching a brand called "60", indicating the percentage of malt whisky.

These days, more than 35 per cent malt would suggest a de luxe blend, although such products are inclined also to derive quality from especially well-matured component

The quality of water used in distilling is often mentioned in the promotion of whisky. The loch above, which is typical, serves the Ardbeg distillery. That whisky features among the samples being nosed by one of Ballantine's blenders, on the left.

whiskies. One of the odder names in this market is Usquaebach, which is sold in replica stoneware crocks. This is claimed to contain some whiskies of 27 years old, with the youngest of its constituents being a mature 18. Most whisky producers have at least one de luxe brand within their range, and good examples are the mellow, smooth Chivas products (the 21-year-old Royal Salute and the 12-year-old Regal). Seagram's owns Chivas, which in turn has several of its own Speyside distilleries, including The Glenlivet. Its is reasonable to conclude that any blending house owning several distilleries will be generous in the use of its own malts.

It is possible to produce a quality whisky with a respectable proportion of malt but. with a relatively light palate. This is achieved by using a high proportion of the softer Lowland malts and by choosing the lightest of the grain whiskies. The classic examples of this style are another Chivas brand, Passport, and two big sellers in the American market, J&B Rare and Cutty Sark. Of the two, J&B has a notably clean palate and Cutty has a little more character. Coincidentally, both of these famous Scotch whiskies are owned by wine merchants with stately premises in St James's Street, London. J&B stands for Justerini and Brooks, who are owned by the major group IDV, itself part of Grand Metropolitan, which has it own malt distilleries in Scotland. Cutty is owned by Berry Brothers and Rudd, a private company specialising in rare malts, and the whisky is blended in Scotland by a Robertson and Baxter subsidiary, Lang Brothers.

Quite separately, Lang Brothers has an outstanding range of blended whiskies under its own name. These Lang's whiskies are

A taste-guide to the principal blended Scotches

The overwhelming majority of the world's Scotch whiskies are blends, running to several thousand brands. Among them are almost all the famous names. Those shown here are, in various incarnations, the principal international brands. Others are even better known within individual regional or national markets.

Bell's "Extra Special" is, in fact, the company's standard brand. It is a robust whisky, with a sweetish start and some astringency in the finish. Not a complex blend, but an everyday favourite in the pubs of England.

Teacher's Highland Cream is, as its name suggests, a smooth, sweetish whisky, at least by the standards of an everyday brand. This derives in part from its having a high malt content for a standard blend.

The Famous Grouse does not have a particularly high malt content, but skilful blending makes for a medium-to-light whisky with roundness and length. It was for a time a "cult" blend in Scotland.

Johnnie Walker Red Label, the flagship brand of D.C.L., is the world's biggest-selling whisky. Its emphatic aroma seems to confirm the blender's use of Talisker as a keynote malt.

Johnnie Walker Black Label, the de luxe version, has – as might be expected – a similar character, but is substantially bigger both in aroma and malty "middle". A good, complex whisky, but with a rather quick finish.

J&B Rare, from Justerini and Brooks, is in the "soft-tasting" style and made its name in the American market. It has a notable fragrance, a lightly sweet palate, and a very long finish, especially evident in the 12-year-old version.

Cutty Sark is better known in the United States than in Britain, though it is an English-owned blend of Scotch whiskies. Of the two basically "soft-tasting" blends, Cutty Sark is slightly fruitier, and arguably more flavourful.

Haig 12-year-old, the de luxe Dimple or Pinch version, has a smooth, malty dryness. The standard blend is now a Whyte and Mackay brand in Britain, but the 12-year-old remains with D.C.L.

White Horse is the peatiest of all the major blends, especially in its aroma. A D.C.L. blend, very popular in Japan, and in some markets offered at a remarkably competitive price.

Black and White is among the smooth, light, dry whiskies made by James Buchanan. In the British market, the standard Buchanan Blend is owned by Whyte and Mackay.

Ballantine's blends, soft in body but complex in palate, have hints of Islay and Highland dryness rounded out in Bourbon aging. Gentle, reflective whiskies, which are very popular in Continental Europe.

Dewar's "White Label", produced by D.C.L. and imported by Schenley, is the biggest-selling blend in the United States. It has a distinctively fresh, clean nose, a beautifully balanced palate, and a medium-to-full body.

Long John blends have a hint of the Islay sea-breezes about them, though this is very subtle in the standard brand. There is more Islay character, in aroma and finish, in the 12-year-old de luxe version.

Chivas Regal has been more successful than any other blended whisky in establishing a luxury image. It is a de luxe blend, with a hint of Speyside smokiness, a mellow but firm palate, and a sweet finish.

Whyte and Mackay make a point of "marrying" their blends in a second period of maturation. There is, indeed, a complexity to their aromatic and delicately sweet whiskies, which have a long, clean finish.

Early, illegal stills were often described as bothies. This word is defined as meaning a small, roughly-built shelter, often in mountain country. It is thought to relate to "booth". The picture seems to be captured perfectly by Landseer in his "The Highland Whiskey Still", painted in the 1820s. At that time, illicit whisky-making was rife in the Highlands. The picture was acquired by the Duke of Wellington, known less as a friend to the distillers than of the brewers.

altogether different in style: full bodied, with a pleasant oily palate and a perfumy fragrance. To complicate matters further, Robertson and Baxter is associated, through an exchange of shareholdings, with Highland Distillers, whose subsidiary Matthew Gloag produces The Famous Grouse, the biggest-selling whisky within Scotland. The definite article and the Victorian flourish is usually dispensed with by devotees, who prefer simply to order "Grouse". It is a splendid blend, with a restrained sweet maltiness and a hint of sherry in its long finish.

Although a soft malt helps make for a light-bodied whisky, the two characteristics are not synonymous. It is not so much lightness as softness, with a touch of Bourbon aging, that characterises the Ballantine whiskies. These are bottled at a number of ages, and the company has several other ranges. The Old Smuggler whiskies are complex and dry; the Lauder and Ambassador brands relatively light, with perhaps more smokiness in the latter. A sister company with its own stocks of malts, Grand Macnish, has whiskies of a fuller flavour, with some spicy fruitiness. Ballantine has both grain and malt distilleries in the Lowlands, at Dumbarton. It also has malt distilleries elsewhere in Scotland. The company is owned by Hiram Walker.

By far the biggest portfolio of blended Scotches was that assembled by the Distillers Company (D.C.L.) between its foundation in 1877, its years of massive growth in the 1920s, and its loss of independence in 1986. What started as a grouping of grain distillers in the Lowlands of Scotland grew to embrace Johnnie Walker, Dewar, Buchanan, Haig, White Horse and scores of other names, owned and operated through a complex of subsidiary companies. When it ceased to exist as an independent company, D.C.L. had more than 100 blended Scotch brands active in world markets.

Since it also owned about half of the distilleries in Scotland, D.C.L. provided more malt whisky than any other company for the thousands of small blends that are owned by drinks concerns all over the world. While all of the drinks companies buy single malts from one another (either directly or through brokers) for blending, D.C.L. has always had the largest and most varied stock of its own. This is reflected in the complexity, balance and fine-tuning of some of its blends. The takeover battles of the mid 1980s began a series of realignments – less initially in the ownership of distilleries than in the control of brands in various markets, though the two are interdependent – that would in the long term influence what went into the glasses of millions of drinkers.

The first shots were fired by Jimmy Gulliver, an international retailing and drinks tycoon. Gulliver's father once owned a grocery store in the whisky-distilling community of Campbeltown. The young Gulliver went on to own distilleries through his companies Argyll, A.D.P. and Barton,

and in the mid 1980s tried greatly to extend his position by bidding for D.C.L. His move was blocked by a counter-bid from Guinness, the Irish and international brewer of stouts and other beers. Wishing to be less dependent on beer, Guinness sought to create one of the world's biggest drinks groupings, in the course of which it had already acquired the producers of the major blended whisky Bell's. When the takeover of D.C.L. attracted an inquiry from the British Government's Department of Trade, Guinness itself became the subject of rumours concerning divestment or merger, with Gulliver again expressing an interest.

At the same time, Hiram Walker – a Canadian company – was also entangled in a protracted takeover deal. Hiram Walker had developed over the years into a conglomerate, and at one stage wanted to divest itself of its original business as a distiller. The question was whether these interests should go to Allied Breweries, of Britain. The other Canadian giant, Seagrams, was simultaneously making headlines in the business pages because of an internal wrangle between members of the controlling Bronfman family as to their respective positions in its management. Among the international giants in whisky-production, only Suntory, of Japan, managed to keep a relatively low profile during this period. Of the Big Four, it was also the only one not to have a substantial and direct involvement in the Scottish industry.

The pedigree of Scotch whisky

The people are Scots (both as a noun and an adjective) or Scottish. So are most other elements of Scotland. Despite its use by Burns and Sir Walter Scott, the contraction *Scotch* is not favoured in the country to which it refers, except to describe phenomena that are both indigenous and special. Scotch mist is special. So is Scotch broth, a barley soup best made with the addition of large helpings of whisky. Of Scotch eggs, the least said the better. Without appendage, *Scotch* means whisky. Even then, the Scots prefer to describe their national drink, without qualification, as "whisky", on the basis that no other country makes a serious competitor.

Certainly, no other nation is as readily and specifically associated with whisky as Scotland. Nowhere else is it quite such an integral part of the national culture and economy. Nor has any other country anything like as many whisky distilleries, or a product as complex and noble.

This despite the art of distilling having arrived late in Scotland, not the easiest of countries to reach in those days and in parts still blessed with inaccessibility today. Distilling was established in Scotland in the 1400s, though – as elsewhere – spirits were at first perceived as being for medicinal use. The Guild of Surgeon Barbers was given a monopoly of manufacture in 1505, though there were soon frequent prosecutions for the infringement of this privilege.

In all countries, early distillers produced spirits too raw to drink without the mask of a flavouring, usually compounded from herbs. Scotland was no exception. As to the raw material from which the spirit itself was distilled, several grains have been used over the centuries but the pre-eminence of malt was recognized even in the 1500s. By the mid 1700s, spirits with and without flavourings seem to have been regarded as two distinct types, the latter being known as "plain malt".

When the Scottish Parliament taxed drinks in 1644, the Act referred in English to "strong waters" and in Latin to *acqua*

Modern distilling might trace its origins from the licence taken out by George Smith, of Glenlivet, in 1824. A century later, the distillery's equipment was much the same as it is today. Wooden fermenting vessels (in Scotland, "wash-backs") are still used. This sequence of pictures from the mid 1920s shows fermentation, distillation and the filling of barrels at Smith's Glenlivet distillery.

vitae. Uisge beatha, usquebaugh, and other Scottish and Irish Gaelic variations had probably been used in spoken language long before that, and corrupted in *usky* or *wusky;* the Irish certainly claim so. However, the word *whisky* finally achieved formal recognition with its entry in 1755 in the dictionary of the pioneering lexicographer Dr Samuel Johnson, otherwise remembered as a verbal scourge of the Scots.

The first "strong waters" in the British Isles were probably grape and apple brandies imported from Spain and France. Such imports were banned by William of Orange, whose Dutch origins helped gin become England's national spirit. The *genever* of Leiden and Schiedam translated into the dry gin of London and Plymouth. Whisky became Scotland's national spirit.

Paradoxically, the Act of Union that joined England and Scotland in 1707 probably did more than anything to identify whisky as being specifically a product of the northern nation. This Union, and the instruments of government and taxation that followed, were not viewed with universal pleasure by the Scots, especially the hardy and isolated people of the Highlands and islands. Among the many efforts to manage, sustain and tax distillation, a measure of 1784 divided the counties of Scotland into the Lowlands and Highlands, and that line persists today in the regional designations given to distilleries. Since the Highlanders and islanders were blessed with mountain streams running through granite and peat, their whisky no doubt had the most character, and legislative separation can only have enhanced its mystique.

Whatever the disadvantages brought about by the Union of England and Scotland, the larger country (in population) provided an excellent market for the products of the smaller one. Since the English generally imagine that the mountains and claymores begin at the border between the two countries, the whole of Scotland's distilling industry was able to exploit that mystique.

The tentative English did, though, find

The word "Highlands" is still felt to evoke the blend of wildness and open-fire warmth that is the setting for a truly Scottish whisky. The Scots also have an affection for colloquial abbreviation such as "Hielanman" ("Highland Man"). "Liqueur whisky" has no real meaning, and such terms are falling out of use. A whisky liqueur is another thing altogether.

the Scotch whiskies a trifle assertive. All Scotch whiskies were at that time, as the greatest ones still are, distilled only from malt, in a simple vessel that is little more than a copper kettle. This type of still is known as a "pot", and produces its malt whisky in single batches. In 1826, a member of the Haig distilling family, Robert Stein, developed a new method of distillation that produced far less assertive and lighter-bodied whiskies from cheaper grains, on a continuous basis. His "patent" still was column-shaped and could be fed with unmalted barley; today, corn is widely used. The whisky industry in Scotland was revolutionised by the patent still and an improved version developed soon afterwards by a man with the odd name Aeneas Coffey. It is thus that the Coffey still is used to produce whisky. Odder yet, Coffey was formerly inspector-general of Excise in Ireland.

The traditional malt whiskies continued to be produced, and a number have always been available in their "single" form, but the bulk of output began to be blended. The practice of blending began on a substantial commercial scale with the Edinburgh firm of Andrew Usher. At first, blending meant the vatting together of several different malts but grain whiskies soon became a significant part of the exercise, producing a less assertive product of broader appeal.

The classic malt whiskies still come from the Highlands and islands, where the water and peat has shaped their palates, but the blander grain distillates are produced mainly in the Lowlands, closer to the markets – the

big Scottish cities and ports, and England. The financial growth of the industry was among the grain distillers and blending houses. It was a grouping of these that gave birth to D.C.L. and began the shaping of an organised and powerful business.

The colourful final episode in the forming of the Scotch whisky industry came in the early 1900s. Its origins were not in Scotland but in France, where the grape louse phylloxera had devastated vineyards, in consequence of which there was a shortage of wine and brandy. British pubs were selling brandies blended from badness-knows-what, and several borough councils in London decided to take action on behalf of the drinking citizen. They did so as part of their responsibility under the Food and Drugs Act to ensure that trading was being properly conducted in pubs within their borough. A test case proved successful and one council, in Islington, a borough on the north-eastern edge of central London, then decided also to look at whisky. A case was mounted in 1905 to establish whether the term whisky meant only pot still products or also included those blended with patent still distillate. The judgment was that only pot still whisky was worthy of the name, and an appeal failed to overturn this. Faced with the prospect that their business might be destroyed by a judgment in a lowly local court, the mighty D.C.L. then lobbied for a Royal Commission. To D.C.L.'s relief, the Commission decided in 1909, after 37 sittings and 116 witnesses, that both pot and patent still whiskies were acceptable. The Commission

defined whisky as a spirit drink distilled from malt, with or without the use of additional cereals. A small proportion of malt has to be used to facilitate the saccharification of other cereal grains, so the definition holds good even for whisky made principally from corn.

The definition was refined six years later by the addition of a provision for a minimum of three years' aging, to include both malt and grain whiskies in blends. If there is a statement of a greater age on the label, this must apply equally to the grain proportion of the blend. The law specifies that aging must be done in casks but does not specify the type of wood to be used. Traditionally, Scotch whisky distillers used sherry butts, often made from American oak. While these are still used to impart their particular character, they have been in short supply since the British began to import sherry in larger tanks. There has been a corresponding increase in the use of Bourbon barrels, also made from American oak. Even a single malt distiller may vat his own product from a calculated mix of sherry and Bourbon casks, of different ages. This is common practice in Scotland.

Scotch whisky must be distilled at less than 94.8 per cent in such a way that the distillate has an aroma and flavour derived from the materials used. Perhaps most important of all, if the whisky is to be called Scotch it must fulfil one clear requirement: it must have been both distilled and matured in Scotland. This was first enshrined in law in 1909.

The Lowlands

Predictably, the Lowlands do not babble with rocky, mountain streams, nor do they altogether wuther with peaty moorlands. The traditional palate of their whiskies, in consequence, owes less to granite springs and peatiness than it does to the soft sweetness of the malt and the fruitiness of the yeast.

Since the image of Scotch whisky is that it issues from dramatic countryside, with the character this imparts, what can fairly be described as a low profile has for years attended the products of the southerly distilleries, at least among drinkers with an interest in single malts. The Lowland malts' reticence of palate has also led to their being used as the background in blends, with whiskies from other regions providing the tonal colour. For both of these reasons, the Lowland malts have less of a reputation than they deserve, and this has begun to be recognized in recent years as drinkers have paid more attention to single whiskies.

The Lowlands landscape may not be massively mountainous but it is neither flat nor uninteresting. The countryside may not have suggested the use of peat but does nothing to forbid it. Distilleries could buy peat from elsewhere in Scotland when they did their own malting; today most of them buy in the malt. Meanwhile, the tradition of the region has, in that soft sweetness and fruitiness of the malts, provided the Lowlands with a style of its own. For the whisky lover wishing to acquire a taste for single malts, those from the Lowlands provide a gentle introduction. The enlightened devotee values them as a regional style and a worthy contrast to the peatier and drier whiskies from other parts of the country.

In so far as there is a small measure of peatiness and dryness in the Lowlands whiskies, the best example of that is to be found in the single malt of the Glenkinchie distillery, near the village of Pencaitland, about 15 miles East of Edinburgh, between the soft, green Lammermuir Hills and the small coastal resorts where the Forth meets the sea. The distillery was founded in the 1830s, largely rebuilt between the two World Wars, and has a small museum. It operates within D.C.L.'s Haig company. The whisky has an aroma that is simultaneously smoky and sweet, faintly reminiscent of a hickory barbecue. The palate is more emphatically sweet, smooth, with a pleasantly dry finish. One or two bottlings are available but none is marketed by the distillery.

Edinburgh itself has only grain distilleries, two of them – and several renowned blenders, of course – but another single malt whisky originates from the ancient town of Linlithgow, about the same distance to the West, close to the Firth of Forth. Sad to say, D.C.L.'s St Magdalene distillery there has not operated in recent years, but the odd bottling of its single malt whisky can still be found. The whisky has a slight smokiness in the aroma, a sweet palate, and is characterised by a lingering and extremely dry finish.

The best known of the Lowlands malts, and the one often cited as the classic example, comes from a little further West, on the edge of Falkirk, a small and very old industrial town where Nelson's "carronade" naval guns were made in the late 1700s. This early industrial theme is sustained by the Forth-Clyde canal, next to which stands the Rosebank distillery, some of its older buildings dating back to the 1850s and 1860s. The clump of distillery buildings straddles a main road. Rosebank uses the town water, which is soft, and mashes in a traditional cast-iron tun with a highly-polished copper top. Fermentation is in beautifully-kept larch washbacks, set into a slatted, wooden floor, in a barn-like hall with exposed beams. It is one of the few distilleries to use the old, three-stage process. Between the normal wash still and spirit still there is an intermediate still. This triple distillation helps create the light, clean, delicate quality that characterises Rosebank. The whisky has a mild nose and palate, lightly fruity, with a restrained sweetness, and a dryish finish with some

In this instance, the waters are not for distillation. They are, somewhat vestigially, the Forth-Clyde Canal. The Rosebank distillery is in the middle of the Central Valley of Lowland Scotland.

The flavourful Lowlands . . . the region is especially well served by its entrant in the "Pride" series of vatted malts from Gordon and MacPhail. Pinwinnie, soft and slightly sweet, is a Lowlands-accented de luxe blend.

sherry notes. Triple-distilled whiskies mature quickly, and the distillery usually markets its single malt at eight years, rather than the greater ages favoured by some of its contemporaries. Rosebank operates within the subsidiary of D.C.L. that markets King George IV blended whisky.

Between the Forth and Clyde, the Central Valley forms the axis of the Lowlands, with sheep farming on the gentle hillsides and industrial towns in the hinterland. In one of these industrial towns, Airdrie, a paper mill was converted to house a grain distillery, and a malt distillery was built, both in 1965, by Inver House, a subsidiary of the American company Publicker. The complex is known as Moffat but a single malt called Glen Flagler was marketed for some years. This whisky, a typical Lowlands malt, with a medium-sweet palate, has not been available for some time. The company has a de luxe blend called Pinwinnie that sells well in the United States.

Hidden in a hollow between the Kilpatrick Hills and the river Clyde, on the northern fringes of the Glasgow metropolitan area, is the distillery that produces an increasingly well-known Lowlands bottled singled malt with the splendid name of Auchentoshan. This is pronounced Och'n'tosh'n, as though it were a derisive imprecation. As a bottled

single malt, marketed by the distillery, Auchentoshan may not have achieved the status of a classic but it is a good example of the Lowlands style. Its fresh aroma, notably light body – sweet but not sticky – and its mellow finish, are exemplified in its five-year-old version. It is also bottled at eight years, when the aroma and palate have matured somewhat and become fuller; at ten, with some dryness; and at 12 and 18, by which time it is very smooth, with some slight woody tones. The local water supply, which comes from Loch Cochno, feeds the distillery; four different yeasts are used; fermentation is in both larch and stainless steel washbacks; and the distillery has an especially rigorous triple distillation procedure, of which it is very proud.

Visitors to the Lowlands who wish to see how the region's single malt whiskies are produced had best go to Auchentoshan. Not only is it an excellent example of a Lowlands malt distillery; it also welcomes parties of visitors. It also has a distillery shop. The scatter of whitewashed buildings dates from a variety of periods. The distillery was founded around 1800, largely rebuilt after the Second World War, and re-equipped in 1974. It has had several owners, and in 1984 was acquired by the Stanley P. Morrison company, complementing their excellent

The quirky Lowlands . . . triple distillation at Auchentoshan, the funky, old distillery at Littlemill, and the pot-column stills at Loch Lomond, a Lowland "Highland" distillery.

Islay and Highland distilleries, Bowmore and Glen Garioch. This energetic private company, originally a whisky broker, moved into distilling in the 1960s.

Another typical Lowlands bottled single malt, and arguably a classic, is produced three or four miles up the old Glasgow-Dumbarton road, at Bowling. This is Littlemill, which is available in the bottle at five and eight years old but expresses its character much better at the greater age. It is also widely used in blends, often at 12 years old. Littlemill has a fresh aroma with an underlying softness in the nose. The palate is very soft indeed, malty and flavourful, with a gentle, slightly oily finish. Littlemill is also below the Kilpatrick ridge, and takes its water from a burn on the wooded hillside. It

has an early form of mechanised maltings on one side of the road and the distillery, set round an open courtyard opposite, in overgrown, cottagey buildings. It is believed to have been founded in 1772 and is a candidate to be Scotland's oldest distillery. It was rebuilt in 1875.

Littlemill was for some years owned by Argyll, and was subsequently bought by its management, trading privately as Barton International. Argyll also owned a sister distillery on an industrial estate at Alexandria, about five miles north in the direction of Loch Lomond. The industrial surroundings belong emphatically to the Lowlands – the distillery is in a converted calico dyeworks – but the site is, by a thread, over the Highland line. The distillery is, romantically, called Loch Lomond.

Both Littlemill and Loch Lomond have unusual stills that combine in a single piece of equipment the traditional pot and a form of rectifying column. These can produce whiskies with varying degrees of body. Loch Lomond produces two malts, one similar to Littlemill and the other lighter and drier. These are not sold as singles, though they may be in the future. Argyll disposed of the distillery to Inver House, who in turn sold it to an independent company called Glen Catrine, which warehouses, blends and bottles whiskies. After its acquisition of Loch Lomond, this company launched a vatted malt called Inchmurrin. This is a light malt, with an aromatic character.

Glasgow is today the dominant city in this part of Scotland, known as Strathclyde; on the other hand, Dumbarton was the capital when Strathclyde was a kingdom. In the marine heyday of the river Clyde, Glasgow built bigger ships than Dumbarton but in the matter of whisky their rival claims are less clear cut. Glasgow is the headquarters for many blenders and brokers but it has only grain distilleries, two of them. One of these, called Strathclyde, has an adjoining malt distillery but that was dismantled (a pity, since the odd bottling of the single malt, called Kinclaith, reveals a seductive, fruity palate, suggesting the appetising combina-

29

The towering edifice of Ballantine's cluster of distilleries guards the river Leven, which itself gives its name to a rare whisky.

tion of a slice of melon dusted with ground ginger). Dumbarton is a far smaller place and more visibly a whisky town, with maturation warehouses ranged along its main roads.

"Dum" or "dun" means "fort". "Barton" is a corruption of Briton. An early tribe of Britons had a fort here, on the volcanic rock by the confluence of the Clyde and the river Leven, which flows from Loch Lomond. Dumbarton Rock was a stronghold at least as early as the fifth century and it is crowned by a castle largely built in the 1600s and 1700s. The rock and the castle dominate the townscape, and in front of them rises the tower of the redbrick, late-1930s building that houses Hiram Walker's Ballantine distillery complex. Within the complex are two distilleries. One distils grain, the other produces two malt whiskies under two different names.

Each of the malt whiskies is produced from the same mash and fermentation but in a different still. Although the difference between the two stills' products is subtle, each has its own name, for the benefit of blenders who want to know exactly what they are getting. One of the stills, which has a passing resemblance to a brandy alembic, produces a whisky called Lomond that has never been bottled for commercial sale. The "alembic" is known as a Lomond still. Its design makes for a heavy, "oily" whisky. The other, a little more conventionally shaped, produces a whisky called Inverleven. Although it is not marketed as a single malt by the distillery, the odd bottling of Inverleven can be found. It has a delicately fruity aroma, a crisp sweetness in the palate and a surprisingly big finish.

While most of the Lowlands distilleries are in the Clyde-Forth belt, two or three are further south. William Grant has two modern distilleries; one for grain, the other for malt, at Girvan, a sandy, seaside resort on the Ayrshire Coast. Offshore is the famous rock called Ailsa Craig, a nesting point for

seabirds, and a source of the granite from which curling stones are made. The area is known for its potatoes, dairy cattle and bacon. Its lightly sweet Ladyburn malt whisky is not marketed as a single by the distillery, although the occasional bottling can be found. The distillery welcomes visitors. There are about half a dozen companies in the whisky business with the name Grant. This one, a family firm, is best known for its Speyside single malt, Glenfiddich, and its Grant's blends.

Visitors to Ayrshire who wish to sample a wide range of single malts can find a good selection at the Turnberry Hotel, just north of Girvan. This Edwardian hotel is also known for its two championship golf courses. The original Johnnie Walker was an Ayrshire man, who blended whisky and sold groceries at a shop in the town of

Kilmarnock in the mid 1800s. Johnnie Walker, the world's biggest selling whisky, is still bottled in Kilmarnock. However, Johnnie Walker whisky today cannot by any means be said to have a Lowlands character, if it ever did.

The southernmost of all the distilleries is Bladnoch, by the river of that name, at Wigtown, on the Machars peninsula of Galloway. This pastoral corner is rich in Celtic history and saw the beginnings of Christianity in Scotland. It also has associations with Robert the Bruce. The distillery was founded in the early 1800s, closed in 1938, reopened in the 1950s, and has had several owners. In 1983, it was acquired by Bell's. The whisky is marketed as a single malt at eight years old. It has a slightly lemony nose, a sweet palate, and an emphatically Lowlands character.

A taste-guide to Lowland whiskies

For the drinker wishing to attempt a gentle entry into the land of single malts, one strategy is to make the approach by way of the Lowlands. The malts of this classic region are, on the whole, soft, sweetish and often light. Their lack of intensity is one reason they often escape notice.

Auchentoshan is one of the principal bottled malts from the Lowlands. It has a fresh aroma, and is lightly sweet without being sticky. It also has a good finish, well manifested in the deftly balanced 12-year-old.

Bladnoch was elusive for years, but became more widely available through Bell's in the mid-1980s. It has a very delicate aroma, with a distinctively lemony character, but becomes bigger in its sweet palate.

Inverleven is only rarely seen in the bottle. It has a delicate aroma – hints of smokiness, and definite fruit – and a crisp sweetness in the palate, developing into a big finish. A Ballantine component.

Rosebank is the malt most widely recognised as being the regional classic. It is a very delicate, subtle, elegant malt, with elements of fruitiness, light sherry sweetness and – in the finish – dryness.

Glenkinchie is the driest of the Lowland malts, with a tasty smokiness. It is not quite as light in body as some of its "neighbours". The distillery does not sell its whisky as a single malt.

Ladyburn is only rarely seen in the bottle. It has a Bourbon aroma and a lightly sweet palate, developing into a surprisingly powerful, long, lingering, dry finish. A Lowland partner to Glenfiddich.

Littlemill is regarded by some as a Lowlands classic. Its palate is very soft indeed, malty and flavourful. Some find it cloying, others might argue that it is a perfect restorative after an afternoon walk.

St Magdalene has a rarity value, since the distillery is closed, but the odd bottling can still be found. This single malt has some smokiness, quite a rich, sweet palate, and a rather bitter – perhaps sappy – finish.

Kinclaith presents a challenge to the ghost-hunters of the spirit world. The distillery no longer stands, but the malt can be found. It has hints of ginger in the aroma and palate, and a melony sweetness.

Campbeltown

Campbeltown whiskies may be few and prized, but the region can also claim the minor bonus of its own liqueur. Sconie is slightly less sweet than some whisky liqueurs.

◆

On the Mull of Kintyre, the mist rolls in from the sea, just as Paul McCartney said it would. Cattle graze by the road to Campbeltown Loch.

Paul McCartney sang to the world about the Mull of Kintyre, where he has a home, but he forgot to mention its classic whiskies. A mull, which has its roots in Icelandic and Gaelic, is a promontory. The pendulous Mull of Kintyre hangs so precariously from the south-west of Scotland that it is almost an island. It intrudes between a group of islands and is for some administrative purposes regarded as being one. At the foot of the Mull of Kintyre, in its heel, is Campbeltown, the smallest of the whisky regions. Although Campbeltown is regarded in the world of whisky as a regional appellation, the place is

nothing more than a small town. It is the only town on the Mull of Kintyre, with a harbour on an inlet called Campbeltown Loch, which a popular Scottish ditty imagines to be full of whisky.

From Glasgow, it is a three-hour drive: north along the bonny banks of Loch Lomond, west through mountain passes at the tip of the Grampians, then south along Loch Fyne, famous for its kippers. Where the last leg of the road runs high above the rocky coast of Kintyre for 30 miles or so, it is possible to look down on to the morning mist, rolling in from the sea, just as the lyric promises. It has a haunting, spectral quality.

If the art of distillation did emerge from the mists of the West, as some believe, then it is reasonable to accept the notion that it arrived first in this part of the country, as has been argued. In its remotest days, Kintyre was a haven of illicit distilling and, with plenty of local barley and peat, it became one of the first centres of the commercial industry. It was the only place in the Western Highlands with a coal mine, to provide heating for the stills, and its sheltered, natural harbour gave it access to steamers. In those days, it enjoyed a brief period of accessibility, before becoming "remote" again in the era of road transport. At its peak, in the

A taste-guide to Campbeltown whiskies

The smallest of the classic single malt regions is Campbeltown. As its name suggests, it comprises just one town, and even that is pretty small. Today, it has only two distilleries, and neither of those has produced for some years. Yet seasoned whiskies argue that Campbeltown should still enjoy recognition.

Springbank has been described as being "Premier Grand Cru Classé". Most lovers of single malts would certainly include this big, profound whisky among their handful of favourites. It is generally regarded as the regional classic.

Glen Scotia is too general a name. Better a meaningless name than one that suggests the whisky could come from anywhere in Scotland. The aroma, palate and finish, however, all speak proudly of Campbeltown. An underrated single malt.

Scotia Royale is a de luxe blended whisky bearing the name of the Campbeltown distillery with which it is associated. It is an elegant blend, with hints of its Campbeltown origins, and with the freshness characteristic of the house.

Longrow is a Campbeltown "single" made entirely with peat-dried malt. Its peatiness is, though, well balanced with malty sweetness. Longrow has the long finish that is characteristic of Campbeltown. A robust revivalist.

Royal Culross has a name that belongs to Fife. That county and former kingdom is on the opposite side of Scotland to Campbeltown. Royal Culross has a Glasgow address, too, but this vatted malt has its roots in Campbeltown.

Old Court is a standard blend that, again, is associated with the Glen Scotia distillery in Campbeltown. For a standard blend, it is quite full bodied. Perhaps it has a hint of Campbeltown in its aroma and palate?

early to mid 1800s, Campbeltown had about 30 distilleries, but it has since suffered severe decline. The coal mine was exhausted, the fashion switched from fully-flavoured western whiskies to the smoother ones from Speyside, and the development of the economy swung against the earliest, small distilleries. Perhaps out of desperation, several Campbeltown distillers dealt themselves a death blow when they took to providing bootleg whisky for the American market during Prohibition. Such was demand that quality was sacrificed for quantity, and the reputation of Campbeltown suffered for it.

The two distilleries that have survived since the Second World War have produced some delightful and distinctive bottled single malts, the character of which suggests that Campbeltown should not have faded as much as it has in the world of whisky. In their heyday, Campbeltown whiskies were famous for their depth of flavour, and that is what they subsequently contributed to blends. It is not only a depth, though; it is a character particular to Campbeltown.

It seems surprising at first, but part of the trick is relatively light peating. This leaves especially unmasked in the Campbeltown malts a quite different taste element: a fresh, salty aroma and palate. That this is picked up from the sea is an explanation not everyone can accept, but the circumstantial evidence is overwhelming. The whiskies do, indeed, have this salty character – and Campbeltown is on a narrow, exposed peninsula. There is no denying the sea mists in Kintyre, and every reason why they should be taken up by the breathing of the barrels in maturation. Some people in the whisky business feel that the salty atmosphere also penetrates the earth floors of the warehouses and, again, that theory seems reasonable enough.

This "sea mist" aroma is at its freshest in Glen Scotia, the single malt marketed by the distillery of that name. Glen Scotia has a magnificent, huge aroma; a smooth, salty palate; and a warm finish. It has been bottled at five years old but is more readily found at eight. The company also has a

big-bodied, flavourful vatted malt called Royal Culross, originally supplied to the burgh of that name in Fife, on the opposite side of the country; a smooth, elegant, lighter-bodied 12-year-old blend, Scotia Royale; a fairly full-bodied principal blend, Old Court; and a whisky liqueur called Sconie, which is slightly less sweet than the best-known example, Drambuie. The Glen Scotia distillery temporarily ceased production in 1983, but continued to maintain its equipment, much of it in cast iron, in smartly red-painted good order. The distillery, founded around 1832, is in a three-floor building, with cottage windows, topped with two small gables for hoists, in a quiet residential street. It is said to be haunted by the ghost of a proprietor who drowned himself in the loch after being conned out of a large sum of money. On the corner of the site there once stood a grocery shop that belonged to the father of Jimmy Gulliver. Although his father never owned the distillery, tycoon Gulliver did until he sold out to Barton International.

From the hillside behind Glen Scotia, it is possible to look across the harbour and toward the town and pick out three or four distillery sites. There are also a large number of churches; several of these were endowed by distillers anxious to book their places in heaven, especially during the temperance era of the mid 1800s. Next to a church, and hidden behind the Gospel Hall, is the Springbank distillery, the only other one still in business. Set round a yard, and with

its own, disused, maltings, this very traditional plant has not produced for some years, but it is still maturing whisky. It has three stills, but is not a triple-distillation plant. It produces a sturdy, stylish single malt.

Springbank's manifestation of the "sea mist" Campbeltown character is round and profound, with a long finish. Springbank is bottled by the distillery in a wide variety of ages, from 5 to 50 years. The principal version is the 12-year-old, and this was unanimously voted "Premier Grand Cru Classé" by a distinguished panel who carried out a blind tasting for "The Times" of London in 1983. A unanimous verdict is rare in whisky tastings, and this included all the classics. The chairperson was wine columnist Jane MacQuitty, one of the most finely-tuned palates in Britain. Springbank is available at conventional alcohol content, and in some markets at barrel proof, which is 57 per cent by volume. The distillery also has a second, peatier malt called Longrow, available in the bottle at 12 years old and 46 per cent. The company additionally has a couple of blends, a premium called Campbeltown Loch and a less expensive bottling named Eaglesome's, after the whisky and grocery shop in the town. The distillery is unusual in that it has its own small bottling line, at which it also fills the Cadenhead range of single malts. Springbank, Eaglesome's and Cadenhead are associate companies. Cadenhead has an outstandingly smooth and malty blend called Putachieside.

Springbank is believed to have been founded in 1828 and has been owned by its present proprietors, a family firm, since the mid 1800s. Among its range of ceramics and miniatures, it has on occasion released vatted malts to commemorate other Campbeltown distilleries like Glengyle, Rieclachan, Springside, Toberanrigh, Longrow and Drumore. They may be gone but they can still be toasted.

Meanwhile, the hilly little stone-built town wraps itself round the harbour, builds and mends fishing boats, and does some trawling. The main hotel on the harbour front has an old photograph showing the jetty laden with hundreds of barrels. It's an impressive sight, but they never did contain whisky; they were herring barrels.

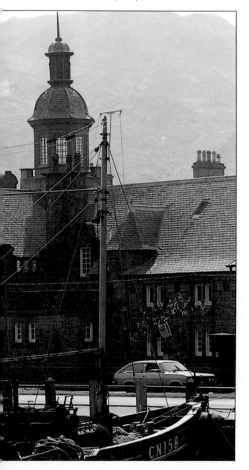

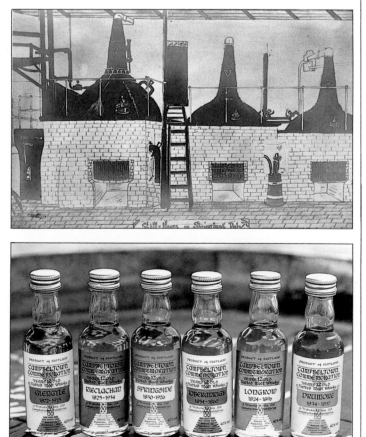

The town on the label . . . Campbeltown (left) remains a proud name in whisky, despite the decline of its industry. It is a one-town region, with the classic ingredients of sea and mountains to create a precarious Western peninsula. Although it may have a primitive quality, the sketch of the stillhouse at Springbank, in coal-fired days, offers a clear impression. Six distilleries of Campbeltown renown live on, if only in their names, in a set of miniatures, complete with dates. The set is bottled by Springbank.

Islay

The most pungent of all Scotch whiskies come from the island of Islay. There are devotees to whom the words "Islay single malt" form the most blessed incantation in the language of whisky. In the English language, Islay is pronounced "eye-la". Gaelic speakers on Islay, of whom there are regrettably few, usually say "eel-uh". Gaelic has slightly different pronunciations, and is more commonly used, in the islands farther north: Skye, Barra, the Uists, Harris and Lewis.

Islay is a Scottish island off the South-West coast, in the Inner Hebrides and, although it is only 25 miles long, it has eight distilleries. Their whiskies have a double pungency, from both the sea and the peat. It is an intense marriage, blissfully consummated. First, the island breezes – with their lightly seaweed aroma – permeate the peat that makes up a large part of the island. Then the water for whisky-making flows in streams across the peat, taking up the earthy aroma and flavour on the way to the distilleries. Then, in some instances, this peaty water is used in the steeping process during the making of the malt. Then the peat itself is cut, taken to the distilleries and burned in the kilning, to impart its tang to the malt. Finally, having entered the whisky through the peatiness of the water and malt, the sea air penetrates the barrels as they breathe in the warehouses. They are delightfully open to this encounter, since all of them lie along the coast, some washed by the sea.

In winter, it blows a gale, and the deposits of brine are measurable on the land. Although some of the streams, or burns, rise in rock, the far greater influence is peat. Distillers joke that Islay water is so full of solids you can walk on it. Or they say the tap water is so peaty that it tastes like whisky. If that were not a joke, it would be a disservice to the wonderful whiskies of Islay.

The marriage of sea, earth and fire, not to mention barley harvested elsewhere, and the life-force of yeast, produces heavily-peated whiskies with a particular, heightened tang. Their nose has been described as "seaweedy", "iodine" or "medicinal". They

are the most phenolic of whiskies by far. A phenolic, peaty nose is found to some extent in most Scotch whiskies, and is one of their defining characteristics, but it is at its boldest in the Islay malts. In that respect, they are the most Scottish of whiskies. That is why they are revered by Scotch whisky zealots and why – in tiny proportion, because of their intensity – they are used in almost all blends. Theirs is the character that makes a blended Scotch unmistakably Scottish, and thank heaven for that. It is also the element that frightens drinkers who have a timid palate.

The Islay malts are to whisky what Lapsang Souchong is to tea. The analogy is perfect. During the early months of the summer "silent season", when the distilleries close for maintenance, some of their workers go peat-cutting on the windswept, boggy, central moorland, starting at daybreak. To refresh themselves, they brew breakfast tea over a peat fire. The tea is rich, sustaining,

at once dry and syrupy, perhaps tar-like. It is a Scottish island's earthy counterpart to the Lapsang Souchong of South China. It is the taste of early summer in the season's progress of whisky-making.

In suggesting that careful whisky-drinking might ensure immortality, James Hogg was being ambitious. Scottish whisky-drinkers probably do cross the great divide, and finish up in Islay. There are more conventional ways to make the journey. The Scottish internal airline Loganair has flights in eight-seat planes from Glasgow, taking about an hour. A car ferry from the Mull of Kintyre takes a couple of hours. Ferries go three times a day, alternating between the Southern and Northern ports on the island, the former providing a quicker introduction to the distilleries.

As the ferry approaches the island, four distilleries come into view, one after the other, their names painted in massive black letters on the white buildings: Ardbeg, pro-

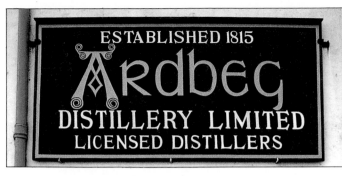

The fishing cobbles and sturdy cottages of Scottish island life . . . bigger vessels make commercial catches of shellfish; there is game, a little farming, some tourism and golf, but whisky is Islay's principal industry.

ducing the most assertive of the island's whiskies, not always easy to find; Lagavulin, with its intensely dry, aristocratic whisky; Laphroaig, probably the best-known name, with its big-bodied, oily whisky, full of the seaweed tang; Port Ellen, with its teasingly bitter-sweet whisky that was never easy to find in the bottle and is now rarer still.

Even this tiny island has regional differences. The more exposed, South side produces the more briny whiskies, and its distilleries all take their water from burns and lochs in a peaty moorland. Where the coastline curves and cuts into the middle of the island, the Bowmore distillery produces what is by Islay standards a "medium-dry" whisky. Round the bay, Bruichladdich is a little gentler. On the North side, Bunnahabhain has a softer whisky but Caol Ila, when it can be found, spoils the progression by being surprisingly peaty and dry.

The sea was the principal access for all of these distilleries when they were built; the interior of the island is sparse in both communications and population (only 4,000 people live on Islay). The distilleries still have, and in some cases use, their own jetties, and all of them are in small bays or coves, on a coastline with a rich history of smuggling and brigandry. Their clusters of buildings are, predictably, weather-beaten, often white-painted and cottagey, sometimes with the drabber, grey rendering that is common on Scottish islands.

The archetypal example is to be found where the South coast road begins to wither and a short track slips down toward the shore to reveal the Ardbeg distillery. It still has its own floor maltings and its pagodas are unusual in that they contain no fans. The advantage of this omission is that the lack of wind helps the peaty phenols better permeate the malt, which has then to be turned during kilning, to prevent it stewing. The procedure that has been followed at Ardbeg is also unusual in that all the kilning has customarily been done with peat fires. It is more common to moderate the peatiness by also having a stage of dry-air kilning from an oil-fired system.

Ardbeg is the most traditionalist of the island's distilleries, though most of them are conservative in their equipment and methods. Ardbeg is believed to have its origins at the end of the 1700s but its official history begins around 1817. Since 1977, it has been owned by Hiram Walker. It has not worked since 1983. At that time, however, Ardbeg as a ten-year-old bottled single malt marketed by the company was becoming more widely available. It is an earthy whisky, with an uncompromisingly peaty flavour, sophisticated by a rich, sherry finish.

A mile back down the road is the Lagavulin distillery. It has smartly cream-painted buildings standing right at the road's edge, on an awkward bend. A sign reminds visitors that Lagavulin is one of the malt distilleries in D.C.L.'s White Horse group. At a glance, the building could be an inn called the White Horse but behind it are red-painted pagodas and a scatter of more utilitarian structures leading down to a harbour.

The malt barn at Ardbeg was in Gothic mood when it was photographed in 1980. Although the distillery ceased production in 1983, it continued to announce itself proudly on its sign.

A taste-guide to Islay whiskies

Among the Western islands of Scotland, only those in the Inner Hebrides make whisky commercially. Within that group, Islay is regarded as being a separate, classic region. Other islands have just one or two distilleries, but Islay is dotted with them – and its intense malts play a character part in many blends.

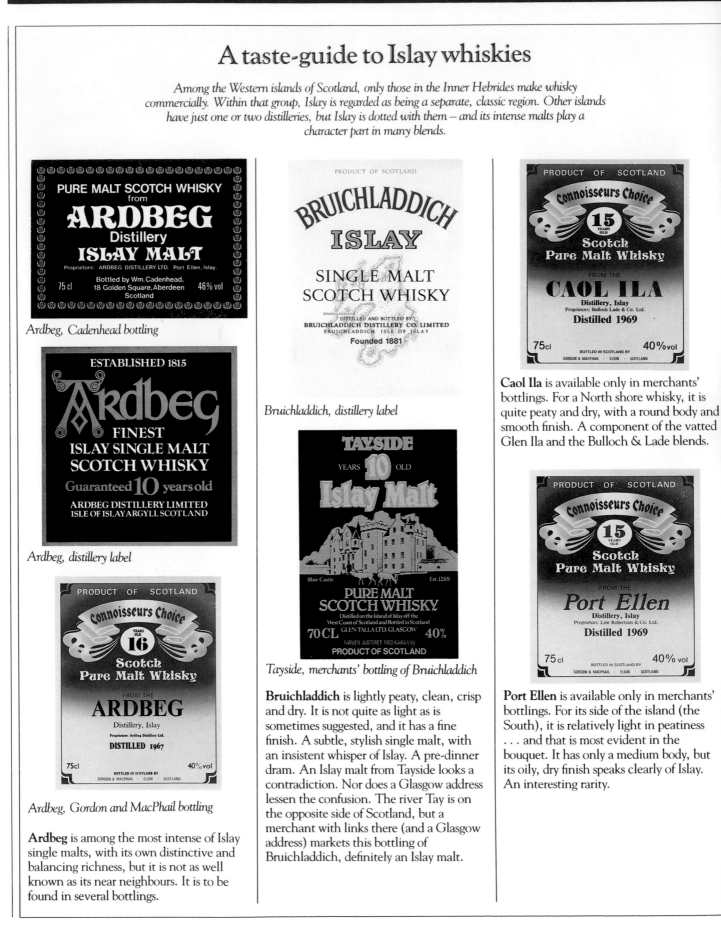

Ardbeg, Cadenhead bottling

Ardbeg, distillery label

Ardbeg, Gordon and MacPhail bottling

Ardbeg is among the most intense of Islay single malts, with its own distinctive and balancing richness, but it is not as well known as its near neighbours. It is to be found in several bottlings.

Bruichladdich, distillery label

Tayside, merchants' bottling of Bruichladdich

Bruichladdich is lightly peaty, clean, crisp and dry. It is not quite as light as is sometimes suggested, and it has a fine finish. A subtle, stylish single malt, with an insistent whisper of Islay. A pre-dinner dram. An Islay malt from Tayside looks a contradiction. Nor does a Glasgow address lessen the confusion. The river Tay is on the opposite side of Scotland, but a merchant with links there (and a Glasgow address) markets this bottling of Bruichladdich, definitely an Islay malt.

Caol Ila is available only in merchants' bottlings. For a North shore whisky, it is quite peaty and dry, with a round body and smooth finish. A component of the vatted Glen Ila and the Bulloch & Lade blends.

Port Ellen is available only in merchants' bottlings. For its side of the island (the South), it is relatively light in peatiness . . . and that is most evident in the bouquet. It has only a medium body, but its oily, dry finish speaks clearly of Islay. An interesting rarity.

Laphroaig, distillery label

Laphroaig, Cadenhead bottling

Laphroaig is the best-known of the Islay single malts. In addition to its renowned "seaweed" character, it has a fullness and oiliness of body that is prized by devotees. It remains a pungent whisky, despite losing a little intensity in recent years.

Lagavulin, with its intense dryness and very firm body, is a noble single malt that challenges its immediate neighbour for the title of regional classic. Some argue that Lagavulin has the most character of all the Islay malts.

Bowmore achieves a confident balance between the intensity of the South shore and the reticence of the North. This is not compromise but character and complexity. The taste of Islay in a lovely, rounded, warming, after-dinner single malt whisky.

Bunnahabhain has barely a hint of peatiness, though perhaps there is some Islay oiliness. A nutty, flowery single malt that, however delicate, has a character all of its own. Delicious as an aperitif or digestif.

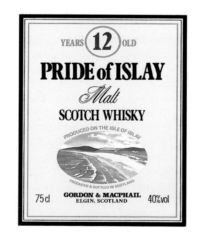

Pride of Islay is a vatted malt. It is one of a series that are intended to represent classic regions or informal sub-regions and districts of malt whisky production. These are vatted by the merchants Gordon and MacPhail.

Glen Ila Vatted Malt has notes of the dryness and peatiness of Caol Ila, its defining "single". The vatted malt is popular in Italy, and is principally available in export markets.

Islay Mist is an eight-year-old de luxe blend from the same house as Laphroaig. Even malt lovers often prefer the restraint of a blend at lunchtime. Islay Mist is, nonetheless, still a weighty, characterful, island whisky.

Above: Black Bottle is a premium blend that has links with Islay through Laphroaig and their mutual parent, Long John. Black Bottle has a hint of Islay in its fresh aroma, along with some Speyside. The brand originated from Aberdeen.

The neat, thriving distillery of Laphroaig (left) produces probably the best-known of the bottled single malts from Islay. Port Ellen (right) has not made whisky for some years, but its malting kilns are visibly busy. Their pungent, peaty aroma is the bouquet of the island itself.

On one side, the harbour is protected by a rocky headland and on the other by a long, wooden pier with small boats moored. The boats belong to distillery employees who in their leisure time catch crabs and lobsters. You have to know the waters to sail here; the sea is booby-trapped with rock reefs, not to mention superstitions. Set into the outer wall of one building at the distillery is a gravestone. This was originally intended to be taken by sea to the graveyard but a chain broke when the stone was being loaded into the boat, and the superstitious crew refused to have anything further to do with it.

With castle ruins offshore, this is an attractive spot, and the distillery has recently opened a visitors' centre. Although Lagavulin no longer does its own malting, it is in all other respects very traditional. The distillery is pleased to receive its water by way of a precipitous, fast-flowing stream that no doubt picks up plenty of peat on the way; its fermentation vessels are made of larch; its stills have distinctively steeply-descending lye pipes; and some of its warehouses are notably sea-swept.

According to the whisky historian Alfred Barnard, there were ten illicit stills in this bay in the mid 1700s. There were certainly two distilleries here in the early 1800s, and they combined in the 1830s. Today, Lagavulin is the only one of D.C.L.'s Islay whiskies to be marketed as a single malt by the company, and it is customarily sold at 12 and 15 years old and 43 per cent. It is a bold but refined whisky, with a fragrant, peaty nose; a big, firm, malty body; and an exceedingly dry finish. Harrods' periodical review of single malts has described it, well, as being "almost Moorish". Most lovers of Scotch would agree that it is a classic. A proportion of Lagavulin goes into the White Horse products, and the family also includes the sweeter blend Logan.

Enthusiasts for Islay malts fall easily to debating the merits of the close neighbours and rivals Lagavulin and Laphroaig. Even their names, both Gaelic, are similar. Lagavulin (pronounced Laggavoolin) means "the hollow where the mill is". Laphroaig (Lafroyg) is a contraction that is no longer clearly translatable, but the distillery renders it, lyrically, as "beautiful hollow by the broad bay". Under previous owners, the two distilleries were locked in a variety of long and bitter disputes. Today, Laphroaig is owned by Long John.

The two whiskies are commonly considered to be similar but they do have distinctly different palates. Laphroaig is less intensely dry but more oily in palate and body, with a "seaweed" tang throughout – in nose, palate and finish, though its pungency has diminished a little over the years. Down a grove of sycamores, past a walled garden, the beautifully-kept spread of the Laphroaig

distillery sits sheltered in the customary bay. Its water, too, is very peaty, and the distillery lays great emphasis on this. The company considers its whisky to be peaty rather than seaweedy, but this is perhaps a simplification. The peat itself may be seaweedy. Having flowed over that peat, the water is used in the steeping process in the maltings as well as in distilling, so its influence is assured.

Laphroaig's floor-maltings is splendidly maintained, though it is not houseproud to the degree of frightening away the traditional sparrows. The bay has the occasional visit from otters, too. In producing its own malt, so rich in the island character, Laphroaig further ensures the individuality of its whisky. To have your own maltings, especially of the traditional, floor type, is not especially economic. That is why several such maltings attached to distilleries no longer operate. Laphroaig's proudly does. A floor maltings cannot meet the capacity of a present-day distillery, but it can provide the "peat reek". If there is enough "homemade" malt to ensure that aroma and flavour, the rest can be bought in.

Devotees argue that Laphroaig is not as peaty as it was in the past, but in the meantime its growth in sales as a bottled single malt has helped Islay whiskies become better known in distant markets. Its still house keeps very busy. There are four pairs of rubicund copper stills in a glass-walled building, visible to parties of visitors, whom the distillery welcomes. The stills are small, and their diminutiveness makes a further important contribution to the whisky, in its full flavour and pleasantly oily palate. Laphroaig's bottled single malt is ten years old. A gentle introduction to the Laphroaig character may be found in Islay Mist, an eight-year-old de luxe blend produced by the company. The Islay constituent is exclusively Laphroaig but its extrovert nature is toned in with two or three of the finest Glenlivet whiskies. There is a hint of Laphroaig, too, in the regular Long John blend, which is also available in a 12-year-old version. The company additionally has a premium blend called Black Bottle.

The most elusive of Islay's whiskies, and one which may be set to vanish from the market altogether, is Port Ellen. This is a complex whisky, with a delicate, dry and lightly peaty nose; a fruity, bitter-sweet palate; a body of only medium weight; and a long, slightly oily, finish. In recent years it has been available only in rare bottlings from merchants – and the distillery, which has not produced whisky for some time, was indefinitely closed in 1984. The Port Ellen distillery was founded in 1825 and has been indefinitely closed before, from 1929 to 1966. Upon being reopened, it was also expanded. It is owned by D.C.L., and operated as part of the Low, Robertson subsidiary. Its white-painted warehouses form an attractive "street" close to the sea in Port Ellen, but the site is dominated by D.C.L.'s large, modern maltings. Outside the maltings, trolleys of peat await incineration, and from the building issues a pungent smoke so that the island smells pleasantly of its famous product.

Port Ellen is one of the three principal villages of Islay. It clanks into activity when a coaster docks with barley or the car ferry disgorges two or three semi-trailers loaded with empty barrels, building materials or supplies. The semis are shunted off by tractor and replaced with full ones, loaded with whisky or shellfish, then peace returns and people wander off for a drink.

Islay has been inhabited since the Middle Stone Age, and over the centuries early settlers included Gaels, Picts and Norsemen. It achieved some political importance in the 1400s as the seat of the Lord of the Isles and, after the defeat of the Macdonalds, became part of the Cawdor Campbells' lands in 1614. It remained in the hands of another branch of the Campbell family until the potato blight and economic crisis of the 1850s, when it was bought by the Morrison family, whose Margadale estate is today the biggest landowner. Although there was a flax-growing and linen-weaving industry in the eighteenth century, distilling is long established on the island. Its geographical position suggests a longer history of distilling than records show, and the quality of its peat and distinctiveness of its whisky has helped to ensure the continuation of the industry.

From Port Ellen, the main road of the island rises quickly to a central moorland of peat, which sits like a saucer, protected by distant ridges. The highest peak is Beinn Bhan, at 1,544ft. The shore birds – eider and merganser ducks, shags, oyster-catchers and a variety of gulls – are left behind, but geese may be seen in flight. More than a hundred species of birds breed in Islay, and it is one of the most important habitats in Europe for Greenland white-fronted geese. The most important breeding spot for these "laughing" geese is a part of the island called Duich Moss, and this is also a potential area of peat-cutting for the whisky industry, a situation that has led to some conflict.

Other birds on the island are cherished for different reasons. Pheasant, like the hare that scamper across the island roads and the deer that, usually, watch from a safe distance, are all liable to finish up on dinner tables in October, November and December. Visitors can sample the local game at modest but comfortable country hotels like the Machrie, the Bridgend and the Dower House. Each has a selection of malt whiskies. Tourism is in its infancy but will undoubtedly grow, and golf brings visitors, too.

March until May or June are the peat-cutting months. In addition to teams of peat-cutters from the distilleries, some with machines and others with hand tools, the people of about 300 households pay nominal rents to farmers or landowners for the right to cut domestic fuel. The peat may not replenish itself at great speed but it is 30ft deep in parts and even the few principal bogs cover more than 16,000 acres. The dark brown, almost black, exposed peat; the strawy-coloured dead couch grass; the purple moor grass; the heather; and the outcrops of quartzite rock provide a shading of colour that changes with the seasons.

Where the peat country tilts to provide sea views over the inlet of Loch Indaal, the waterfront reveals the island's "capital", the village of Bowmore, with its busy distillery. The shape and style of Bowmore, an early example of a planned village, is very distinctive. Its more singular feature is its circular church, designed by a French architect. The shape was traditionally held to eliminate any corners in which the Devil might hide. The church is in a dizzyingly dominant position at the top of the steep, wide main street, which leads down to the jetty and harbour. They enwrap the loading dock of the distillery and much of the village in a tight knot of buildings at the water's edge.

Bowmore village was established in 1768 and the distillery reputedly had its beginnings in 1779. One of the original stone-and-lime buildings still stands. In the Second World War, the distillery, jetty and harbour of Bowmore were occupied by Coastal Command as a base for flying boats. In

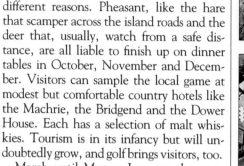

Scotch not quite on the rocks at Bruichladdich (above), with a courtyard layout like that of Bunnahabhain (far left). Sea air . . . and golden sun reflected in lochs of whisky-worthy water.

So sudden are the hills that Lagavulin (above and left) can appear to be wrapped in them, yet it backs on to the open sea, with its own pier and small boats. It's easy to see how the revenue men might have been led a dance in the days when the cove at Lagavulin hid the illicit distillery.

Bowmore (left) is the island's "capital", but it comprises little more than a couple of streets. Its sheltered harbour was a handy base for flying boats in the Second World War, but Bowmore has long resumed the more peaceable role of distilling. With its own maltings to feed the mill and (above) mashing machine and tun, it is an efficient, successful distillery.

The most evident catch at Port Askaig (left) are lobsters, but there is whisky galore in the nearby coves, with Caol Ila to one side and Bunnahabhain to the other.

1963, its revival as a distillery began with a takeover by Stanley P. Morrison. Since then, it has become an interesting mix of tradition and innovation. The water used rises from, and flows over, peat, in the river Laggan. The distillery has its own floor maltings, and has achieved the rare feat of making them economic, thanks to inventive techniques of energy conservation, funded with the help of government grants. The still-house overlooks the sea. Visible through its window are barrels on the dock, waiting to be filled, and warehouses that are doused with four or five feet of water on a high tide. Bowmore welcomes parties of visitors, and hopes in the future to use its dock as a starting point for cruises to other islands. Meanwhile, the company is making its product much more widely available as a bottled single malt. It is a medium-peated whisky, with a lovely, rounded body and an emphatic warming finish. It has enough of

the Islay character to be a good introduction to the style without being overwhelming. Bowmore has been bottled at 5 and 8 years, but is more commonly found at 12.

From Bowmore, the coast road curves round the sheltered bay of Loch Indaal, where the land becomes flat and in places marshy, and there are beaches on the peninsula called the Rhinns. Facing Bowmore across the water is the Bruichladdich distillery. For the character of its whisky, Bruichladdich is held in high esteem by the other distillers on the island. It is a clean, crisp, dry whisky with an unmistakable but *sotto voce* peatiness. The distillery's water comes from a hillside spring that does, indeed, flow over peat. However, its journey is less peaty than that encountered by the waters of some other distilleries on the island. The distillery has not made its own malt since the mid 1960s but is otherwise very traditional, with equipment that is in general old but ex-

tremely well maintained. It has lovely cast-iron brewing tanks dating from its foundation in 1881, an open mash-tun of the same material, fermentation vessels of Oregon pine, and one of its two stills is riveted rather than being welded. The stills have tall necks, producing a relatively light, clean spirit. Most of the warehouses are of the old, earth-floored type, creating the dark, damp atmosphere preferred by traditionalists. The low, white-painted buildings are set round a courtyard, and the distillery faces across the coast road on to the seafront, where it has a pier. Bruichladdich is the most Westerly working distillery in Scotland, though there is a defunct one a couple of miles down the road at Port Charlotte, the third of Islay's villages. Students of whisky will also want to visit Port Charlotte to see the Museum of Islay Life.

Bruichladdich is marketed with the distillery label as a bottled single malt, and under the confusing names of Tayside and Glen Talla by a firm of merchants in Ayrshire. The distillers' and merchants' versions are both usually ten years old. Bruichladdich is part of the Invergordon group, which also owns several Highland distilleries and is itself part of a British conglomerate. The distillery claims that its whisky is the lightest of the Islay malts but this is open to question. Nor is lightness necessarily a virtue among Islay malts, though neither is it a fault. This is another instance of similar whiskies with names which might confuse the non-Gaelic speaker. Bruichladdich, pronounced "brook laddie", means "brae on the shore". A brae means a bank or brow. The other light Islay malt is called Bunnahabhain, pronounced "boona hav'n", which means "mouth of the river". Bunnahabhain comes from further north, on the mountainous coast where the Margadale river flows into the Sound of Jura.

The main road north runs through another surprising change of scenery, the deciduous woodland of the Margadale Estate – soft, and looking more like Southern England – before it reaches the dramatically steep and rocky coastline. Just before the end of the road, a spur runs off, winding down and round the hillsides to Bunnahabhain. The road was first cut in 1881 by the company that was at the same time establishing the distillery, though access from the sea is still used. So truly isolated is this spot that the custom of building houses for distillery workers was in this case essential. The company also built "villas" for the Excise officers, a reading room and a school. Like many Scottish distilleries, Bunnahabhain is set round a courtyard, but this one is so beautifully planned that it looks like the Northern counterpart to a château in Bordeaux. It began life with its own maltings but now imports its raw material. The distillery's water comes from streams on the Margadale Hills but it is piped to Bunnahabhain. It is thus less peaty than most water used for distilling on the island, though on Islay that is a matter of degree.

Bunnahabhain is a traditionally-minded distillery, emphasising care and attention to detail. Its spirit stills have an unusual pear shape, and produce a whisky that is oily but light in body. The whisky has a nutty palate, with undertones of flowery sweetness. It is marketed with the distillery label as a bottled single malt, usually at ten years old. Because of its delicacy, it also is a flavoured component of some blended Scotches that are popular in the American market. Since Bunnahabhain is owned by Highland Distilleries, it might be expected to find its way into Cutty Sark. In line with this maritime theme, the company uses in its publicity the traditional ballad "Westering Home". In the words of the song, it was to Islay that the sailors were "Westering Home". Strangers have been less lucky; there have been 250 recorded wrecks or strandings round Islay, and an ocean-going trawler has lain off the coast near Bunnahabhain since 1974.

The cove that accommodates Bunnahabhain is separated by about two miles of cliffs from Port Askaig, which on the map has the appearance of being the principal

Island fisherman kindly lend a romantic touch to the brusquely-modernised Caol Ila distillery

Northern village of the island. Port Askaig is a busy and important harbour for ferries, but the village comprises little more than the pier office, a general store and a hotel, at the foot of a steeply winding hill. On the coast close to Port Askaig is the Caol Ila distillery, again in an isolated cove. This is pronounced in several different ways, though "cull-eela" is most usual locally. Caol is the Gaelic word for "kyle", or narrow passage of water. "Sound" is perhaps better understood. Caol Ila means "Sound of Islay". The distillery was built in 1846, subsequently acquired by Bulloch and Lade, and rebuilt in 1879. It is still operated by Bulloch and Lade, a subsidiary of D.C.L. In the 1970s, what was an attractive distillery, with its own maltings, was remodelled without a great deal of aesthetic sensibility. The whisky, however, remains worthy of investigation, when it can be found. It has a characteristically Islay peatiness, with the typically medicinal notes, and is very dry. It is bottled by one or two merchants, but is not marketed as a single malt by the distillery. In some markets, it may be found within a vatted malt called Glen Ila.

The enigma of the Islay malts is that they share the island's characteristics yet are also distinctly different from one another. There are enough of them to make Islay malt a style to explore, yet few enough for the drinker to try every one. Each is in its own way a distinguished whisky, and the classics do not nominate themselves as clearly as they do elsewhere in Scotland. The drinker unable to choose one from among the singles might enjoy a vatted malt called Pride of Islay, at 10 years old. This has a hint of Islay's "seaweed" character but also a smooth, slightly sweet, malty palate, with some sherry notes, and a long warming finish. It is one of several such vattings devoted to regions of Scotland by Gordon and MacPhail.

Such is the pungency of its whiskies that Islay sometimes wonders whether it has been blessed with too much of a good thing. It has not. Islay should, indeed, be proud and a growing number of drinkers in far off places are beginning to realise that.

The Western Islands – *Jura*

It cannot be overlooked that the island of Jura is best known for the mountain peaks known as the Paps. The word, which is of Scandinavian origin, is still used in some parts of Scotland and Northern England to mean breasts. Viewed from across the Sound of Islay, the Paps have the shape of an old-fashioned, heavily-engineered brassiere. From other angles the ribaldry is spoiled by the fact that a third Pap comes into view.

The highest of these quartzite peaks is 2,571ft., and they are along a ridge that covers most of the island. There are forest lands inhabited by 6,000 deer but the 225 people of the island almost all live in half a dozen hamlets dotted along the Eastern coast. The island is eight miles wide at its broadest, and has just one road – a single track, with passing points for cars – clinging to the East coast for thirty-two and a half miles.

The Paps are said to have been the home of a lovesick witch, and the island is pervaded with bloodthirsty folklore concerning deer-hunting, cattle-theft, whisky-smuggling, robbery and clan raids. One hamlet, Cnocbreac, was abandoned during the 1840s, allegedly because its inhabitants were falsely accused of poaching the laird's salmon; several of its people emigrated to North Carolina.

Apart from its Paps, its whisky and its own gloomy stories, Jura is known for its link with George Orwell. He went there to write his last book, "Nineteen Eighty-Four", not long before his death in 1950. The scenario depicted in the book could not be more remote from windswept Jura, but this urban man was able to write with a clear mind there.

On the map, the islands of Islay and Jura look at a glance like one. They are separated by a narrow sound that is only about half a mile across at the ferrying point. The ferry is a simple diesel vehicle comprising nothing more than an open platform deck for three or four cars. The two islands are so closely linked that no one would visit Islay without taking a look at Jura. Neither is a large

Impenetrable Jura . . . but who would visit these islands without taking a look, being tempted to investigate, and making the crossing?

island, and they are not so different in land area, but Islay seems metropolitan in comparison with impenetrable Jura. In the matter of whisky, Islay is noted for the number of its distilleries and their stylistic contribution; Jura has but one distillery, producing a pleasant but diffident whisky. In style, it is less of an island malt than a Highland one.

From the ferry, it is about eight miles to the distillery, in the hamlet of Craighouse, though the steep, winding road makes more of the journey. A modern, distillery warehouse is accused of spoiling the view on the approach to Craighouse, by local guide Peter Youngson in his booklet "The Long Road", but the place is barely a beauty spot. The distillery, a pier, a shop, a church and a scatter of houses comprise the village, which overlooks Small Isles Bay. Across the bay is a chain of tiny islands, of volcanic origin, uninhabited by humans but with animal life including a colony of seals.

Water for the distillery comes from 1,000 feet up in the hills, passes through a cave that was once a haunt of smugglers, and runs over more rock than peat, although it does pick up a little of the "island" character on its way. The distillery is said to have been founded in 1810, rebuilt later that century, and apparently abandoned at the time of the First World War. A couple of buildings dated back to its early days are still in use but the present distillery was constructed in the late 1950s and early 1960s, and enlarged in

the 1970s, by Mackinlay's, the whisky subsidiary of Scottish and Newcastle Breweries. It is now owned by Invergordon. The slate-roofed, grey-rendered buildings have a utilitarian, perhaps agricultural, appearance, and their harsher edges have been flattened by the weather. The distillery has no maltings. The malt it imports is only lightly peated, and the other important influence on flavour is the high necks of the stills. The heavier oils produced in distilling cannot ascend such high necks, and the result is a light, clean spirit. The company began to market its Isle of Jura whisky as a bottled single malt in the mid 1970s. The whisky, which is marketed at eight and ten years old, has a hint of island character in its nose, but is very clean and light, with a fresh, flowery finish.

Naturalists might like to know that, on the edge of the hamlet, the Market Loch Burn supports unusual mosses and liverworts in its depths. Many other visitors drive almost to the end of the island to visit, out of curiosity or reverence, the cottage where George Orwell lived, at Barnhill. "Orwell does not seem to have made a very deep impression on Jura", records Peter Youngson. "Nor it on him".

We shall never be sure of that. He was already ill during his time on Jura, but told friends that he wished to write more books after "Nineteen Eighty-Four". That was not to be.

The Western Islands ~ *Mull*

Beautiful though the island of Mull undoubtedly is, most visitors are on their way somewhere else. Where could they go from a Hebridean island? To its offshore islets of Iona (where St Columba began to establish Christianity in Scotland) and Staffa (where Fingal's Cave is). Lyricizing about this part of Scotland, the writer and whisky-lover Derek Cooper found exactly the right note... "islands with magic and often mystic names... Iona, Eriskay, Canna, Staffa, Tiree..."

Iona seems to have been a sacred spot even before St Columba, but he made the island a haven of learning. Erudite drinkers will point out that he came from Ireland, where his name has since been given to the waters from which Bushmills whiskey is made. However, there is no evidence that he brought the art of distillation to Scotland. Nor is there anything to say it was brought across the Giant's Causeway, though that phenomenon of Northern Irish whiskey country is echoed in the basalt columns of Staffa.

Fingal (*Fion na Gael*) was a Gaelic hero honoured in the popular epics produced by the 18th-century Scottish writer James Macpherson. These writings provoked the scorn of Dr Johnson, who visited Mull with Boswell, but they engaged the interest of Mendelssohn, who went to Staffa in 1829. Three years after Mendelssohn wrote his "Hebrides Overture", Turner depicted Fingal's Cave in one of his most evocative paintings.

The grumpy Johnson found Mull "dolorous" but Boswell liked it: "Mull corresponded exactly with the idea I always had of it: a hilly country, diversified with heath and grass, and many rivulets". Keats caught a cold on Mull, and Wordsworth found it crowded: he must have gone there in the holiday season. Sir Walter Scott, Robert Louis Stevenson (in "Kidnapped") and John Buchan all used Mull as a setting for stories, and Siegfried Sassoon had a home there for many years.

The island still has summer and retirement homes, tourism and farming, though it is no longer the major base that it once was for fishing fleets. Mull stretches for 26 miles at its widest point, has 2,700 people, 80,000 sheep (mainly Scottish blackface), 5,000 cattle and more than 3,000 deer. It offers a wide range of recreations, including deer-stalking, angling (in lochs, rivers and the sea) and sailing. And it has a whisky distillery.

From the Scottish mainland at Oban, in the middle of the West coast, the principal car ferry route takes only 45 minutes to Mull, to the village of Craignure. From there, the island's main road runs 36 miles West to the point where sailings leave for Iona. In the opposite direction, it heads 24 miles North to Tobermory, which is the main village on the island as well as being the home of the distillery.

As the road descends a wooded hill into Tobermory, the distillery appears before the rest of the village, which is built round a broad bay. "This hill is relieved by masses of the greenest foliage, which here and there seem to hold some fantastically shaped rock in their soft embrace", Barnard reported. "At its base, shrubs and ferns grow in wild profusion". It hasn't changed much in a hundred years.

On top of the hill is a quarry, and stones were rolled down to build an impressive four-storey whisky warehouse with windows like arrows slits; it was an armoury in the Second World War. The distillery itself, with maltings that are no longer used, stands round a hexagonal courtyard. It was founded in 1798 and the present buildings were erected during its first period of operation, which continued until 1826. The distillery was "silent" for long periods in the mid 1800s and mid 1900s, and was twice revived during the 1970s, for some time being known as Ledaig. It again temporarily stopped production in 1980, but was kept in condition to re-start, and continued to market its whisky under the Tobermory name. The distillery is owned by a private company.

Two rivers running over peat flow into a reservoir to serve the distillery. It uses medium-peated malt, has an attractive, high-domed mash-tun, Oregon pine fermentation vessels, and stills of the high-necked type, producing a light, clean spirit. Tobermory's malt whisky has some peat in the spirity nose, a dry palate and a light, sweetish finish. It is marketed by Tobermory as a bottled single malt, with no age statement, at eight years old. It is also available in some markets at 12 years. The company additionally markets a blended whisky comprising 40 per cent malt, at five years old.

At one stage, the distillery was owned by D.C.L., and their John Hopkins subsidiary just across the water in Oban still has as its main blend a brand called Old Mull. This is a pleasant, flavourful blend, of medium weight, with a hint of peatiness in the nose.

Even by the standards of this intermittent industry, Mull has had some difficulty staying in the whisky business and, though it is a fine tribute that a brand should be produced on the mainland, that is not quite the same thing. There was a stage when maps of distilleries ceased to show Tobermory and it would be a shame for an island as proud as Mull if that were to happen again.

Along with looking smart, Mull is brightened by touches like the cherub with the water bottle (bottom right). She was presented to the island in 1883 by the engineer who had just laid the island's water-mains. The distillery (right) dates from 1798. Duart Castle (left) is older, having been a stronghold of the Lords of the Isles in the 13th century.

Below: the Castle gives its name to a whisky, the label of a mainland merchant. Mull also inspires a whisky-based cream liqueur named after St Columba.

47

The Western Islands ~ *Skye*

Carry the lad that's born to be King
Over the sea to Skye
　　　　　　– the Skye Boat Song

Every Scottish island is mentioned in legend or song, but Skye is probably the most romantically celebrated. It is an island rich in tales of magic and bravery, and is especially associated with Bonnie Prince Charlie. It is also the birth-place of a whisky-based drink that owes its renown to the Prince – Drambuie.

Bonnie Prince Charlie may be a misty figure to the rest of the world but Scots fondly recall that his attempts to re-establish the royal house of Stuart did include a briefly successful military expedition into England. The Scots still enjoy giving a black eye to the English, whose history has a habit of forgetting such a recent invasion, especially since it took place after the Act of Union between the two countries.

When he was driven back to Scotland as a fugitive, the Bonnie Prince sought safety on the island of Skye. While he was there, his hosts were a family called Mackinnon, and they are said to have served in his honour a drink prepared from whisky, heather honey, and herbs or spices. At that time, distilled spirits were not especially refined, and were commonly flavoured with plants of one sort or another, and there are a number of accounts of heather drinks in various Western parts of the British Isles. In her delightful book "The Scots Cellar", Marian McNeill scorns another version of the story, in which the formulation for the drink is said to have been a gift to the family from the grateful Prince, who had learned the recipe in France. It's true that he lived in exile in France, and drank away his later years there, but his tipple then was brandy. The British, in so far as they concern themselves with such matters, perceive the liqueurist's art, rightly, as being Continental European and that may explain the more romantic version.

According to "The Scots Cellar", the Mackinnons' liqueur was made on Skye and bottled privately in the course of the next century. The name Drambuie, loosely trans-lated as "the drink that satisfies", was registered in 1892. Then, in 1906, a member of the family decided to put the drink into commercial production. In order to do this, he set up a business in the capital city, somewhat closer to the markets. The company is still owned by the family and the liqueur continues to be produced in Edinburgh. It is based on both malt and grain whiskies, heather honey and other, secret ingredients.

During the boom in sweet drinks in the early 1980s, the company also launched a "Scotch Apple" liqueur, but Drambuie remains its principal confection and by far the biggest seller among products of this type, although numerous others have been launched at various times. Although some of them claim to have as many as a dozen secret ingredients, their similarities are far greater than the differences between them.

When enthusiasts for single malts talk vaguely of the "island" whiskies, without offering a specific indication of style or origin, they often have in mind a wonderful product called Talisker, which is made on Skye. The island whiskies do not in themselves represent a style, but a number are characterised by being big-bodied and flavourful, and Talisker is a good example. Talisker is one of the best-loved island whiskies, from a well-established and successful distillery operated by a subsidiary of D.C.L. The whisky is readily available as a single malt under the distillery label, usually at eight years old and 45.8 per cent alcohol. Drinkers with a truly analytical capability might be able to detect a hint of its character in the Johnnie Walker blends.

From the short ferry crossing at Kyle of Lochalsh, it is 30-odd miles to the opposite, West, coast to the site of the distillery. After a number of false starts on other sites, the distillery was established in 1831 and extended in 1900. For much of its life, it used triple distillation, and in those days Robert Louis Stevenson ranked Talisker as a style on its own, comparable with the Islay and Glenlivet whiskies. It switched to double distillation in 1928, was partly rebuilt in

Above: there may be a longer story to Drambuie, the liqueur of Skye, but the island's classic is its single malt: Talisker.

The Talisker distillery (right) now has a reception centre for visitors.

1960, after a fire and, sad to say, demolished its floor maltings in 1972.

It stands, as Derek Cooper puts it, on the "seaweed-tangled shores of Loch Harport", with the wildness of the Cuillin Hills behind. A good whisky needs no bush, but Talisker deserves Cooper's frequent flourishes. He has a home on Skye, and his writings on Hebridean and gastronomic topics; in books, for the B.B.C. and for various magazines and newspapers, include some of the best reporting on malt whisky. He mocks himself in his book "The Century Companion to Whiskies":

"I remember some years ago being pole-axed by hyperbole when confronted with a particularly potent dram of Talisker: 'The pungent, slightly oily, peaty ruggedness of the bouquet mounts into my nostrils. The corpus of the drink advances like the lava of

the Cuillins down my throat. Then voom! Steam rises from the temples, a seismic shock rocks the building, my eyes water, cheeks aflame, I steady myself against a chair . . . ' ''

He could have said that Talisker has a nose that is seaweedy but also peppery and spicy, with both sour and sweet notes, and has a huge, warm, peaty, finish. Somehow Cooper's interpretation, however histrionic, better communicates the excitement of this characterful whisky.

As for the lava of the Cuillins, those Skye hills are not to be underestimated, either. They prompted H.V. Morton to his own histrionics in his book "In Search of Scotland": "When you come suddenly for the first time on the Coolins your mouth opens and you gasp. Imagine Wagner's 'Ride of the Valkyries' frozen in stone and hung up like a colossal screen against the sky".

Amid all this drama, it is easy to forget that, though it has only one distillery, Skye has a couple more whiskies. There is on the island another whisky company, marketing a blend and a vatted malt. Both are full bodied, with some malty sweetness and a little peatiness. Each contains some Talisker, though both have more Speyside whisky. The vatted malt, which is 12 years old, is called Poit Dhubh, pronounced "potch dhu". The "dh" is a soft guttural. The name is Gaelic for "black pot", meaning an illicit still. The blend is called Té Bheag nan Eilean, pronounced "Chey Vek nan Yellan", which means "the little lady of the islands". This is an allusion to a dram of whisky.

There are some mongers of Gaelic myth who insist that the language on the label makes these into finer whiskies. Perhaps there is something in that. All drinks and foods taste best in the region of origin – their natural habitat – and the native language adds a comforting credibility. Poit Dhubh and Té Bheag are whiskies intended to resound not only across Skye but also to be heard in the Gaelic-speaking islands of the Outer Hebrides, which have no "uisge beatha" of their own. They are also available elsewhere in Scotland but are harder to find in England. In the New World they are, appropriately enough, marketed in Nova Scotia, whence they have been known to seep into Ontario. There is also a blend called Isle of Skye, from the Edinburgh merchants Ian Macleod and Co. This is a dry, perfumy whisky with a light-to-medium body.

If only that dashing, hard-drinking prince had used whisky as his weapon, he might have subverted more than the English.

A taste-guide to Western Island and Western Highland whiskies

While Islay is a classic region, the other Western islands are not. Malt lovers use the term "island whisky" to suggest intensity; that hardly characterises the products of Jura or Mull, though it certainly fits Talisker, from Skye. All of these whiskies can be grouped informally with those of the Western Highlands and classified as Highland malts.

Jura

Isle of Jura has a hint of peat in the nose but is light in the palate for an island malt. It is a clean-tasting single malt, with a flowery, round finish. A component of the excellent Mackinlay blends.

Mull

Tobermory has not only a hint of peat but also fruity and spirity notes in the nose. It has a dry, gentle palate and a soft, sweetish finish. It is available as a single malt, and has a sister, blended whisky.

Skye

Talisker evinces the kind of intensity and power that whisky lovers have in mind when they talk of an "island malt". It is the famous whisky of Skye, with no greater region to call its own. A classic single malt.

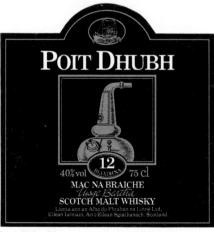

Poit Dhubh is a Gaelic-speaking vatted malt from a company called Praban na Linne, on the island of Skye. They say that it contains Talisker, along with several Speyside malts. A good islands-and-Highlands malt.

Té Bheag is a blended whisky with a Skye address. It identifies itself in the language of the outer islands and the craggy, North-Western Highlands. It is a medium blend with hints of its regional origins.

Isle of Skye is a blended whisky from an Edinburgh company. It is a perfumy-tasting blend, of light-to-medium weight. An enjoyable whisky with which to honour Skye, but with no pronounced island character.

The Western Highlands

Glengoyne just about qualifies geographically as a Western Highland whisky. Although it is not a famous malt, it is well-respected and is gaining in admirers. It has a light-to-medium body with a rounded fruitiness.

Oban is a single malt named after its little hometown, the "capital" of the Western Highlands. This whisky exemplifies the style of the region, with its peaty aroma, smooth body and balancing sweetness.

Glencoe is a vatted malt bearing one of the most haunting names in a land that echoes with violent history. MacDonald's appropriately bold whisky offers a defiant shot of "Scottish courage".

Glenlochy, Cadenhead bottling

Glenlochy, Gordon and MacPhail bottling

Glenlochy is a single malt available only in merchants' bottlings, and with some rarity value, since the distillery is now closed. A good Western Highlands' character, with a typically light-to-medium body.

Ben Nevis single malt was for years available only in merchants' bottlings. In that form, it is an aromatic, fruity-flowery dram. Malt lovers look forward to a new series of "vintages" from Ben Nevis.

Ben Nevis, Scotland's (and Britain's) highest mountain (at 4,406ft), gives its name to a blend. At the foot of the mountain, in Fort William, is the distillery whose whisky contributes towards this characterful blend.

The Western Highlands

From the biggest cities of Scotland, you don't have to travel far to the Highlands. They are called Highlands because they are high; they are mountainous but they are not all remote or Northerly. Only 20 miles from the centre of Glasgow are the banks of Loch Lomond, from which point Scotland becomes largely a land of lakes and mountains. A loch is a Scottish word for a long, narrow, slit-shaped stretch of water that may be a lake or an inlet from the sea. Loch Lomond is more than 20 miles long but in most places only about a mile wide. It is dotted with picnic spots, launching jetties for small boats and sailing dinghies, and little hotels. At either side of the loch, the land rises immediately, and steeply, covered in fir trees, sloping away to interleaved peaks – shallow, broad, triangles of mountain in smooth, regular shapes and proportions, their colours softening through dark green, grey and mauve as they are filtered through the Scottish light.

These are the Western Highlands, and whisky merchants or bars sometimes use that term to bracket loosely the single malts from this side of Scotland, whether they are products of the mainland, the peninsula or the archipelago. The Westerners quite properly like it to be known that they, too, have whiskies, and there are several Highland and island malts that do not specifically fit into the Campbeltown or Islay styles.

On the mainland, the most accessible Western Highland malt whisky distillery, and one that is well organised to receive visitors, is Glengoyne. There are five tours each day at Glengoyne during the summer, and no appointment is necessary. It is just over a dozen miles from the centre of Glasgow, near a hamlet called Dumgoyne, six or seven miles from Loch Lomond. It is barely the Highlands, but the distillery is just over the imaginary line that marks their beginning. It straddles a country road, and in spring is surrounded by daffodils. Behind it are the rough, rounded hills called the Campsie Fells, and the distillery is in the valley of a small river that eventually flows into Loch Lomond. Sheep graze on the hills,

Right: the Colosseum, high above a Scottish port? It's one of the odder flourishes among many that decorated Scottish towns in the Victorian and Edwardian eras. Oban is an eccentric little town, with grand memories. It has enjoyed its position as a gateway on the road to the isles . . . and it still produces a definitively Western Highlands malt whisky. No Colosseum at Glengoyne (left), just a well-tended pagoda. A remarkably exotic country, Scotland.

and streams flow into a well-tended glen, forming a waterfall into the red sandstone hollow where ducks swim in the distillery's dam. Though Glengoyne no longer does its own malting, the white-painted buildings still sport an ornate pagoda. With its copper-domed mash tun, Oregon pine fermentation vessels and lacquered stills, it is an establishment of proud smartness. Glengoyne whisky is bottled as a single malt under the distillery label and can be found at 8, more often 10, and sometimes 12, years old. It is not an especially fashionable malt, but it is one that is steadily gaining admirers. It is a smooth, rounded malt, flavourful and slightly fruity, with a fresh, sweetish finish. Glengoyne is owned by Robertson and Baxter.

From Glengoyne it is an 80-mile drive along the banks of Loch Lomond and through a mountain pass in the Grampians to Oban, the main town on the central West coast of Scotland and the ferry port serving Mull and a number of other Hebridean islands. Oban is the capital of the Western Highlands, and is rich in

architectural flourishes that seem eccentric in such a small town. It is a hilly town, with several eye-catching views, but it is best seen from a boat in the bay. The waterfront is lined with hotels in a colourful mix of architectural styles – the Scots of Victorian and Edwardian times were fond of Gothic flourishes, and here they stand side-by-side with Flemish and Elizabethan allusions. High above the town is its oddest building, a turn-of-the-century replica of Rome's Colosseum; this one was built as a family monument by a local banker called McCaig. Below McCaig's Tower, set into a hillside close to the centre of the town is John Hopkins' Oban distillery, a chunky, tall, group of stone buildings. This distillery is said to have been founded in 1794, though the present buildings probably date from the 1880s. It is operated by a subsidiary of D.C.L. and, like many of their distilleries, has no facilities for tours. Oban's whisky is marketed under the distillery label as a single malt at 12 years old. It has a faintly peaty aroma, a smooth body of medium-to-full weight, and a fla-

vourful, slightly sweet palate and finish. The company also has a number of blends, including Glen Garry and Glen Royal.

About 30 miles North of Oban is Glencoe, scene of the massacre by the Campbells of the Macdonalds in the 17th century. The road runs through this wild glen, between mountains of more than 3,000ft, and there is a bridge over Loch Leven to take traffic farther North. Despite the gracelessness of the Campbells, there are still Macdonalds living in the area, and one of them founded a company in the village of Glencoe to market a vatted malt whisky. This product, called Glencoe, is sold at eight years old and 57 per cent alcohol. It has a peaty, spirity, nose, a big, flavourful palate, and a smooth, sweetish, malty finish.

The Glencoe company's founder is the great grandson of "Long John" Macdonald, a man who in both literal and figurative senses was a larger-than-life figure in the history of Scotch whisky. Long John was a descendant of a King of Argyll and of a Lord of the Isles (Argyll was a kingdom embrac-

ing the Western Highlands). He stood 6ft. 4in., "which was considered an unusual height 150 years ago", as Philip Morrice observes in his "Schweppes Guide to Scotch", a book comprehensive even in such details. Long John was a distiller and a publicist. In 1825, he built a distillery on the slopes of Ben Nevis at Fort William. This was the first legal distillery in the area, and produced a whisky called Long John's Dew of Ben Nevis. The distillery and the Long John brand name became separated in their subsequent history, passing to different companies, but were reunited in 1981. At that time, there had been no production for some years, and the whisky had become hard to find, though through one of its past ownerships it remained available at the Inverlochy Castle Restaurant, Fort William. This is widely agreed to be one of the best restaurants and hotels in Scotland, though it is very expensive and usually has to be booked long in advance. In 1984, moves began toward the resumption of distilling at Long John's old establishment, which has both

grain and malt stills. The malt whisky distilled there in the past has had plenty of character, with a sweet, malty nose; a pleasantly oily, firm, body; a slightly aromatic palate; and a long, floral finish.

The reunion of the Long John name with a revived Ben Nevis distillery was one of the happier stories in Scotland during a difficult period for the whisky industry. Sad to say, Fort William's other distillery, Glenlochy, was indefinitely closed by its owners, D.C.L. This distillery, built in 1898, produced a whisky with the same pleasantly oily texture but a great deal of dry peatiness all the way through: in nose, palate and finish. If anything can be said to be typical of the Western Highlands, it is this combination of a malty, oily character with some peatiness. All the sadder that this fine example should now become a rarity.

North of Fort William, a system of manmade and natural waterways links up with the monstrous Loch Ness all the way to Inverness and the Moray Firth. Beyond this line are the Northern Highlands.

Orkney

Sternly reminding visitors that the company was founded in 1798, Highland Park's iron gate arch stylistically betrays its origins. It would also be happy on a Yorkshire woollen mill.

The most Northerly of whiskies are Orcadian. That is to say that they are distilled in the Orkneys, a group of islands that were for 500 years ruled by Norway and Denmark, and remain strangers to Gaelic culture though they passed to Scotland in 1468. King Christian I of Norway pawned the Orkney and Shetland islands in lieu of a dowry on his daughter's marriage to James III of Scotland.

There are 65 islands in the Orkneys, 30 of them inhabited, and just over 18,000 people. The principal island is known to Orcadians as "the mainland", and its capital is the small town of Kirkwall. That is where

the Orkneys' two distilleries are. One of them, Scapa (named after a nearby stretch of water famous in Naval history) produces a pleasant but unexceptional single malt. The other, Highland Park, distils an outstanding whisky that deserves wider recognition. Apart from the making of whisky, the Orcadians' principal occupation is farming, and they are noted for their beef.

Fifty miles North of the Orkneys are the Shetland islands, 100 of them, 15 inhabited, with just under 18,000 people. They have no distilleries, and earn their living from rich fishing grounds. The Shetlands are especially well blessed with prehistoric sites, and gave their name to a breed of pony and a

type of wool. Halfway between the two groups is Fair Isle, with an ornithological observatory and a craft of knitting in intricate, traditional patterns. To the West, half way to Iceland, are the Faroe Islands, a self-governing dependency of Denmark. All of these North Atlantic islands are linked by tourist ferries operated by one or two shipping lines in association with British Rail.

From the Scottish mainland, the principal sea route to Orkney is from Thurso Bay, from the port of Scrabster. The car ferry to Stromness, on the Orkney mainland, takes two hours. There are 20-minute flights in eight-seater planes to Kirkwall from Wick, and routes from several other Scottish airports.

From the tiny airport of Kirkwall, the road into town passes the Highland Park distillery on the left. The distillery, which welcomes visitors for a number of tours at set times each day, is half-hidden in a fold in farming fields. Behind its handsome, wrought-iron gate, it has long, low warehouses of the local Walliwall stone. Stratified like sandstone, this has flashes of vivid yellow and brick-red as well as granite grey. The distillery has two pagodas, and still operates a floor maltings.

Highland Park is said to have been founded in 1795 and enlarged in the 1890s. Its oldest buildings are from the latter date – some of those Walliwall warehouses, which have the traditional, earth floors. Walliwall features in the water supply, too. The water, which is very hard, rises from a rock spring on a hill half a mile from the distillery, and is held in a disused Walliwall quarry. The peat for the maltings is from Hobbister Moor, on the other side of Scapa Flow. The beds there are shallow, so the peat imparts a distinctively "young", heathery, rooty flavour. This is the character that some maltsters traditionally tried to achieve by throwing a bunch of heather into the burning peat. A heavily-peated malt is used at Highland Park. A shining, stainless steel mash tun of the modern, semi-lauter type, is the only untraditional piece of equipment in the place. The washbacks are wooden, and three yeasts are used. The stills are set low into the floor, curving sharply underneath into a broad, rounded onion shape. The whisky sold under the distillery label as a single malt is all aged in sherry butts, though some are used several times.

The whisky has a most distinctive aroma, with almost the sweetness of a garden bonfire in that combination of peat smoke and heather-honey. The palate is cleanly sweet, with a succulent, medium-weight body. Then that heathery and peaty aromatic quality returns in a smooth, lingering finish. As a bottled single malt, it can occasionally be found at eight years, but more commonly at 12. It is a slow maturing whisky, and perhaps should also be marketed as a 15-year-old. It might also be better showcased than in a "modern" bottle that looks as though it might contain a urine sample.

Highland Park was the only product ever to have scored 100 per cent when it was rated by the regular tasting team of "The Scotsman" newspaper in 1984. This was no mean feat, since that publication is the national newspaper of Scotland. As it happens, Highland Park was sampled last, after half a dozen other malts, at a time when the team's palates might have been expected to be jaded. The report of the tasting said that Highland Park "prompted expressions of ecstasy of a kind our cynical team felt almost ashamed to admit to. It also drew such comments as 'superb, subtle, varied but integrated', 'long and golden, with many shades of flavour' and 'deep and lingering'". In fairness, it should be recorded that the sample being tasted was at barrel strength, more than 60 per cent alcohol. At a standard strength, the whisky loses something in the finish.

Tastings like that, and coverage in the respected "Decanter" magazine in London, have helped spread the renown of this whisky, but it is still not one of the more widely-known names among bottled single malts. It surely should be regarded as a classic island malt. It has long been well regarded by blenders, and for them it performs a special function. It is said to be a catalyst in blends,

The lattice windows of Kirkwall's Old Town . . . with a museum through the arch. Remoteness, more than conservation, has protected Kirkwall, though it is beginning to attract some tourism. It can only be helped by the growing, and justified, reputation of its single malt whisky.

bringing out the flavours in other whiskies. The owning company is part of Highland Distilleries, so it has a family relationship with Lang's and The Famous Grouse.

Highland Park is the most Northerly Scotch whisky distillery but, despite the remoteness of the Orkneys (or, more likely, because of that), the islands have a significant history in this field of endeavour. The water supply to Highland Park was allegedly first used by a famous distiller called Magnus Eunson, in the days before whisky-making was legal. Orkney was one of several remote parts of Scotland where *bere*, a primitive predecessor of barley, was used in whisky-making. The grain is still ground on the island and used in the baking of bannocks, a girdle-cooked variation on oatcakes. Orcadian peat is so highly regarded in whisky-making that it was once exported to distilleries in mainland Scotland. There were in the past another two distilleries in the Kirkwall area and possibly three at Stromness.

Highland Park's claim to be the most Northerly distillery is close run. Less than half a mile South is the Scapa Distillery. Highland Park was built to have access to the sea, but Scapa is slightly closer to the waters whose name it shares. Scapa was founded in 1885, and has two original warehouses, now used for the storage of empty casks. The company has restored a waterwheel that once powered the distillery, but most of the rest of the fabric dates from

1959, when the place was rebuilt. Scapa has an unusually small mash tun, with a conical top, cast-iron fermentation vessels, and a "Lomond" wash still, contributing to a slightly oily spirit. The distillery stopped malting at about the time of its rebuilding. It is unusual in that it uses a wholly unpeated malt. However, the water supply, from a nearby hill, is very peaty. The whisky has some peatiness in the nose; a clean, light, rounded palate; and a slightly oily, dry finish. It is aged in Bourbon casks for bottling as a single malt. Scapa is owned by a Hiram Walker subsidiary but the whisky as a single malt is available only with the Gordon and MacPhail label, at eight years old.

Gordon and MacPhail also produce a vatted malt and a blend to an Orkney character. In their regional series of vatted malts, Pride of Orkney, at 12 years old, has some peatiness and a "chewy" palate. Their Old Orkney blend has a faintly bitter-sweet finish.

These whiskies are not always easy to find outside the far North, though they are – of course – readily available in the small hotels of Kirkwall's paved old town area, between the harbour and the unusual, red sandstone cathedral of St Magnus. The cathedral was founded in 1137, and during renovations in 1919, the skull of St Magnus was found, sealed into a pillar. It was split across – St Magnus was murdered with an axe, according to a Norse saga.

A taste-guide to Orkney and Northern Highland whiskies

Far from the other whisky-producing islands, Orkney is in every sense isolated. Its two distilleries both produce whiskies with heathery tones, and this flowery-spicy character finds an affinity in the distillates from the Northern mainland. Island or mainland, the far North makes some outstanding Highland malts.

Orkney

Highland Park is a powerful malt full of "island" character, and with a smooth, heather-sweet succulence that makes it a magnificent after-dinner drink. A malt to challenge any Cognac or Armagnac.

Pride of Orkney is a vatted malt in the regional series from Gordon and MacPhail. Orkney may not be a classic region, but as a district it is becoming better appreciated. This is a peaty, flavourful malt.

The Northern Highlands

Old Pulteney is a single malt from the Northernmost distillery on the Scottish mainland. Does its "Manzanilla" character come directly from the sea air or at one remove, through the wood of the barrels?

Scapa is a single malt with its own heathery tones, especially in the aroma; a medium, rounded body; and a firm, smooth finish. Its palate speaks of Orkney, but more quietly than its neighbour.

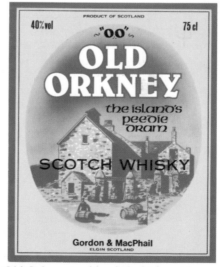

Old Orkney is a blended whisky with a local accent, again from Gordon and MacPhail. It is a peaty blend, with the typically Orcadian sweet smokiness that can dry intensely in the finish. A pre-dinner blend.

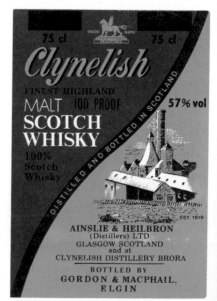

Clynelish is a single malt of great character. It embodies all the qualities of a Northern Highlands malt, and does so more assertively than any other. It is not widely known, but it has a cult following.

Glenmorangie is one of the best-known single malts. It clearly belongs to the Northern Highlands, but does not wear its origins on its sleeve. It is a subtle, teasing whisky, with a character of its own.

Balblair, distillery label

Glenordie is a perilously drinkable single malt, especially after dinner. It was previously known simply as Ord. How strange that the label of this enjoyable product does not identify its source.

Dalmore is a splendid single malt that deserves to be more widely known. A rich, smooth, flavourful whisky, with its suggestion of sweetness restrained to the end, it is delicious as an after-dinner drink.

Balblair, Gordon and MacPhail bottling

Balblair is a dry, spicy, slightly sharp single malt, of some delicacy. A pre-dinner whisky. It contributes to the Ballantine blends, is bottled as a single mainly for export, and in Britain by Gordon and MacPhail.

Teaninich is a single malt that is available only in merchants' bottlings. Nor has the distillery operated for a year or two. The whisky is worth seeking out, for its complex of light peatiness, fruit and softness.

The Northern Highlands

From Cape Wrath, the mountains swing across the most remote part of the Scottish mainland in an almost severed chunk, a rocky haven for wildcats and golden eagles but a less comfortable place for the indulgences of humans. Yet, hanging by their fingernails on to the East coast, there are ten distilleries. The whiskies of the Northern Highlands have in general plenty of flavour, often with earthy, flowery or spicy tones. Some of the local peat has a crumbly character that imparts its own earthiness, and in the past that may have helped shape local palates. Some of the local water is hard, bestowing an unusual character to Scotch whisky, though it is prized by beer brewers – and there has always been some interplay between the two industries as economics have favoured one or the other. The sea air again plays its part, too.

In the world of whisky, this segment of the Highlands is not quite the most revered, but it has some excellent and individualistic malts, including one of the best known.

From the Northernmost village, John O'Groats, it is less than 20 miles to the first distillery: Pulteney, in the ancient town of Wick. This produces a very distinctive whisky, with an earthy, salty nose. The whisky, called Old Pulteney, has been compared to a Manzanilla, a character that must derive in part from its being aged in casks from that part of the world. The "Manzanilla of the North" is available as a bottled single malt at eight years old under the Gordon and MacPhail label. The distillery was founded in 1826 and sold in 1955 to Hiram Walker, who rebuilt it in 1959. Although it doesn't have tours, visitors are welcomed (this is often the case with Hiram Walker distilleries). The Wick area has a Neolithic burial chamber and several castles, and the town once imposed prohibition in its wild days as the gathering-place for itinerant crews of herring fishermen.

The fishing and golfing resort of Brora, 40-odd miles down the coast, has two distilleries side by side, both owned by D.C.L. One, simply called Brora, was founded in 1819, rebuilt by a firm of brewers in the 1890s, and closed indefinitely in the early 1980s. The distillery had in earlier times been called Clynelish, but that name is now used for its new neighbour, built in 1967. The D.C.L. subsidiary that operates Clynelish markets the whisky as a bottled single malt under the distillery label at 12 years old. It is a characterful whisky – very dry, earthy, spicy, with a hint of saltiness and a full body.

Where the coast curls inland to accommodate the Dornoch Firth, the Balblair Forest gives its name to a pretty, little distillery at Edderton. The Balblair distillery has its origins in the 1790s, but the present site dates from the 1870s, since when it has changed little. With its single malting tower (no longer used, sad to say), conservatory windows on its gables, and buildings that could belong to a farm, it sits in a hollow among fields full of sheep, with mountains behind. It belongs to Hiram Walker, and its whisky is sold as a bottled single malt under the Gordon and MacPhail label. It is a dry, delicately spicy whisky, with a slightly sharp finish.

Nearby, close to the pretty little town of Tain, is the Glenmorangie distillery, producing the best-known of the Northern Highland whiskies and the biggest-selling single malt in the Scottish market (in England, Glenfiddich has greater sales). Tain, a Royal Burgh since 1066, is one of several claimants to being the oldest town in Scotland. It has a population of only 4,000, some of whom work in the building of oil rigs several miles away in the Cromarty Firth, others of whom are in mixed farming or whisky. "The Sixteen Men of Tain" have been featured in handsome, woodcut illustrations in advertisements for Glenmorangie: Archie Murdoch the Mashman, Ken Murray the Brewer; Ian Macleod the Stillman; Stuart Thomson the Cooper, and so on. Tain is built from the mustard-coloured local sandstone, which is very durable, and through which flows the water from Glenmorangie's spring.

There is some argument about the pronunciation of Morangie. Sassenachs tend to

emphasise the last two syllables, as though it were something to do with a woman called Angie. Highlanders stress the "o", as in orange. Morangie as in "orangey". There is uncertainty, too, about the meaning of "Morangie" but the company translates it as "great tranquillity". Whisky-induced, no doubt.

The Glen of Great Tranquillity is just outside the town, running into the Dornoch Firth. From the road, the short private drive to the distillery passes between an assortment of trees and a dam shaped like a millpond; beyond can be seen the waters of the firth. It's a solid-looking stone building that could be an early woollen mill (and still retains a watermill), though the premises were a brewery until 1843, and much of the present exterior dates from 1887. The giveaway is the pagodas, though they have a flat, utilitarian shape that is less romantic than most.

Like many distilleries that have retained their pagodas out of a good instinct for conservation and for their image, Glenmorangie no longer does its own malting. The company buys malt from a number of sources, though it favours local barley, and it specifies only a light peating. This is one contributor to the character of the whisky,

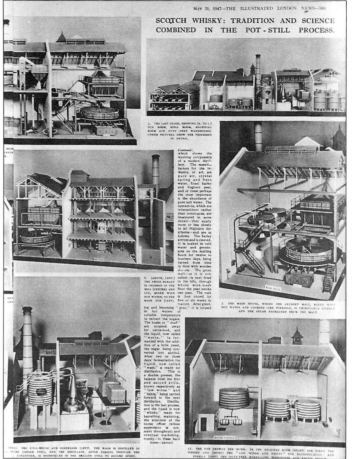

Balblair, a pretty and unassuming distillery (above), is set in Northerly but relatively gentle Highland countryside. It's a pastoral scene, hardly marred by the single-track railway that runs beside the distillery.

The millpond calm of Glenmorangie (facing page) fits the mood of a distillery that advertised by telling whisky lovers about the daily routines of its workers in the small town of Tain. The company also cherishes an article from the "Illustrated London News" of 1947 (right) . . . another exposition of the way in which whisky is made. Mashing (centre, right), distilling (bottom, left) and filling (bottom, right) are especially clearly shown.

and the hard water of Tain is another. Then there is the yeast. While many distillers feel that the use of both beer and whisky yeasts ensures the best fermentation, Glenmorangie opts for only the latter, in two pure cultures. Their house yeasts impart an estery character that may have something to do with the whisky's distinctive bouquet.

Glenmorangie's stills are the tallest in the Highlands, at 16ft.10¼in., to be precise, and the company makes much of this. It isn't a tall story – they do, of course, produce a very clean and rather light spirit. The distillery also ages all of its whisky in Bourbon barrels and makes a point of this, too. Others may favour the tradition of sherry, with the richness it imparts, but Glenmorangie opts without compromise for the softer, slightly vanilla tones of the New World.

It is a delightful and complex whisky of the lighter, drier type. It has a very pale colour (like a fino sherry, though that hardly seems an appropriate comparison). Its most individual characteristic, though, is its very flowery nose, followed by a light, dancing, dry palate (but with the sweet tones of the malt elusively in there somewhere). The finish is long and rounded. This is surely

more of an aperitif whisky than the digestif that the distillery suggests, but it would be a gentle delight on either occasion.

Glenmorangie is very unusual in that almost all of its output is sold as a bottled single malt – with the distillery label, at ten years old. The only proportion used for blending stays within the owning family firm of Macdonald and Muir, whose several subsidiaries produce a wide range of labels, the best known probably being the various Highland Queen whiskies. The company also owns the Glen Moray distillery, on Speyside.

On the same peninsula between the Dornoch and Cromarty Firths, there are a further five distilleries, one of which produces an outstanding whisky that deserves a far wider recognition. First down the road are the Ben Wyvis malt and Invergordon grain distilleries, sharing an ugly, modern complex. Ben Wyvis began distilling in 1965, and its whisky has as yet not been made available as a bottled single malt. It is owned by the Invergordon company, which is named after the town, an important port. Much of Invergordon's output goes into importers' own labels in other countries.

The outstanding single malt of the Dal-

more distillery is produced just down the road, near the village of Alness. Dalmore Highland Malt may be found under the distillery label at eight, more often 12, and occasionally 20 years old. It has a profound orange-marmalade colour, which perhaps predisposes the nose and palate to detect similar tones in the whisky. It certainly has a full, fruity aroma. It has a velvet-smooth dryness of palate and a very full body that is firm and malty without ever being sweet or sticky. Its finish is long, with a gently orangey bitter-sweet tone. An after-dinner whisky as noble as the greatest of Cognacs.

The Dalmore distillery is down a steep, wooded, winding lane, at the top of which are ruins of old warehouses. The distillery offices bear a passing resemblance to a country railway station. Inside, they are partly panelled with carved oak that once graced a shooting lodge. Behind lies the Cromarty Firth. Inland, the view is of the Ardross Forest, and of mountains rising to well over 2,000ft. On one of the closer hills is a mock-classical monument built to provide work for local people during the corn famine of the 1820s.

Beyond lies the loch that is the source of the Alness river, which in turn provides the

In the days when a diary was a record of the immediate past rather than a programme for the future, it left open a door through which we can still glimpse another world. At the Dalmore whisky distillery today, there is still a Mackenzie to open the diary of his grandfather, and to read of a world in which there was time each day to record even the weather, along with the smearing of hogs. In October 1867, Mr Mackenzie bought Dalmore. By January 1868, "samples of our new whisky pleased well".

water for the distillery. The water is soft and clean. The distillery buys in its malt, lightly peated. The fruitiness of the whisky must derive in part from the yeasts used, and its distinctive texture from stills of two unusual shapes. The wash stills have a narrow waist broadening into a neck that is shaped like a cone, narrowing to a flat top. The spirit stills have a reflux chamber shaped like a flask. It is also unusual that there are sets of stills in different sizes. The individualistic whisky that issues from them is largely aged in sherry butts, some used more than once.

The distillery is said to have been founded in 1839, and was acquired by a distinguished local family, the Mackenzies, in 1867. A diary recording, day by day and step by step, the Mackenzies' production of their first whisky, is still in the family's possession. It shows clearly and simply the role that the distilling of malt whisky played in local agriculture and commerce, and is a remarkable social document. The original Mackenzie's grandson still manages the distillery, though the family no longer own it. From their

earliest days in the business, the family were friendly with the merchant James Whyte, whose partnership with Charles Mackay created a famous name in whisky. Eventually, the companies merged as Dalmore, Whyte and Mackay. Subsequently, the whisky business became a part of Scottish and Universal Investments, under another famous Scottish name, Sir Hugh Fraser. Scottish and Universal became a part of Lonrho. In addition to Dalmore, the Tomintoul Glenlivet and Fettercairn distilleries are part of the Whyte and Mackay group. Their whiskies are thus among the components of the various Whyte and Mackay blends.

Also close to Alness is the Teaninich distillery, operated by a subsidiary of D.C.L. Teaninich was founded in 1817 but most of its present buildings were constructed in the 1970s. The stills can be seen, through large windows, from the road. The whisky, which is lightly peated, is used in R.H. Thomson blends like Robbie Burns, but merchants' bottlings can occasionally be found. The

distillery has not produced since 1985.

There is another D.C.L. distillery a few miles further South at Muir of Ord. This one was licensed to the Peter Dawson subsidiary but is now operated for Dewar's. The whisky is marketed as a bottled single malt at 12 years old under the name Glenordie. It is a slighly peaty, full-bodied whisky, with a dry, smooth finish, and is perilously drinkable. The distillery was founded in 1838, and has some old warehouses in the pinkish local stone but the modern still-house dates from only 1966. There are also open-sided barns full of peat on the site, which has modern Saladin and drum maltings.

In the distance behind the distillery are the mountains of the Northern Highlands. Immediately South is the Moray Firth, biting into the side of Scotland. The road winds round the Firth towards Inverness, and ahead lies Speyside, the world's greatest whisky-producing region. As whisky is a spirit, perhaps Speyside should be compared to Cognac, though in the variety of its products Bordeaux seems a closer parallel.

Speyside

The stretch of the river Spey that forms a broad valley, or "Strath", runs for 20-odd miles, and has as many distilleries. This one is Speyburn, producing a characterful whisky that is hard to find as a single malt.

The world's greatest whisky-making region, in the number of its distilleries, the diverse palates of their products, and arguably in quality, runs between Loch Ness (or, in close focus, the Moray Firth), the Grampian Mountains (better still, the Cairngorm range) and the North Sea. It spreads between the Highland cities of Inverness and Aberdeen. In this broadest interpretation, bounded by natural features, it is 80 miles across. Its principal centres of whisky production, the small towns of Elgin, Rothes, Dufftown and Keith, have a span of only 15 miles.

The mountains water this region with rivers like the Findhorn, the Lossie, the Spey and the Deveron, flowing North into the sea. That water, often rising in granite and flowing over peat, is the parent of the region's thoroughbred whiskies. The clean, mountain water picks up enough of the region's peat to impart the smokiness that is their particular characteristic. Often it is not considered necessary to peat the malt heavily as well. With light or medium peating, the malt's own character presents itself firmly. In addition to being smoky and firm, some of the region's classics also speak eloquently of maturation in sherry wood. Smoky, firm-bodied, with more than a hint of sherryish sweetness, they are the most complex of whiskies, and the most elegant.

Of the 100-odd malt distilleries in Scotland, more than 60 are in or around the region, and more than 50 are commonly agreed to belong to Speyside. By no means all of them are near the river, but a remarkable number are, and its valley is the backbone of the region. Hence the term Strathspey; strath is the Scottish word for a broad valley. Rising to the South and West of Cairn Gorm (4,084ft.), the Spey flows by Aviemore and Grantown as it approaches whisky country, and reaches the sea between Elgin and Buckie.

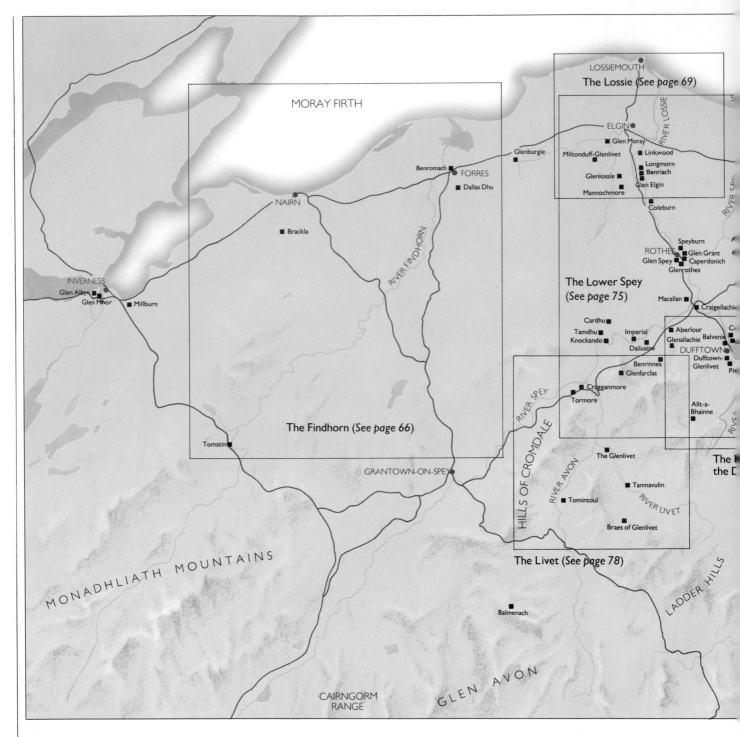

The Lossie (See page 69)

The Lower Spey (See page 75)

The Findhorn (See page 66)

The Livet (See page 78)

One of the Spey's tributaries is the small river Livet. The Glen of the Livet is the heart of whisky country. If Speyside is to be compared with Cognac, the appellation Glenlivet corresponds to Grande Champagne. About 20 distilleries use the appellation Glenlivet, or have done in recent years. All of them are close to the glen but only three or four can claim actually to be in it.

One of the gateways to Speyside, the city of Inverness, has three distilleries of its own, all belonging to D.C.L. Of these only one,

Millburn, has operated in recent years, and it temporarily ceased production in 1985. It produces a lovely whisky typical of the region: with a rich aroma; a smooth, dry, full body, with some fruitiness; and a long finish, with undertones of peat. Merchants' bottlings of this whisky can occasionally be found but it is not marketed by the company as a single malt. It is, though, a major component of a 12-year-old vatted malt called The Mill Burn, and of the Macleay Duff blends. Although it was founded in the

early 1800s, Millburn was rebuilt in 1876, and again in 1922, after a fire, and has been considerably modernised since. Glen Albyn, founded in 1846, rebuilt in 1884, and closed indefinitely in the early 1980s, produced a whisky with a light taste, faintly sweet, but with a bigger body than might be expected. Bottlings can be found, though the whisky was not marketed as a single malt by the company. Glen Mhor, built in 1892 and closed in the early 1980s, produced a light, sweet, nutty whisky that has been

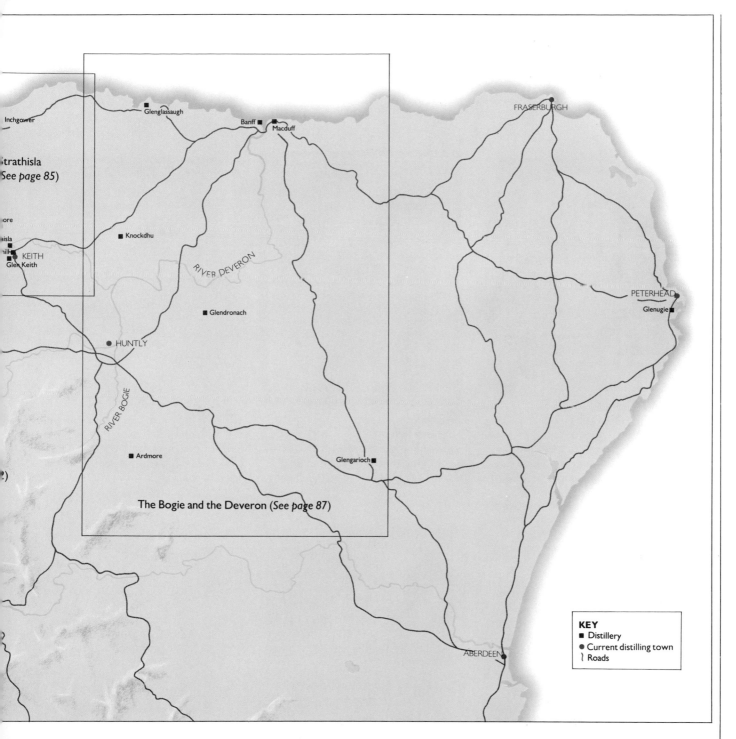

The Bogie and the Deveron (See page 87)

KEY
■ Distillery
● Current distilling town
⌇ Roads

bottled by Gordon and MacPhail.

Yet another D.C.L. distillery, producing an excellent whisky, lies just to the East of Inverness at Cawdor, on the way to Nairn. The Brackla distillery was founded in 1812, and has been permitted to style itself "Royal" since 1835 – because King William IV enjoyed the whisky. The distillery was rebuilt in 1898 and again in 1966, and extended in 1970, though it temporarily ceased production in 1985. Royal Brackla single malt whisky is occasionally bottled by merchants but is not marketed under the distillery label, though it does find its way into the Bisset blends. As a single malt, it is a perfect example of a Highlands Scotch whisky. It has just that complex balance of peaty smokiness and firm maltiness, but without any of its own eccentricities or flourishes. It has a big smoky-sweet nose, almost a hint of molasses; firm, slightly chewy, body; hints of fruitiness and peatiness in its palate; and a long, dry, peaty finish. A pleasant prelude to the symphonies from Speyside.

Flowing from South to North, the river Spey and tributaries like the Livet and the Dullan provide the axis of a broad region. In the South, the ranges of mountains adjoin; the valleys share a mild climate that no doubt helps, in aging, to create a Speyside character; the rivers flow to a single coastline that, from the Findhorn to the Deveron, arguably defines an imprecise region.

A taste-guide to Inverness area whiskies

Everywhere is the gateway to somewhere. Britain's Northernmost town of any size, and the overall "capital" of Scotland's Highlands, Inverness can say without irony, and with justifiable pride, that it is the natural Gateway to Speyside.

Millburn (one word and no article) is the track-side distillery that greets sleepy-eyed travellers as the night-train from London ends its eleven-hour journey in Inverness each morning. A rich, delicious single malt, but hard to find.

Glen Mhor is described on the label as being "rare". Such epithets come easily to label-writers, but this one is valid, since the distillery is closed. Bottlings can, though, be found of this enjoyably nutty single malt.

Glen Albyn is an elusive single malt: hard to find, and subtle in character. It has a light palate but a well-rounded body and a full finish. It is faintly sweet, with some smokiness.

The Mill Burn (two words, with article) is a vatted malt with the company label. It reminds drinkers of the single's rich aroma, full body, and long finish.

Royal Brackla is a good, big, after-dinner single malt, with a complex of peatiness, sweetness and fruit. It comes from a distillery in Nairn, East of Inverness. Regrettably, the whisky is hard to find.

Old Inverness is a local blended whisky from a wine and spirit merchant in the town. The company is called H. D. Wines. The whisky is very aromatic, perhaps with a hint of cloves, and quite full-bodied for a blend.

A taste-guide to Findhorn whiskies

Is the Findhorn river and valley the Western border of Speyside, or is it already in that classic sub-region of malt distillation? Speyside is not precisely delineated, except to say that it extends well beyond its own river valley, and is embraced on either side by parallel rivers flowing North to the same coastline.

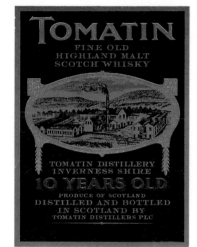

Tomatin is from Scotland's biggest malt distillery. Its output has to be welcomed in large quantities by many blenders. It has to be broad-shouldered, rather than idiosyncratic, but it is a pleasant "single".

Old St Andrews is named after the golf-course in Fife. However, this quality blended whisky is associated with Tomatin, and has the flavour of the Findhorn.

Glenburgie is a single malt with a distinctive palate almost reminiscent of bison-leaf vodka. Perhaps whisky-makers do not wish their product to be compared with vodka, but this is a delightful dram.

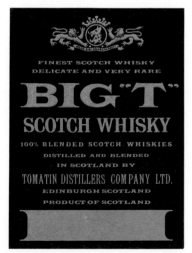

Big "T" identifies the Tomatin distillery rather than a Texas cattle-ranch. It is the brand-name of the house blended whisky of the Tomatin company. It is a clean, sweetish, medium-bodied blend.

Dallas Dhu has nothing to do with Texas. Its name has gaelic origins. This powerful, peaty whisky should be sampled while it lasts. The distillery is to become a museum.

Benromach is a subtle, flowery single malt, available only in merchants' bottlings. Historically, the distillery is associated with The Antiquary, a de luxe blend.

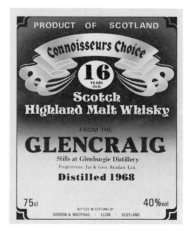

Glencraig has a positively exotic character. Were it easier to find as a bottled single malt, it would make an interesting after-dinner drink. It is produced in Lomond stills, as a second whisky, at Glenburgie.

Speyside ~ The Findhorn

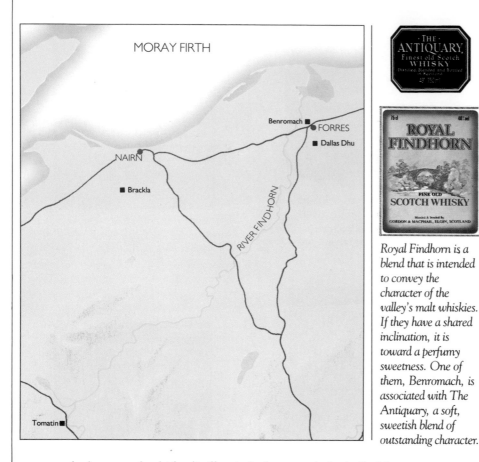

Royal Findhorn is a blend that is intended to convey the character of the valley's malt whiskies. If they have a shared inclination, it is toward a perfumy sweetness. One of them, Benromach, is associated with The Antiquary, a soft, sweetish blend of outstanding character.

The largest malt whisky distillery in Scotland is Tomatin, which has a production capacity approaching that at Suntory's Hakushu distillery, in Japan. With its 23 stills (oddly, one fewer than at Hakushu), Tomatin makes a remarkable sight, high in the foothills of the Monadhliath Mountains. At 1,028ft., it is, too, one of the highest distilleries in Scotland.

Tomatin, founded in 1897, was steadily extended during the 1950s and 1960s – boom years for Scotch whisky – and even into the 1970s. Because of its size, the distillery's fortunes are tied to those of the whole industry, and in the late 1970s and early 1980s it suffered accordingly. Malt whisky produced in such large volume has to be saleable in considerable quantities to blenders with big-selling brands. During

that period, the hall of the mountain spirits faced silence; the whole nation of Scotland had its own "whisky mountain". Tomatin was at the time a public company; at one stage 20 per cent of an enlarged capital was taken up by Heineken, the Dutch and international brewer (which also had distilling interests, in the production of *jenever* gin). Despite the involvement of such a powerful international drinks company, Tomatin went into liquidation in 1985. A sad condition for any company, not least one producing drink.

If the distillery were to be bought, Japan looked the most likely source of a buyer. Japan had long bought large quantities of Scotch whisky, both to retail as an import and to use in its own blends. Japanese companies had previously tried to buy distilleries in Scotland, though her atten-

tions had sometimes fallen foul of the patriotic sensibilities. Attitudes were perhaps a little different on this occasion.

At the time the Tomatin distillery became available for purchase, Japanese whisky-producers were themselves suffering from falling sales, due to competition from *shochu*, their own local spirit. Tomatin might have seemed a natural purchase for Suntory, but they already had sufficient capacity to produce high-volume malt. The distillery was, in due course, acquired by another Japanese company, Takara, Shuzo and Okura. They had long been substantial importers of Tomatin whisky but, ironically, their bigger business in Japan is in *shochu*.

Despite its role as a "filler", Tomatin is a most enjoyable whisky as a single malt, in which form it can be found at five, and more often ten, years old under the distillery label. It has never been a fashionable malt, but its previous proprietors were perhaps needlessly modest about it. Tomatin has a fresh, clean aroma and palate, and is an expressive whisky. There is a well-struck balance between light peatiness in the nose and finish and a sweet maltiness in the palate. For the drinker wanting to become familiar with the elements of Scotch whisky, this is a good one in which to taste the malt.

The same character is to some extent apparent in Tomatin's Big "T" blend at five years old. In the ten-year-old version of the blend, the malt seems to have rounded out and the peat to have emerged more strongly. The Tomatin whiskies have a definite character of Bourbon aging, though that is hardly reason to use a name like Big "T", a brand that might more happily sit on the hide of a steer or cow. (A related brand called Old St Andrew's sounds more Scottish, though it surely belongs to the Kingdom of Fife.)

The distillery is named after the nearby hamlet of Tomatin, which is about 15 miles South of Inverness. The name is pronounced T'matin, rhyming with satin, and in Gaelic means "hill of the bushes". It has been suggested that the name was inspired by juniper bushes, which are common in the Scottish moorlands, and which should have

The still-house at Tomatin is the biggest in Scotland and one of the largest in the world. Its malt is found in a great many blended Scotches.

made any visiting Dutch distiller feel at home. A Continental European might also note with satisfaction Tomatin's German-style, semi-lauter, mash-tun, the first to be installed in a Scotch whisky distillery.

As well as being Scotland's largest malt distillery, Tomatin has also been one of the most innovative. The whole still-house can be run by two workers, and the distillery's penchant for technical development has led throughout to savings in both labour and energy. At times, the warm water exhausted from the condensers has been used as a medium in which to farm eels and trout. The distillery buildings, in pebbledash and iron, are less interesting, despite their grand setting.

Tomatin's distillery water comes from a burn that rises in granite on the Monadhliath Mountains and picks up a light peatiness before flowing into the Findhorn. The river itself wanders on through some fine beef country before reaching the coast at Findhorn Bay, just West of Forres, the town mentioned in Macbeth as the site of King Duncan's court. The area has also become known in the present day as the home of the Findhorn Foundation. This might be described as an alternative spiritual community, though not of the kind concerned with distillation. There are, however, two distilleries at Forres and one just to the East of the town.

At Forres, the distillery of Dallas Dhu (which might sound American, but derives from the Gaelic for "black water valley") was built in 1899 and reconstructed in 1939. It has not distilled since the early 1980s, and is being converted into a museum by the Historic Buildings Department of Scotland. The distillery was operated by Benmore, a D.C.L. subsidiary. Benmore has several blends and a vatted malt. The Dallas Dhu single malt has been marketed by its proprietors as Dallas Mhor and under its own name by merchants. It has a full, peaty nose: a rich palate, with an underlying malty sweetness; and a dry, aromatic, peaty finish. It is a big whisky, with a powerful resonance in that counterpoint between peatiness and maltiness. The other Forres distillery is D.C.L.'s Benromach. This was built in 1898 and underwent reconstruction in 1966 and 1974. Its whisky as a single malt is found only in merchants' bottlings. It has a lovely, perfumy, slightly sweet bouquet; a flowery palate; and a long, emphatically dry finish. A subtle and characterful whisky.

Also in the neighbourhood of Forres, to the East at Alves, is the Glenburgie distillery. A distillery was founded on this site in 1829, subsequently fell into disuse, was revived in 1878, acquired by Hiram Walker in 1930 and extended in 1958, with the addition of two of the company's favoured Lomond stills. Its single malts have appeared in a number of bottlings. The original, conventionally-shaped, stills produce a whisky with a distinctive nose (sweet, grassy, almost bison-leaf); a light, dancing palate; and a dry, crisp finish. The whisky from the Lomond stills was in their first decade or so separately identified by the name Glencraig. It has a similar character, but with an even more exotic aroma (guava?); a firmer, oilier body; and a long, dry finish.

The distillery suffixes itself Glenlivet. Among those that do, it is one of the farthest from the glen, but its whiskies are delightful all the same.

Speyside ~ *The Lossie*

It may be one of the shorter rivers in the region but the Lossie flows through some of the most fertile barley-growing country in Scotland, has on its banks the elegant market town of Elgin (an important centre for the bottling of single malt whiskies) and boasts nine distilleries within its hinterland. Such a concentration of distilleries is not unique in this part of the country – there are another three or four similar clusters – but the Lossie and Elgin area is the first to confront many travellers on one of the main approaches to Speyside, from the South and West. For the whisky-lover, it is in more senses than one a potentially dizzying encounter, even though none of the distilleries in the Lossie area is among the very best-known names.

To the South and West of Elgin is one of the better-known, Miltonduff-Glenlivet. This distillery produces a bottled single malt under its own name, but in hyphenated form: Milton-Duff Glenlivet. It's an aromatic, smooth malt, with the delicacy of palate that is often found among the lightest of "Glen" whiskies. Though the appellation may in this respect seem fair enough, Miltonduff is about 20 miles from the Livet.

The Miltonduff site was "almost certainly" that of an illicit still, according to the whisky writer Philip Morrice, who believes many of the original features were then incorporated into the legal distillery of 1824. The distillery was drastically modernised in the 1930s and again in the 1970s. It is owned by Hiram Walker, and has in addition to its conventional stills a couple of their Lomond type, the product of which has on occasion been bottled separately under the name Mosstowie. While there are a number of Hiram Walker distilleries that have both conventional and Lomond stills, the difference between their products seems especially pronounced in this instance. As might be expected, the Mosstowie whisky is much bigger, but it also has a very assertive, expressive palate. In its bone-dry aroma there is a great deal of smokiness, which returns to a lesser degree in the finish.

The only other distillery on this West side of the river Lossie is Glen Moray, which also uses the suffix Glenlivet. This, again, is one of the lightest "Glen" whiskies, with a very fresh aroma and palate, and a notably pale colour. It can be found as a bottled single malt under the distillery label at eight, ten and more often 12 years old.

Converted from a brewery in 1897, the distillery still has a steam engine. It was extended in 1958, and in its ownership is a sister distillery to the better-known Glenmorangie, in the Northern Highlands. Glen Moray has in the market place become something of a companion label, perhaps a junior one, to Glenmorangie. It stands therefore to become better known with the success of the company in the marketing of bottled single malts.

To the East of the Lossie, the distillery farthest up river is Coleburn, which is licensed to J. and G. Stewart, the D.C.L. subsidiary that owns the Andrew Usher label. The Coleburn whisky can occasionally be found in merchants' bottlings. It has a light bouquet and a flowery, pleasantly oily palate, with a rather weak finish. The distillery was built in 1896, and seems to have had an uneventful history until its temporary closure in 1985. Close by is another D.C.L. distillery, operated by the White Horse subsidiary. This one, Glen Elgin, produces a flavourful whisky, with a fruity, sweetish palate, a smooth body and some smokiness in the finish. Glen Elgin is marketed as a bottled single malt at 12 years old under the distillery label. The distillery was built in 1898 and reconstructed in 1964.

Another pair next door to each other are Glenlossie and Mannochmore, both operated for D.C.L.'s Haig subsidiary. Glenlossie was built in 1876, reconstructed in 1896 and extended in 1962. It produces a malt whisky prized by blenders but, sad to say, not marketed under the distillery label. However, merchants' bottlings can be found. Glenlossie has a full, fruity nose; a light, spirity palate; and a long, dry, aromatic finish. Mannochmore was built relatively recently, in 1971, and closed temporarily in 1985, without its whisky having been bottled as a malt.

It is not unusual for distilleries to be built relatively very close to one another. If the available water suits one distillery, it may also accommodate another. The same is true of other resources, the skills of local labour, and access. In times of prosperity in the industry, proprietors have often augmented a successful distillery by building next door.

Yet another pair, built in the 1890s, long associated with each other, and now owned by Seagram's through its subsidiary The Glenlivet Distillers, are Longmorn and Benriach. Both were extended in the 1970s, though neither is wholly modern. Longmorn has a water-wheel and a steam engine, and Benriach has a floor maltings.

Longmorn's whisky is much appreciated by lovers of single malts, and in recent years has become more readily available, especi-

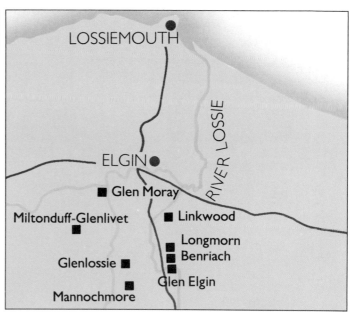

Since these pictures were taken, some modernisations have been carried out at Gordon and MacPhail's shop in Elgin, but it is still a family business, with its own warehouses for the maturation of whisky. The founding families employed a Mr Urquhart, who succeeded them as owner. The second and third generations of his family now run the business.

ally in a 15-year-old, 43 per cent, version, under the distillery label. It has a full aroma and body; a fresh, assertive palate; and a nutty, dry finish. Longmorn is in demand by blenders, as is Benriach, the latter especially for its ability to mature quickly. For that reason, it is harder to find as a single malt, though there have been bottlings by merchants. Benriach's whisky has a dry nose, a malty palate and a big, sweet finish.

The farthest down river of the Lossie distilleries is Linkwood, producing a whisky greatly admired both by blenders and drinkers. Linkwood is one of the smokiest Speyside malts, in both its palate and its long finish, with a big, assertive, malty body. It is marketed as a bottled single malt under the distillery label at 12 years old. Linkwood is owned by D.C.L. through one of its less well-known subsidiaries, John McEwan, whose blends include Abbot's Choice and Chequers. The distillery was founded in 1824, and rebuilt in 1872, 1962 and 1971. Despite its growth, it has a proud tradition. Philip Morrice recalls that at one stage the management forbade even the removal of spiders' webs in case a change in the environment should affect the whisky.

The rarer Lossie malts: smoky, assertive Mosstowie; and dry-and-sweet Benriach.

69

A taste-guide to Lossie whiskies

In the valley of the river Lossie stands the town of Elgin, an important centre for the malt-whisky industry. Elgin bottles a great many "singles", and is the principal market town and trading centre for the whole of Speyside. The immediate area is dotted with distilleries, including several distinguished names.

Linkwood is by general agreement one of the classic Speyside malts – in its smokiness, elegance, balancing sweetness and full body. The associated D.C.L. brand, Abbot's Choice, is an important blend in some markets.

Glenlossie is not easy to find, but it is a single malt well worth seeking out. It has a full, sweet, fruity nose; a light and softly spirity palate; and a long, dry, aromatic finish.

Coleburn is a light, flowery and pleasantly oily single malt that is hard to find. Its associated brand, Usher's Green Stripe, is an important blended whisky in many international markets, including the U.S.

Glen Moray is from a single malt distillery owned by the same company as the similar-sounding, and better known, Glenmorangie. The "junior partner" is fresh and light, with a pleasantly clean maltiness of palate.

Milton-Duff is much closer to the Lossie than to the Livet, but it is no less a single malt for that. This aromatic whisky, with its light-to-medium palate and delicate finish, is an excellent malt in its own right.

Longmorn is a nutty, complex single malt that used to identify itself as a Glenlivet, but is now ceasing to do so. Despite Longmorn's bigger body, it is not a thousand miles from its sister product The Glenlivet.

Glen Elgin is a single malt from a distillery in the White Horse group of D.C.L. The Elgin malt is smooth, with a heather-honey sweetness and a powerfully balancing smokiness. A good, solid, typical Speyside malt.

Speyside – *The Upper Spey*

Both the quality and romance of Scotch whisky depend upon mountains, rocky streams, peat moors and fresh air, so it is hardly surprising that many distilleries like to regard their locations as being remote. Few though, are as remote as Dalwhinnie, at 1,073ft above sea level, in a high glen, with the Monadhliath Mountains to one side, the Forest of Atholl, the Cairngorms and the Grampians to the other.

Dalwhinnie is Gaelic for "meeting place", and it stands at the junction of old cattle-droving routes from the West and the North down to the Central Lowlands. Clan armies have clashed there, and much whisky smuggling has passed along the route. There is peat in the moors, and pure water in the small, mountain lochs. To the South is a large stretch of water, Loch Ericht; passing in front of the distillery and flowing North, the river Truim is one of several that feed the Spey. At a stretch, Dalwhinnie is a Speyside distillery, though it is 25 miles or more from the beginning of dense distillery country to the North.

The Dalwhinnie distillery was called Strathspey when it opened in 1897. It was badly damaged by fire in 1934, reopened in 1938, and is operated for the D.C.L. subsidiary that produces the James Buchanan blends. There have been various bottlings of Dalwhinnie as a single malt, and it is a most enjoyable whisky. As might be expected, it has a decidedly peaty, Highland character, especially in its powerful nose, and to a lesser extent in its dry finish. It is big-bodied, very smooth and full of flavour.

A good 25 miles down the road is the village of Aviemore, Scotland's main centre for skiing, with facilities for ice-skating and curling. In the fullness of time, Aviemore stands also to become known as a centre for the sampling of malt whiskies. Since the beginning of the 1980s, it has been the home of the Cairngorm Whisky Centre and Museum (tel 0479-810574), which has its own shop and tasting-room and mounts a festival for a week each November. The centre also operates guided walks, farm tours

and trout-fishing. Aviemore also has the rock of Craigellachie, remembered in the "Stand Fast!" war cry of the Clan Grant. However, neither the Craigellachie distillery nor those of any of the Grants, are especially nearby.

The nearest distillery is a further 15 miles or so down the road, beyond Grantown-on-Spey, and in the stretch of land known as the Haughs of Cromdale. The Haughs are a series of valleys, forming a ribbed plain, irrigated by seven or eight small rivers that flow in parallel series into the Spey from the Cromdale Hills. This area was well-known for the illicit production of whisky before distilling was legalised in the Highlands. The distillery at Cromdale that was licensed to James Macgregor in 1824 was one of the first in the Highlands to become legitimate. In the year of its being made legal, it already had a reputation far and wide for the quality of its whisky, according to Mr Macgregor's great-grandson Sir Robert Bruce Lockhart, in his warmly entertaining book "Scotch". Sir Robert was better known for more distant essays in his "Memoirs of a British Agent", among his baker's dozen books, but his thoughts seem never to have been far from Scotland. In "Scotch", he devoted a chapter to his family connection with the Macgregors' Balmenach distillery at Cromdale. The distillery, which has been modernised over the years, is now operated by the D.C.L. subsidiary that produces the Crabbie blends. There have been merchants' bottlings of the Balmenach whisky as a single malt. It has a big, perfumy nose; a dry, clean, flowery body, with a blossomy palate; and a lightly fruity finish.

The Spey reaches the heart of whisky country when, after miles with barely a building, there is suddenly the sight of the remarkably elegant Tormore distillery, near Advie. With its ornamental curling lake and fountains; its pristine, white buildings, decorative dormer windows, belfry and musical clock; its topiary, and the huge hill of dense firs forming a backdrop; Tormore might be a spa, offering a cure of mountain water and piney air. Instead, it offers the

water of life, *uisge beatha*. When was it built? Perhaps the mid 1800s, or the turn of the century? No, it was erected in 1958, as a showpiece for Scotch whisky. Tormore was designed by Sir Albert Richardson, a past President of the Royal Academy, and built by Long John Distillers. It was the first completely new malt distillery to be built in the Highlands in the twentieth century, though several others were opened during the prosperous years of the late 1950s and early 1960s. Tormore's whisky is bottled under the distillery label as a single malt at ten years old. It is an excellent whisky, with almondy notes in the aroma and palate, smooth and firm but not at all heavy, with a long finish.

Near the point where the Spey accommodates the Avon (into which has already flowed the Livet), is the distillery of Cragganmore, producing a whisky held in high esteem by blenders. Cragganmore's whisky has a dry aroma; a very firm, malty, palate; and a smoky finish. An austere, haughty whisky that can sometimes be found as a 12-year-old single malt under the distillery label. Cragganmore is operated by the D.C.L. subsidiary that produces the McCallum blends. The distillery was founded in 1869, rebuilt in 1902 and extended in 1964.

From this point on, the distilleries come thick and fast.

The "strath" of the Spey embraces parts of both the upper and lower stretches of the river. The whole valley is honoured in this vatted malt: clean, elegant and medium-bodied. The label shows a landmark on the lower Spey, at Craigellachie. The bridge was designed by the great Scottish engineer Thomas Telford.

A taste-guide to Upper and Lower Spey whiskies

The river Spey rises amid the mountains, on the roof of Scotland. The upper reaches of the river have only a handful of distilleries. As the Spey descends towards the sea, there are suddenly distilleries at every bend. The Lower Spey is not commonly defined as a district, but there are more malt whiskies here than anywhere else.

The Upper Spey

Dalwhinnie is an aromatic and dry single malt, with a firm body. The different bottlings that have found their way on to the market over the years have varied somewhat, no doubt due to age and the wood used.

Balmenach is an aromatic and flowery single malt from a very old distillery with an interesting history. Its associate blended whisky is from the firm of John Crabbie, also known for its green ginger "wine".

Tormore is a single malt from the most elegant distillery in Scotland. It is a distinctive whisky, with light almondy notes and a medium body. It is not far from the Livet in either miles or style.

Cragganmore is a haughty single malt, with a smoky character. A good Highland whisky, well regarded by blenders. Its own associate blends, the McCallum's, are especially popular in Australasia.

The Lower Spey

Glenfarclas, at its various ages, is one of Scotland's greatest malts. It would be the obvious classic of the Lower Spey if it did not have to compete in this regard with The Macallan. Two big, sherryish malts.

Cardhu is being marketed as its principal single malt by Johnnie Walker, the D.C.L. subsidiary. It is clearly hoped that Cardhu's light-to-medium weight and gentle sweetness will please a broad market.

The Singleton of Auchroisk has a velvety smoothness and a great deal of finesse. It has notes of smokiness and fruitiness, but a lightly sherryish character eventually wins through.

The Macallan, as it likes to be called, is one of Scotland's great single malts, and the favourite of many whisky lovers. Famous for its big body, "Calvados" tones and – especially – its sherry finish.

Glen Grant is the Rothes classic. It has been available as a bottled single malt for many years, and can be found in a variety of ages. It is a light, dry whisky, with hints of hazelnut in its complex character.

Tamdhu is a delicate, soft, rounded single malt. It has hints of smokiness, but its final accent is toward sweetness. A typically Livet-leaning Speyside malt of excellent quality.

Glenallachie is an elegant single malt, aromatic, complex, on the light side, but with a beautifully sustained finish. It is one of those Spey malts that lean toward the Livet in their light complexity.

Knockando is, despite its comical-sounding name, a very serious single malt. It has a light-to-medium body and nutty palate (one taster mentioned sugared almonds). A malt that gains a lot of character with age.

Inchgower is at the lowest part of the Spey: its bay. This is enough to qualify it as a Speyside single malt. It has peat, malt, and perhaps some sea-salt, in its distinctive, assertive character.

Glen Spey is an aromatic single malt with a smooth palate and a light-to-medium body. Although the distillery is old-established, the whisky has not been available for long as a single malt.

Aberlour is a single malt in a rich, rounded, after-dinner style. The distillery is under French ownership, and the whisky is popular in its adoptive country. The Auld Alliance could cause furrowed brows in Cognac.

Glentauchers is a very pleasant single malt either before or after dinner, but is perhaps at its best as a digestif, with its fruitiness of both aroma and palate, balanced by a dry finish.

Speyside – The Lower Spey

On the main road along the East side of the Spey valley, the Glenfarclas distillery stands beneath Ben Rinnes (2,759ft), whence its water flows. Geographically, it might claim to occupy the commanding heights of Strathspey and, with the growth of interest in bottled single malt whiskies, it has emerged as one of the most respected and prominent producers. The whiskies of Glenfarclas have a rich, sherryish aroma; a big, fruity palate; and a long, mellow finish. They are available as bottled single malts under the distillery label at a variety of ages from eight to the much-enjoyed 15, and even 25, and at several strengths, from the conventional 40 per cent to a potent 60. They tend to feature among the ten or a dozen favourites of most malt lovers.

The distillery is one of the few licensed to sell whisky on the premises, and it welcomes visitors. The reception room is decorated with panelling from an ocean liner, and there are on display a number of items of historical interest to the whisky-buff. Although some of the buildings date from the mid 1800s, Glenfarclas no longer has its own maltings, and its tun-room and still-house are very modern, as is much of the plant. The stills, the largest on Speyside, are replicas of the originals.

What started as a farm distillery in 1836 was acquired in 1865 by its present owning family, John and George Grant. They are proud of the Glenfarclas herd of Aberdeen Angus pedigrees, as well as their distillery – and of their independence. The firm has no connection with the several other companies called Grant in the whisky business, though family relationships could no doubt be traced.

Down this stretch of the Spey, on both sides of the river, are some of the most famous names in malt whisky. On the same side as Glenfarclas are Dailuaine, Benrinnes, Glenallachie, and Aberlour. Then comes the village and distillery of Craigellachie, the river skirts Rothes, and near Mulben are the distilleries of Glentauchers and Auchroisk. On the coast in Spey Bay is Inchgower. On the West side of the Spey are Knockando and Tamdhu, Cardhu and Imperial, then Macallan – perhaps the most revered of them all – and the five distilleries of Rothes.

Dailuaine, founded in 1852 and rebuilt several times, most recently in 1960, is operated by the D.C.L. subsidiary Scottish Malt Distillers. It has a long association with D.C.L.'s Talisker distillery on Skye, which suggests that its whisky might find its way into the Johnnie Walker blends. The whisky – which is fruity, with a full palate and a crisp finish – is not generally bottled.

Benrinnes has an unusual system of production which largely, but not completely, uses a triple-distillation method. Unlike the Lowland triple-distillation system, this hybrid arrangement produces quite an intense spirit – Benrinnes has an uncompromisingly Highland character. The whisky has a smoky nose and palate; a big, pleasantly oily body; and a powerful, dry finish. It is a whisky of character, much respected by blenders, though available as a single malt only in merchants' bottlings. The distillery may have been founded as early as the 1820s, but its more definite history begins in the 1860s and it was rebuilt in 1956. It is operated by the D.C.L. subsidiary that produces the Crawford blends.

Glenallachie is a subtle and delicate whisky very much in the "Glen" style. It has an aromatic, smoky nose; a light, perfumy, faintly oily palate; and a surprisingly firm, long finish. The whisky can sometimes be found as a bottled single malt under the distillery name, though the lion's share goes into the Mackinlay blends. Glenallachie is a modern distillery, dating from only 1967, and is somewhat utilitarian in appearance.

Aberlour, founded in 1826 and rebuilt a couple of times in the late 1800s, still has much of its Victorian exterior, despite a refit in 1973. The distillery is one of two in Scotland (the other being the tiny Edradour) that are controlled by Pernod Ricard, the French-based, international drinks company. The Aberlour whisky is marketed under the distillery label at 12 years old. It has a full, rich aroma; a rounded, fruity palate; and a clean finish. A pleasant after-dinner whisky. The group has a considerable range of blends: full-bodied and sweet under the White Heather label; the full-bodied and drier King's Ransom; light-bodied and sweet House of Lords; light-bodied and drier Clan Campbell; and several others.

Craigellachie, founded in 1891 and rebuilt in 1965, is operated by the D.C.L. distillery that produces White Horse whisky. Craigellachie's whisky as a single malt can be found only occasionally, in merchants' bottlings. It is a big, fruity malt. Beyond Craigellachie, the main road swings away from the Spey, through the Rosarie Forest to Mulben, on the way to Keith. In the Mulben area there are two distilleries. One of them, founded in 1898 and rebuilt in 1965, is Glentauchers, operated for the D.C.L. subsidiary that produces the Buchanan blends. Glentauchers whisky can occasionally be found under the distillery label or in merchants' bottlings as a single malt. It has a pronounced fruitiness in both its fragrance and its palate, and a dry finish. A very pleasant after-dinner whisky. The distillery closed temporarily in 1985.

The other distillery at Mulben, Auchroisk, was opened as recently as 1974, by I.D.V., and is operated by their subsidiary Justerini and Brooks ("J&B"). With its steeply-pitched roofs leaning into the moorland, the Auchroisk distillery is a handsome and innovative building that has won several architectural awards and one from the Angling Foundation "for not incommoding the passing salmon", as Derek Cooper politely puts it in his "The Whisky Roads of Scotland". Its whisky, first made available as a single malt in 1986, has a medium-to-full body, a sherryish sweetness, and a great deal of finesse. It has the contrived name The Singleton of Auchroisk. "Singleton" is meant to suggest straight malt. "Auchroisk" was thought too difficult a name to stand alone.

About 20 winding miles down this particular whisky road, the Spey flows into the bay that bears its name and, near Buckie, the distillery of Inchgower stands alone. Although this is some distance from the rest of the Speyside distilleries, it was once an area noted for illicit distilling. Inchgower was established in 1871 and is now owned by Bell's. Its whisky is sold as a bottled single malt under the distillery label at 12 years old. It is a big whisky, with a peaty nose, assertive palate, and powerful finish.

Justerini and Brooks, again, has a distillery on the West side of the Spey, at Knockando. This might seem a comical name, but it is said to be derived from the Gaelic for "the little black hillock". (There is some academic dispute, though, about the derivation.) The distillery was built in 1898 and reconstructed in 1969. The whisky is bottled as a single malt under the distillery label, at a number of ages, with the dates of production and distilling separately indicated. Because it is very light for Speyside, it is not always given credit for having a considerable character, but it is an especially smooth whisky, with subtle, nutty tones in the finish.

Close to Knockando is Tamdhu, producing a soft, rounded whisky, with a smoky nose and a gently sweetish finish. Tamdhu is marketed under its own label by its proprietors, Highland Distilleries. The Tamdhu distillery was founded in 1896 and largely rebuilt in the 1970s. At the entrance to the distillery, the disused railway station has been turned into a reception centre for visitors.

Just down the road from Knockando and Tamdhu is Cardow, home of Cardhu whisky. This is a light-to-medium malt in aroma and body, with a sweetish palate and finish. It is one of those malts that are relatively easy on the palate of the uninitiated, and is widely marketed, at 12 years old, by its parent, the Johnnie Walker subsidiary of D.C.L.

D.C.L. has another distillery, closer to the river, at Carron. This distillery, called Imperial, produces a whisky with the unusual combination of a sweetish aroma and a smoky palate. The whisky is not generally available as a single malt, but it has occa-

Glenfarclas is an increasingly popular malt, and one that has always been well respected. It signs itself with a flourish and the customary reminder of its great age, though the disillery itself has been much modernised.

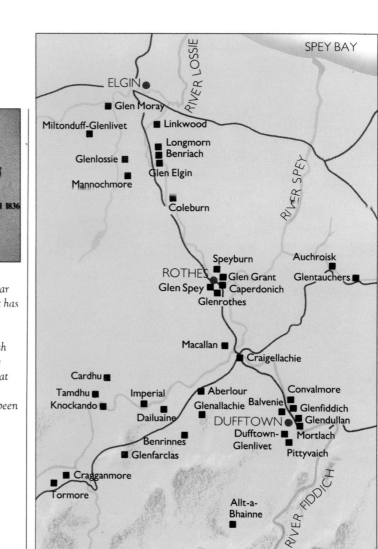

sionally been bottled by merchants. It has nothing to do with one or two blends called Imperial that have been introduced to the market at different times by unrelated companies. Like most malt, that from Imperial no doubt finds its way into many blends, perhaps again including Johnnie Walker. The distillery has family links with Dailuaine and Talisker. It closed temporarily in 1985.

Two or three miles down the river is Macallan, one of the great distilleries of Speyside. Macallan was for many years a "cult" whisky known only to devotees of single malts but in the 1980s the company began to acknowledge its own status in a series of small, monochrome Press advertisements that feigned modest embarrassment at the product's success. These advertise-

ments, with thumbnail cartoons by well-known illustrators, affected a ponderous prose style, and referred to the whisky as *The Macallan*, perhaps to distinguish the distillery label from merchants' bottlings of the distillery's whisky, which do not have the definite article.

As the whisky was more enthusiastically marketed, it began to challenge Glenmorangie's title as the biggest selling malt within Scotland. The Macallan at 17 years old came top in a blind-tasting held in the mid 1980s by the "Sunday Times" of London, and repeated the performance in the hands of Americans soon afterwards. That event, described as New York City's first comparative tasting of single malts, took place at Keens, the famous old bar and

GLENALLACHIE DISTILLERY

Not every distillery has a rustic beauty, though the utilitarian style of Glenallachie is softened by its dam. The famous Glen Grant distillery is among the five tucked away in the town of Rothes (right). Huddled in its glen, where the Rothes burn looks for the Spey, this little town might escape notice, and slumber like some alcoholic Brigadoon – were it not for the signal of steam. A plume of steam is one of the signs of a distillery. As the stills drive off their own alcoholic vapour, it has to be cooled back to condensation. The cooling waters of the condenser are a prime producer of steam. In modern times, though, it may also issue from a "dark grains" plant. This dries the spent grain that has been left behind in the mash-tun of a distillery. The dried grain is used as cattle feed. Happy herds are a by-product of whisky-making (and of beer-brewing); excellent milk and best Scottish beef.

chop-house near Herald Square. The Macallan, in fact, featured twice in the list, its 12-year-old version being rated ninth among the 22 malts to be found in the city at that time. The judges included such experienced palates as Harriet Lembeck, of "Grossman's Guide", and Robert Lawrence Balzer, of the "Los Angeles Times".

The Macallan has been bottled in small quantities at 50 years old, and a number of dated editions have been issued to mark especially good "vintages". It is more readily available at 25, 18, 12 (especially in international markets), ten (popular in Britain) and eight (in Southern Europe) years old. Those who claim that The Macallan has reminders of Calvados in its palate find that characteristic especially in the 18-year-old. When the Soviet leader Nikita Kruschev visited London, he was served with The Macallan as an alternative to Cognac at a dinner in his honour.

Debates about the best ages of The Macallan, and allusions to other drinks, are based on a firm foundation. So is the insistence about the definite article, however derivative that literary flourish might be. The Macallan, under the distillery label, is entirely aged in sherry. It is the only bottled single malt that, at all ages, offers that guarantee. In that respect, it is a most traditional Scotch whisky, and the pronounced sherry aroma and finish are two of its defining characteristics.

Since the shipping of sherry in the wood has declined, Macallan has made a special arrangement to ensure supplies. The company buys its own new butts in Spain, and has them filled for two season's fermentations of sherry. After these fermentations, from September to February, the butts serve two years in the solera system before being shipped to Scotland. Although fino, manzanilla and amontillado butts have played their part, oloroso is the principal sherry wood used. The butts are sometimes used only once for whisky, and never more than twice, though that might already represent

25 or 50 years.

Apart from its sherry character, The Macallan is notable for its dryness. It contrives somehow to be simultaneously rich and dry. The richness comes in part from the use of very small stills. They are the smallest on Speyside, and Macallan has insisted that "small is beautiful", building three such still-houses to cope with growing demand. Small stills make for a big-bodied whisky, but in this instance one that is also very firm. That firmness perhaps has a drying effect. So does the peatiness, which is definite but restrained.

Macallan no longer does its own malting, and most of the distillery buildings are modern. It does, however, have its own farm, on which a 1700s house has been restored as a reception centre for invited guests. The distillery is believed to have been founded in 1824, and has been controlled by the same family since 1892, though it does have a stock market quotation. It is the subject of takeover speculation from time to time.

The rarer Lower Spey malts: Dailuaine is a fruity, full whisky; Caperdonich is also fruity and fragrant, with a smoky finish; Imperial is smoky, sweetish and very rich; Speyburn has a heathery aroma, a malty palate, and notes of honey in the finish.

Finally, on the West side of the river, there is Rothes, with its five distilleries. Rothes is a one-street town. It is possible, just, to stand in the middle of that street without seeing a single distillery, because most of them are tucked off the road.

In Rothes, D.C.L. owns the Speyburn distillery, through the company that produces the Robertson blends. The Speyburn whisky as a single malt may occasionally be found in merchants' bottlings. It has a heathery bouquet and a big, malty palate, with a sweetish finish. Speyburn was built in 1897, and is one of the most handsome old distilleries.

Highland Distilleries own Glenrothes, which was built in 1878 and enlarged in 1963 and 1980. Its whisky, prized by blenders, is bottled as a single malt under the distillery label, at eight years old. It has an emphatically fruity nose; a well-rounded body; and a dry finish. A pleasant digestif.

Although they are now a part of I.D.V., the London wine merchants Gilbey's were

an independent company in 1887 when they observed the potential of Scotch whisky and bought the Glen Spey distillery in Rothes. The distillery had existed for only two or three years at that time, and has prospered ever since. It was, however, completely rebuilt in 1970. Its notably fragrant whisky, light and smooth, is bottled under the distillery name at eight years old. It also contributes to Strathspey Vatted Malt and a pleasant blend called Spey Royal.

Seagram's own two distilleries in Rothes. One of them, Caperdonich, founded in 1898, was rebuilt in 1965 and extended in 1967. Its whisky is not sold as a single malt under the distillery label, but merchants' bottlings can be found. It has a light bouquet, a very fruity palate, and a long finish. Caperdonich has from its beginnings been the Number Two distillery for Glen Grant, which is just across the road.

Glen Grant is highly-rated by blenders and is popular as a bottled single malt. It is marketed under the distillery label in a wide

range of ages, up to 25 years. However, an even greater array – about a dozen versions – are bottled by the merchants Gordon and MacPhail, and these on occasion go up to 50 years, with some aged exclusively in sherry wood. Glen Grant is one of Gordon and MacPhail's favourites. It, too, has a light bouquet, but with elusive, herby tones that some tasters have described as "hazelnut".

Glen Grant was founded in 1840 and some of the original buildings remain. The distillery is set around a small courtyard, with turreted and gabled office buildings in the "Scottish baronial" style, probably dating from the 1880s. It is a quirky place, traditional in style despite expansions in the 1970s. Pine fermentation vessels are used, and the stills have bulbous, irregular shapes. The older stills are coal-fired. The newer ones, dating from 1977, may be returned to coal, though they were installed with gas heating. Unlike the other distilleries in Rothes, Glen Grant has facilities for tours of its premises.

Speyside – *The Livet*

For lovers of elegant whiskies, the search for the holy grail narrows itself down as follows: within the nation of Scotland, the largest number of famous distilleries is in the broad sweep of the Highlands; in that half of the country, the greatest concentration is beside the river Spey and its neighbouring valleys (the broad *straths* and high-sided *glens*); within that region, the most famous district is that around the Livet.

The Livet is a river, little more than a creek, that flows first into the Avon and then into the Spey. From the heart of whisky country, the lower part of the glen of the Livet is broad and grassy, but it quickly rises to the South in forest and moorland, on the fringes of the Grampian mountains. Up the glen are passes through the mountains, and by these routes whisky was, in the days of illicit distilling, smuggled to the more populous Central Lowlands of Scotland, to entrepôt cities like Dundee and Perth. Whisky "from Glenlivet" no doubt enjoyed a cachet farther South. There are said to have been a couple of hundred illicit stills in the wild, mountain country around the glen in the late 1700s and early 1800s.

At that time, partly because of grain shortages but also for reasons of political vindictiveness, the Highlanders were permitted to distil only on a domestic scale. The idea was that farmers would use some of their own grain to make whisky for local consumption. The modern distilling industry began after the Duke of Gordon successfully proposed more accommodating legislation. With his encouragement, one of his tenants, a farmer, distiller and whisky smuggler, became the first to apply for a licence under the new law, in 1824. This swashbuckling character was a member of a family who had supported Bonnie Prince Charlie, and had subsequently been obliged to change their name, which until then was Gow. They avoided anything too Scottish and chose the anonymous "Smith". George Smith, assisted and succeeded by his son John Gordon Smith, founded the distillery that established precedence as *The* Glenlivet.

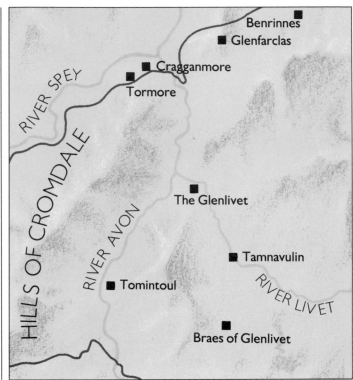

The Glen that produces Scotland's most famous malt whisky. With the Hills of Cromdale on one side, the Ladder Hills on the other, and itself rising steeply into the Grampian Mountains, this was both a hiding place and a route South. The Glen looks perhaps less cluttered today than it did when the picture on the right (centre) was taken. The distillery has suffered some new buildings, though it retains its older face. That is hidden in the big picture (top right), like the Livet, which is masked by trees.

The designation *The* Glenlivet was granted in a test case in 1880. Other distillers who wished to proclaim their proximity to The Glenlivet either geographically or in style were permitted to add the appellation in only hyphenated form. There are today four distilleries in the immediate area of the glen but elsewhere, along the system of rivers to which the Livet and Spey belong, so many more use the hyphenated form that it indicates little.

After distilling on two other sites, the Smiths moved in 1858 to the present location, not far from the hamlet of Glenlivet, but at a point where the grassy valley is already beginning to steepen. Some original buildings remain, and the offices occupy a handsome 1920s house, though at a distance the distillery is masked by a dark grains plant. Several distilleries have such plants, which dry the spent grain so that it can be used as cattle feed. The company remained independent until 1953, and is still called G. and J.G. Smith, although it has since 1977 been owned by Seagram's.

The whisky is sometimes described on merchants' bottlings as "Smith's The Glenlivet", to indicate doubly its proud provenance. It is available in a wide variety of ages from Gordon and MacPhail, while the distillery label accommodates the occasional one-off special bottling as well as the 12-year-old, which is the principal version. The distillery label carries Smith as the company name but identifies the whisky simply as "The Glenlivet". There is only one "The Glenlivet". The whisky can be sampled at the distillery, which has a reception centre and mini-museum for visitors.

Perhaps The Glenlivet is one of those cases where the water is the dominant factor. The water comes from a nearby well, but academic research has indicated that rain can take two years to reach that point. Where has it been in the meantime? No one is exactly sure. It seems likely that a large

Right: the much newer Braes of Glenlivet distillery.

number of underground streams feed the well but no one has been able to trace them all or identify their sources and catchment areas. A mix of lightly and heavily-peated malts is bought-in by the distillery; a stainless steel semi-lauter mash tun is used; the fermentation vessels are all made from Oregon pine; the wash stills are very large, with long, descending necks; about a third of the whisky is matured in sherry wood; but none of these features is extraordinary.

Nonetheless, in addition to enjoying an historic significance, The Glenlivet is respected as the most elegant of whiskies. It is a delicate malt, though one of considerable complexity. Its bouquet is lavishly flowery, with hints of a herbal smokiness; its body is light to medium; its palate clean but sweet; its finish a soothing caress.

This elegant, delicate manner characterises to a greater or lesser degree all four of the malts from the Livet district and a good many others that are sometimes loosely described as being of the "glen" style.

Seagram's also owns the Braes of Glenlivet distillery, high in the valley, with the mountain ridge behind. The distillery is on a fast-flowing, rocky stream that feeds the Livet. It is just beyond the isolated, Catholic hamlet of Chapeltown. Appropriately, the distillery has the look of a monastery (Spanish, perhaps?), with its modest, latticed windows framed in arches against its pristine, cream-painted walls. It is a most attractive

building, and a modern one – constructed in the mid 1970s by the Seagram's subsidiary Chivas. A fair share of its whisky no doubt finds its way into the Chivas products, but it has yet to be bottled as a single malt.

Not far away, Invergordon owns the Tamnavulin distillery, which is impeccably situated in the steep embrace of the glen of the Livet. It is in the hamlet of Tomnavoulin, but the two differ on the spelling. This is also modern, built in the mid 1960s, but it is a much less attractive, more utilitarian, distillery. It began, however, to present a less stern face to the outside world when the company decided, in the mid 1980s, to open a reception centre for visitors, in an adjoining building that was once a water-powered mill for the carding of wool. Tamnavulin means "mill on the hill". The Tamnavulin whisky is very much in the delicate, Glenlivet style: it is smooth, rather light in body, with a sweet start and an almost lemony finish. It is marketed under the distillery label at eight years old.

Tamnavulin, in either spelling, and

Tomintoul are neighbours whose names might confuse the non Gaelic-speaking visitor. Tomintoul is the highest village in the area, at the foot of Carn Meadhonach (1,928ft), and is a centre for climbers and walkers, with small hotels and shops. It is still something of a hill "capital", and was once an isolated haven of illicit distilling. Today's legal Tomintoul distillery is a good five miles down the hill, on the edge of the Glenlivet Forest. It is in the parish of Glenlivet but on the river Avon, near the hamlet of Ballindalloch. This distillery, too, was built in the 1960s, and is in the Whyte and Mackay group. It is a modern-looking distillery producing, again, a typically elegant Glenlivet whisky: with a delicate, hesitant bouquet; a lightish but smooth body; and a sweet palate. It is marketed as a single malt without an age statement, and at eight and 12 years old, under the distillery label in what looks like a perfume bottle.

More than one whisky-lover has been moved to think that is taking elegance a little far.

Steam wagons trucked The Glenlivet whisky to the nearest railway in the 1920s. Sparkling smokestacks and barrels breathing spirit seem a perilous combination, but the Smiths were used to living dangerously. When George (left, top) founded a legal distillery in 1824, he was harassed by his erstwhile smuggling comrades. Smith protected himself with a pair of hair-trigger pistols. His son John Gordon Smith (left, bottom), the "J.G." of the company name, also looks to have been a sturdy character.

A taste-guide to Livet whiskies

Within the broad embrace of Speyside is the smaller district around the glen of the river Livet. The whiskies produced in and around this valley are famous by association. The appellation "-Glenlivet" is loosely used. Nor does it indicate a style, though perhaps it should, suggesting a lightish, elegant, complex malt.

Glenlivet, Gordon and MacPhail bottling (40%)

Glenlivet, Gordon and MacPhail bottling (57%)

The Glenlivet, distillery label

Glenlivet, Gordon and MacPhail bottling (46%)

Glenlivet, Gordon and MacPhail bottling (40%, Distilled 1938)

The Glenlivet is the "official" label on this most elegant and complex of single malts. The names of the original producers, George and J. G. Smith, are tucked away at the bottom. Versions in different ages and proofs from the merchants Gordon and MacPhail make more of the Smith name, to indicate clearly exactly which Glenlivet they are selling.

Tomintoul is produced in the parish of Glenlivet. The distillery is also pleased to proclaim a telephone number on the Glenlivet exchange. It is not an old-established distillery, but its single malt is in the elegant style appropriate to the location. It has a good bouquet and an interesting palate, accented toward sweetness. It is a touch lighter all round than The Glenlivet.

Tamnavulin is, indeed, in the heart of the glen, as its label insists. It is sweeter in the nose than The Glenlivet, but with a most definite geographical affinity of style.

Speyside ~ *The Fiddich and the Dullan*

On the other side of the hills from Glenlivet, to the East, is Glenfiddich. From Corryhabbie Hill (2,563ft), the river Fiddich flows through a forest and a glen, both of which take its name. From the same hill, and from the brooding Ben Rinnes, the waters of the Dullan also flow, meeting the Fiddich at Dufftown, then joining the Spey.

The glens of the Fiddich and the Dullan, and their meeting place, Dufftown, form another of the classic whisky-distilling districts of Speyside. People in the whisky business who dismiss single malts as too "difficult" for the everyday drinker forget the Glenfiddich label, which has extended itself far beyond the constraints of Highland exotica. It is the most widely marketed, and biggest selling single malt worldwide, and in the important market represented by airport duty-free shops it outpaces all other whiskies. Glenfiddich has achieved this status because it has been marketed with what can only be described as single-mindedness, and vision, and not only because it is one of the "easier" malts to appreciate.

The distillery is in the glen of the Fiddich, on the edge of Dufftown. It was founded by William Grant in 1886, and is still in the family, which is also known for its blended whiskies and as an aggressive company in the business of marketing spirits and other drinks. At Glenfiddich, original buildings in honey-and-grey stone remain, beautifully maintained, and the style has been followed in considerable new construction. Although the distillery no longer produces its own malt, pagodas have been added to some of the newer buildings as a salute – however coy – to tradition. Glenfiddich uses lightly-peated malt; has an open, cast-iron mash-tun; employs fermentation vessels of Oregon pine; and is especially proud of its coal-fired stills. The large, airy still-house is noisy with the rumble of screws and the snap of ratchets as the stills are mechanically fed and the clatter of rakes as stokers clear the ashes. Inside the stills, "chain-mail" rummagers rotate to stop the wash from sticking. The stills are small, some rounded and others

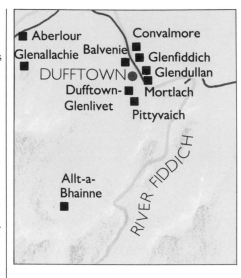

shaped rather like lampshades, with large condensers.

The whisky is principally aged in plain oak, though about ten per cent goes into sherry casks. No Bourbon casks are used, and no caramel colouring. Whisky aged in different woods is married in plain oak, then passes through a solera system to ensure Glenfiddich's consistency. The distillery is unusual in that it has its own bottling line. (The only other malt distillery with bottling facilities is Springbank, where a very small line is used also for the Cadenhead range). Glenfiddich is, naturally enough, bottled under the distillery label. The whisky can be bought at the distillery, which has its own shop. Glenfiddich was the first distillery in Scotland to have a reception centre for the public. The company employs two dozen tour guides, and has an audio-visual presentation in six languages.

The whisky, labelled as Glenfiddich Pure Malt, has traditionally been bottled at eight years old, though the distillery has in recent years dropped the age statement. The argument for this is that age matters less than maturity. Glenfiddich has a very gentle peatiness in the nose; a light, smooth, sweetish palate; and an aromatic finish. There is enough dry peatiness to balance the sweetness, and the company likes to prom-

ote Glenfiddich as an aperitif whisky. There is some canniness in this, since their suggested digestif is The Balvenie, from the distillery next door, which they have owned since its foundation in 1892. In 1982, the company started to package their principal Balvenie whisky, "Founder's Reserve", in a corked, smoked-glass bottle that speaks soothingly of after-dinner relaxation.

The Balvenie Founder's Reserve, immodestly labelled as "Probably the Finest Highland Malt", is vatted from distillates of between seven and 12 years old. It has a smoky but mellow aroma; a smooth, mature palate; and a clean, dry, long finish, with just a hint of sherry. A version called The Balvenie Classic, in an even more gastronomic-looking flask, is 12 years old. However, this is vatted with more sherry-wood whiskies, some matured in fino butts, others in sweet oloroso. The whiskies spend their last year being "married" in sweet oloroso butts. The result is a highly distinctive and delicious

Dufftown is not in the Glen of the Livet, but neither are many of the distilleries that cling to the same designation. At least the town gets top billing in the name of the older of Bell's malt distilleries there (left). As a bottled single malt, its whisky is marketed as Dufftown Glenlivet. Steeply-pitched roofs of grey slate are an architectural feature of many Scottish malt distilleries. The well-tended examples (above, right) house the much-visited Glenfiddich distillery,

at Dufftown, where the world's best-known bottled single malt is produced. Grant's (right), a blend, and The Balvenie, from the distillery next door, are family.

whisky, with honey tones as well as its sherry finish. The Balvenie whiskies are increasingly popular in Scotland. The distillery, which grows barley on its own farm and still operates a floor maltings, is close to Balvenie Castle, which had its origins in the 1300s and was occupied during the Jacobite rising in 1746.

More recent, and less meaningful, battlements are to be found on the little clock tower of Dufftown. It is a hilly, stone-built town, set round a crossroads, dipping at all points toward distilleries. The town is encircled by pagodas peeping through the trees, and the steam of distillery condensers billows out of the glens.

D.C.L. has three distilleries in Dufftown: Convalmore, Glendullan and Mortlach. Convalmore, founded in 1894, is today dominated by modern buildings. It produces a dry, assertive whisky that can be found in the odd merchant's bottling as a single malt, but most of which goes into blends, includ-

ing the Lowrie's label. The distillery temporarily ceased production in 1985. Glendullan, founded in 1897 and modernised in 1962, still has a handsome pagoda, and is set in a pretty location among trees by the water. It produces a substantial malt with a fruity bouquet; a smooth, mellow palate; and a firm finish. The whisky is marketed as a single malt under the distillery label at 12 years old, and is a component of the premium blend Old Parr. Mortlach is an attractive, very old distillery, built in 1823 and modernised in 1903 and 1964. It produces a whisky very highly regarded both by blenders and as a 12-year-old bottled single malt under the distillery label. For a whisky that is said to be only lightly peated, it has a profoundly flowery bouquet; its palate is rich and intense, fairly quickly moving to a long, dry finish. The subsidiary that operates this distillery, George Cowie, produces the John Barr blend but has a long association with Johnnie Walker.

Another big name in blended whisky, Bell's, owns two distilleries in the town. One is called Dufftown-Glenlivet, the other Pittyvaich. Dufftown-Glenlivet was converted from a meal mill in 1896, bought by Bell's in the 1930s, and twice extended during the 1970s. It is an attractive, old waterside distillery, producing a malt that is light in aroma and body, but with plenty of flavour. The whisky has a smoky aroma; a smooth, slightly fruity palate; and a rather abrupt finish. It is marketed as a bottled single malt under the distillery label, at eight years old. Pittyvaich, next door, was built in 1975. It produces a similar whisky that has yet to be bottled as a single malt.

Another new distillery that has yet to bottle any whisky as a single malt is Allt à Bhainne, just outside Dufftown. This is an imposing, tile-hung building of 1975 that has some architectural references to its contemporary Braes of Glenlivet. Both belong to Chivas, a subsidiary of Seagram's.

A taste-guide to Fiddich and Dullan whiskies

It may not be widely realised outside Scotland that the glen of the Fiddich is a place. The two rivers Fiddich and Dullan meet at Dufftown. Both valleys feature in the names of individual single malts, and the Dufftown district is one of the principal centres of distillation in the broader Speyside region.

The Balvenie, distillery label

The Balvenie Founder's Reserve, distillery label

The Balvenie single malts, in their various forms, are sweeter than Glenfiddich, with honeyish tones. They make natural after-dinner malts, and offer a further gentle step in sophistication for the Glenfiddich graduate.

Convalmore is an aromatic, dry, assertive single malt. All round, quite an interesting whisky, but available only in merchants' bottlings. The distillery has not produced for a year or two, but is in working order.

Glenfiddich became the world's biggest-selling single malt because it was the first to be marketed with sufficient conviction. Its amiably light and smooth character introduced malts to a larger and broader market.

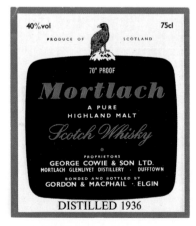

Mortlach is widely regarded as one of the Highlands' leading malts, though it is not very actively marketed as a bottled "single". It has a profound, flowery aroma, a rich palate and a notably long finish.

Dufftown-Glenlivet is one of those single malts that seem uncertain where their loyalties lie. On balance, its character belongs to Dufftown rather than Glenlivet. It has a smoky aroma and a smooth, fruity palate.

Glendullan is a smooth, firm, big malt, worthy of wider recognition. Its associate blended whisky is the excellent de luxe brand Old Parr, also big, firm and smooth. Old Parr is especially popular in Japan.

Speyside ~ *Strathisla*

The oldest distillery in the Highlands is Strathisla, sometimes also known by its earlier name of Milton, and founded in 1786. The *strath*, or broad valley, of the river Isla wraps itself round Keith, a pleasant town with several points of historical interest – and four distilleries. There are several more distilleries in the surrounding countryside, and the Strathisla district is known for whiskies that are robust and often seem a little woody. Why the Strathisla whiskies should often have this characteristic woodiness is not clear. It may be something to do with the micro-climate, but there is nothing that obviously distinguishes Strathisla from the other valleys of Speyside.

Accounts of the production of "heather ale" in this district as early as 1208 are mentioned by Philip Morrice, but that was not unique in Scotland. A reference in 1545 mentions a warehouse, presumably for grain, on the site subsequently occupied by the Strathisla distillery.

The Strathisla distillery (1786) is the oldest in the Highlands but some in other regions were established earlier. In the East of Scotland, in Perthshire, Glenturret was founded in 1775. In the Lowlands, Littlemill can trace its history back to 1772. On Islay, Bowmore dates from 1779. Many distilleries trace their histories back to illicit stills, so dates of foundation cannot always be sure. In some instances, production has ceased on a site for many decades, after which a largely new distillery has been constructed there.

Having been originally a farm distillery, Strathisla began to take its present shape during the 1820s and throughout that century, especially after a fire in 1876. In the 1940s, it was owned by a financier who was convicted of tax evasion, and in 1950 it was acquired by the Chivas subsidiary of Seagram's, who have taken great care to maintain it, unspoiled, as a showpiece. It has small stills, two of them coal-fired. Visitors are welcomed. The whisky is marketed under the distillery label. It isn't always easy to find, and has been bottled at a variety of ages and strengths. Strathisla is a considerable whisky: pungent and fruity, with a very big finish. A taster for the Harrods Book of Whiskies found a 15-year-old to have a trace of "fresh ivy leaves" in its bouquet.

On the opposite bank of the Isla, the same company in 1957 bought and largely reconstructed a corn mill to create the Glen Keith distillery. Even-handedly, this distillery was the first in Scotland to have gas-fired stills. Its whisky can rarely be found as a single malt but there has been the odd merchant's bottling. It is a tasty, satisfying whisky, almost chewy, sweet without being sticky, and becoming drier in the finish.

Corn mills and distilleries seem to overlap in Keith. It's not clear whether there was a corn mill or a distillery first at Strathmill, since the two may have alternated. Certainly in 1891 a building then serving as a corn mill was converted into a distillery. This was partly rebuilt in the late 1960s and is now operated by Justerini and Brooks. It does not have a reception centre but visitors can often be welcomed. The whisky appears never to have been bottled as a single malt.

The Keith area also has a D.C.L. distillery, operated by the J. and R. Harvey subsidiary. This distillery, a couple of miles out of the town, is called Aultmore. It was built in 1896 and reconstructed in 1971. Its whisky, which is well respected by blenders, is marketed as a 12-year-old bottled single malt under the distillery label. It has some peatiness in its big, fresh aroma; a flavourful, fruity palate; and a mellow finish. D.C.L.'s Glentauchers distillery may be disputed between the Spey and the Isla, but the latter would probably claim Knockdhu. This has the distinction of having been the first malt distillery to be built by D.C.L., in 1892. It was established to provide malt whisky for the Haig blends. Although there have been occasional merchants' bottlings, the Knockdhu whisky has never been easy to find as a single malt, and that is a matter for regret. It is a characterful whisky with a dry, fruity, almost pear-like aroma; a very full, expressive palate, with a smooth, sweet fruitiness; and a long warming finish. Sad to say, the distillery closed indefinitely in 1983.

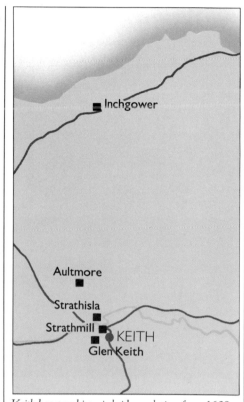

Keith has two historic bridges, dating from 1609 and 1770 – and four distilleries, representing a distinct whisky district. There are more around the river valley, though Inchgower probably relates less to the Isla than to the Spey. It is all, of course, Speyside.

A taste-guide to Strathisla whiskies

*Speyside, too, has Isla whiskies (same pronunciation, but no final "y" and no "seaweed").
Strathisla is an important whisky valley. Not everyone would agree that its malts are characterised
by a faint woodiness, but in this instance that is not a criticism. The dryness is a part of their
distinctive style.*

Strathisla, distillery label (8 years old)

*Strathisla-Glenlivet, Cadenhead bottling of
Strathisla*

*Glenkeith-Glenlivet, Cadenhead bottling of
Glen Keith*

Glen Keith, Gordon and MacPhail bottling

Strathisla is the name not only of the
region but also of one specific distillery and
hence single malts. They are pungent, on
the dry side, fruity, and have a big finish.
They are available in quite a wide variety
of ages. Strathisla-Glenlivet is a
merchant's bottling. The whisky, and the
sobriquet, derive from the full-title of the
Strathisla distillery. In its business name,
the distillery confusingly styles itself
Strathisla-Glenlivet.

Glen Keith is a satisfyingly chewy single
malt, with a typically Strathisla dryness in
the finish. The Glen Keith distillery stands
on the banks of the river Isla.
Glenkeith-Glenlivet is a Cadenhead
bottling. The whisky is the single malt of
the Glen Keith distillery. The distillery
itself uses two words for Glen Keith, but
adds the one word *-Glenlivet* in the
company name.

Knockdhu is a single malt with a
distinctive aroma, lots of fruit, a medium
body and a long finish. It is hard to find,
and will over the years become a rarity,
since the distillery is closed.

Aultmore is a single malt with a big, fresh
aroma, a fruity palate and a mellow finish.
It is a most pleasant malt, but not
especially well known. Its associate
blended whisky is Harvey's.

Speyside ~ *The Bogie and the Deveron*

Loosely though it is defined, Speyside is usually considered to end in the East around the valley of the oddly-named river Bogie, which flows through the Clashindarroch Forest before joining the Deveron and reaching the sea at the old county town, port and resort of Banff.

On the Eastern side of the valley are two malt distilleries owned by the company that produces the Teacher's blends. William Teacher was a wine and spirit merchant during the 19th century, and he was noted for his blended whiskies. His company was among those that developed well-known labels in the early days of branding. Teacher's Highland Cream remains a major brand, especially in the English market, and the company also has its "60", as well as de luxe versions which are 12 and 18 years old.

In order to ensure a good supply of malt for the company, Teacher's built a handsome distillery called Ardmore, at Kennethmont, in 1898. The distillery is close to the river Bogie and not far from the Clashindarroch Forest. It has retained some of its original features, despite extensive expansions and modernisations in the 1950s and 1970s. It has preserved its steam engine, and still uses coal-fired stills. Its whisky is hard to find as a single malt, but there is the occasional merchant's bottling. It has a light aroma but a very big, emphatically sweet and malty palate, with a crisp finish.

The aroma is much more a feature of Glendronach, the other local malt in Teacher's palette. It has a very fresh, heathery bouquet and is again notably sweet, but crisply so. It has some smokiness in the finish. Glendronach is marketed as a bottled single malt under the distillery label at eight and twelve years old. Some critics have found the younger version a little sharp, but the older Glendronach can only be described as rich and delicious. The Glendronach distillery was founded in 1826 but was not acquired by Teacher's until 1960. It has a floor maltings (and coal-fired stills), and remains a very attractive building, revealing

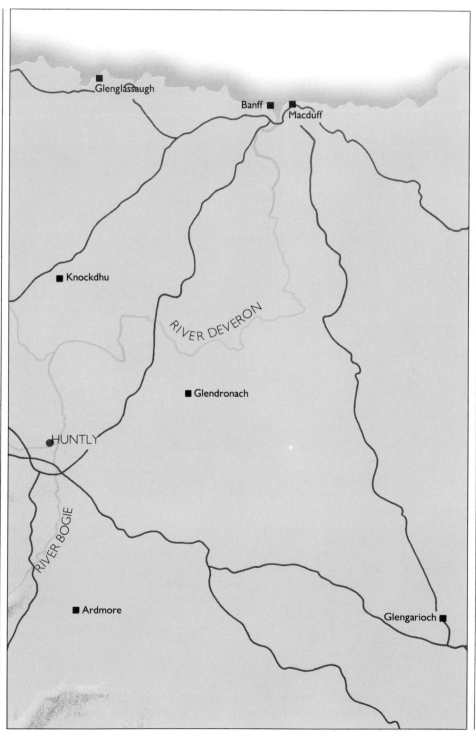

little of its 1966 expansion. It is set in a fold in farmer's fields to the East of Huntly.

Down the river Deveron, the town of Banff gives its name to a distillery. The Banff distillery was founded in 1863, and is the subject of much local folk history. It was badly damaged by fire in 1877, bombed in the Second World War, and once provided whisky for Members of Parliament. In recent years, its whisky has not been available as a single malt and in 1983 its owners, D.C.L., closed it indefinitely.

Facing Banff across the Deveron is the rocky headland of Macduff, which also gives its name to a distillery. The Macduff distil-

lery is modern – built in 1962 – and is operated by William Lawson Distillers, which has links with the international Martini and Rossi group. The whisky no doubt finds its way into Lawson blends like Gow's, Lismore and Royal Heritage. It can be found in merchants' bottlings, and is very pleasant. It is a big, smooth, after-dinner whisky, with a crisp, dry finish.

Just along the coast is Glenglassaugh, founded in 1875, bought by Highland Distilleries in the 1890s, and completely rebuilt by them in 1960. It is the only one of the group's distilleries that does not market its whisky as a bottled single malt.

The rich textures of Aberdeenshire farming country enfold the Glendronach distillery. The whisky is rich, too, especially at 12 years old.

The Eastern Highlands

Scotland's third largest city, Aberdeen, dominates the North-Eastern bulge of the Highlands, and provides a convenient base from which to explore the distilleries on its coastline and inland toward the valleys of Speyside. The granite city was once a stern and ascetic place, but the development of the Scottish oil industry in the late 1970s and early 1980s made it more cosmopolitan, for a time prosperous, and therefore rather expensive for the visitor. The influx of outsiders also brought a curiosity about the malt whiskies of the region, which were in the past often taken for granted. Several bars and hotels in Aberdeen and the surrounding countryside began to stock large ranges of malts. A good example is the Bridge Bar, in the shopping centre, and a very large selection of malts is held by the Ferryhill House Hotel, in Bon Accord Street.

The city once had its own distillery, a handsome place, but that has long been defunct. However, there are nine distilleries within a radius of about 40 miles. The flat-topped mountains of the Grampians try to form an Eastern Highland region here, then succumb to the fertile valleys of the Don and the Dee, both salmon rivers. Aberdeen Angus cattle graze in rich farmland. On the coast are fishing ports – in the past the home of large fleets of whalers and later herring trawlers – and sandy resorts. The whiskies of the region are not regarded as being in a style of their own, though several of them do have an especially rich fruitiness.

The Northernmost among the distilleries is Glenugie. The river Ugie flows into the sea at the port and boat-building town of Peterhead, and the distillery is nearby, close to the vestiges of an old fishing village. There was first a distillery on the site in the 1830s, but this was converted into a brewery, and the present buildings date from 1875. The smart little distillery, in pinkish stone, with a preserved mill tower, was most recently operated by Long John. However, in 1982 it stopped distilling. Under Long John's management, its whisky was not marketed as a single malt, but merchants' bottlings can still be found. The whisky has a ripe fruitiness in the nose; a smooth, firm, malty body; and a quick, dry finish.

About 20 miles South and ten further inland, at the quaintly-named market town of Old Meldrum, is the distillery of Glengarioch (pronounced Glen-geery). This is in the sheltered Garioch valley, traditionally the grain-growing district for this part of Scotland. The distillery, founded in 1798, is a chunky, stone building that looks in parts like a village school. It is very traditional in that it has floor maltings but innovative in that it has experimented with several ways of avoiding the waste of heat generated in the distilling process. This has included the recovery and use of heat to warm greenhouses in which cyclamens, tulips, lettuce, cucumbers and, especially, tomatoes have been ripened. The distillery is owned by Stanley P. Morrison, and visitors are welcomed. The whisky is marketed as a single malt under the distillery label. It has a light, raisiny nose; a clean, spirity palate; and a quick, dry finish. A pleasant, light, after-

The mountain of Lochnagar inspired a children's story by the Prince of Wales. The Scottish distillery of the same name inspired the appetite of Queen Victoria.

dinner whisky. Glengarioch also makes a major contribution to the Rob Roy blend.

Although the Don and the Dee bracket the city of Aberdeen, the latter is its principal river. About 45 miles up river, the valley runs between the Grampians to the North, and Balmoral Forest and the mountain of Lochnagar (3,789ft) to the South. Balmoral is the Scottish private home of the Queen, and nearby Braemar the scene of the annual Royal Highland Gathering. Lochnagar has inspired the writings of the Prince of Wales, as well as Lord Byron. Just east of Balmoral is the distillery of Lochnagar. Its founder, believed to have been already an illicit distiller, acquired a licence to make whisky at Lochnagar in 1826.

The present distillery was built in 1845 and visited soon afterwards by Queen Victoria and Prince Albert. Victoria was said to have been fond of Lochnagar whisky, and to have laced her claret with it – thus ruining two of the world's finest drinks. Over the years, the distillery has been rebuilt three times, most recently in 1967. In its early days, Lochnagar was owned by a well-known distiller called John Begg, and his name survives in the D.C.L. blends to which its whisky makes a significant contribution. Lochnagar is marketed as a bottled single malt under the distillery label at 12 years old. It has a big, fruity aroma; a fresh, clean, flavourful palate; and a sweetish finish. For more than a century, the distillery was known as Royal Lochnagar, but in the late 1970s this prefix was dropped, for reasons that the company is unwilling or unable to make clear. The whisky writer Derek Cooper believes the decision may have resulted from intepretations placed on a public speech by the Duke of Edinburgh concerning industry and the ecology. In the mid 1980s, the royal flourish was restored.

A royal suffix is assumed by the Glenury distillery, on the coast South of Aberdeen and close to the fishing port and resort of Stonehaven. The distillery takes its name from the glen running through the Ury district. It was built in 1825 by Captain Robert Barclay, the local Member of Parliament, who was also an athlete and marathon walker. This flamboyant character had a friend at court, referred to coyly as "Mr Windsor", through whose influence he was given permission by King William IV to style his whisky "Royal". The distillery was rebuilt in 1966, and operated for the D.C.L. subsidiary Gillon's, whose blends include King William IV. Glenury Royal Highland Malt is marketed as a single under the distillery label at 12 years old. It is fairly light and medium-dry in both aroma and palate, with a faintly smoky finish. The

The neat and trim Glenesk distillery has an insouciant look, considering the changes it has seen. It was among the batch of distilleries that were "mothballed" by D.C.L. in 1985, when Scotch whisky reserves were high. D.C.L. hoped to re-start production soon.

coming a malt distillery in 1897, being re-equipped to produce grain whisky around the time of the Second World War, converted back in the 1960s, and extended in the 1970s. It is operated for D.C.L.'s Wm Sanderson subsidiary, which produces the VAT 69 blends. The whisky is marketed as a 12-year-old single malt under the Glenesk label but in small quantities and in limited export markets.

The other Montrose distillery, Lochside, also has an interesting history. It was originally a brewery, belonging to the well-known firm of James Deuchar, and was converted to become a distillery as recently as 1957. In 1973, it was acquired by the Spanish company Distilerias y Crienza, whose principal brand is the blend DYC. The company also has a malty blend in the Scottish market, called Sandy Macnab's. Lochside's whisky is marketed under the distillery label as a single malt at eight and 12 years old. It has a big, "soft fruit" aroma; a smooth, firm palate; a medium-to-big body; and a dry, long finish.

Up the South Esk, there is a further pair of distilleries at Brechin, a very old town built mainly from red sandstone and noted for the round watchtower on its church. Both of the distilleries are very old. One, Glencadam, is said to have been founded in 1825. It was bought by Ballantine's, and extensively modernised, in the 1950s. Most of its whisky goes for blending, but it can occasionally be found as a single malt under the distillery label. It has a very fruity aroma and a smooth, almost creamy palate; a most unusual and characterful whisky.

The other Brechin distillery, North Port, is even older, having been founded in 1820. It is now owned by D.C.L., and was for some years operated by their Mitchell Brothers subsidiary, whose brands include Heather Dew, and a vatted malt called Glen Dew. North Port's whisky can be found as a single malt in some merchants' bottlings. For this part of the country, it is a surprisingly peaty, smoky whisky, with a light-to-medium body and a very dry finish. Sad to say, the distillery closed in 1983.

distillery closed temporarily in 1985.

The next important rivers are the North and South Esk. Not far from the glen of the North Esk is the village of Fettercairn, in a fertile moorland plain known as the Howe o' the Mearns. The nearby hills around Cairn o' Mount (this is apostrophe country) were once whisky-smuggling country, and the first Fettercairn distillery is believed to have been there. Having apparently been founded in 1824, the present Fettercairn distillery is itself one of the oldest in Scotland, though it has some of the most modern

equipment since an expansion in 1966. The distillery is owned by Whyte and Mackay. Its whisky has been marketed as a bottled single malt under the Old Fettercairn label at a variety of ages. It is a light but smooth whisky with a nutty palate and a dry finish.

At the mouth of the South Esk is Montrose, historically an important town in the region and today a centre for sailing. It has two distilleries: Glen Esk (sometimes still known by its earlier name of Hillside), and Lochside. The first has had a colourful history, having started life as a flax mill, be-

A taste-guide to Bogie, Deveron and Eastern Highland whiskies

Speyside just about straddles the rivers Bogie and Deveron. East of their valleys, there are still more distilleries, albeit thinner on the ground, making good Highland malts. There are some sweet, malty whiskies from the valleys of the Bogie and the Deveron, and a variety of palates are to be found among the "singles" of the Eastern Highlands.

The Bogie and the Deveron

Glendronach, distillery label (8 years old)

Glendronach, distillery label (12 years old)

Glendronach is a deliciously sweet single malt, with some heathery, smoky, dry notes to balance it. A hearty after-dinner whisky that is surprisingly little known.

Ardmore is a big-bodied single malt, its sweetness balanced by a good, crisp finish. It is available only in merchants' bottlings, and is one of the component malts of the Teacher's blended whiskies.

Glen Deveron, distillery label for Macduff

Macduff, Cadenhead bottling

Macduff is a heartily named after-dinner whisky. A single malt with a fresh, welcoming aroma and smooth palate. Bottled under the distillery name by merchants, and more elegantly as Glen Deveron by the proprietors.

Glenglassaugh is a firm, smooth single malt, with a sweetish palate, drying slightly in the finish. A good example of the regional character, but hard to find. Available only in merchants' bottlings.

Banff is a single malt with a lightly smoky aroma, an assertive palate . . . and rarity value. The distillery has an interesting history, but is now closed. It was associated with the Slater Rodger blends.

The Eastern Highlands

Lochnagar, distillery label

Lochnagar, Gordon and MacPhail bottling

Lochnagar is a full-bodied single malt, with plenty of fruit, flavour and complexity, and a sweetish finish. It is said to have been a favourite of Queen Victoria, and is now becoming more widely available.

Glenugie, a ripe, fruity single malt, is still sometimes sighted in merchants' bottlings. Glenugie was once the most easterly distillery in Scotland, but closed in 1982.

Glen Garioch has a slightly fruity aroma, in which some tasters also notice a smokiness. Light-to-medium in palate, it is perhaps best after dinner.

Glencadam is a fruity, creamy single malt. A most unusual and characterful whisky. It is hard to find under the distillery label. This bottling is from Cadenhead.

Glenury-Royal is a light, medium-dry single malt, best before dinner. The royal suffix did not save the distillery from temporary closure in 1985, but the whisky can still easily be found. A pleasant dram.

Old Fettercairn is a light, dry, smooth single malt, with a nutty palate. Similar to the Livet whiskies, though its proprietors – Whyte and Mackay – have, in Tomintoul, their own entrant in that category.

Lochside is a single malt with a big "soft fruit" aroma and a smooth, firm palate. A pleasant after-dinner whisky, but hard to find under the distillery label. This bottling is from Gordon and MacPhail.

North Port is quite a peaty and dry single malt, and one of those with rarity value. The distillery is closed, but merchants' bottlings can be found.

The Scottish Midlands

Stewart's Cream of the Barley is, as its romantically appetising name suggests, quite a malty-tasting blend. Stewart's, of Dundee, belongs to Allied Breweries. Beneagles is a sturdy, well-balanced blend, owned by a Scottish wine-and-spirit merchant. Tayside is a minor brand. It is a sweetish blend from the Glen Talla company.

The pivotal point of the whisky trade could be said to be neither in the Highlands (where the greatest number of distilleries are) or in the Lowlands (where the largest cities, Edinburgh and Glasgow, make for the biggest domestic markets) but between the two, in the Midlands of Scotland. The principal city in this region, Dundee, is the fourth largest in Scotland, but its neighbour Perth has emerged as the more important in the whisky business.

Both are on the Tay, Scotland's longest river, and each is an entrepôt town, with a history of importing whisky from the Highlands, blending and bottling it, then exporting it through the Central Valley to the main areas of population, or by sea to foreign markets. In both respects, Perth is better situated: deeper into the country and closer to the mountain passes whence whisky was at first smuggled; yet close to the point where the river opens into the Firth of Tay, its estuary to the sea.

Some of the best-known blended whiskies come from the Midlands. In world markets, the Dewar's and Bell's blends (both from Perth) and Haig (from the county of Fife) are the most famous Midlands whiskies. In Scotland, The Famous Grouse and Beneagles (both from Perth) are especially popular examples. One well-made Midlands blend, Stewart's Cream of the Barley, is widely enjoyed but at some time in the distant past established a particular following in Northern Ireland. No one is any longer sure why.

Dewar's, of "White Label" fame, claims to have been the first company to sell a branded bottled Scotch. The company was founded in 1846 and a buccaneering member of the family, Tommy Dewar, helped put Scotch whisky on the world map with his international selling exploits in the 1890s. The company has since 1925 been a part of D.C.L. Arthur Bell also founded his firm in the mid 19th century. Bell's is the classic case of a Midlands-based company using its strategic position to build sales in the Central Valley, and it has a strong hold on the industrial towns and cities of Scotland. In recent years, its hard-driving management increasingly looked to export markets, with a success that made it a very desirable property to Guinness.

The Famous Grouse is the biggest-selling whisky within Scotland. The grouse was originally just a drawing, a trademark, on the label of Gloag's whisky, which was marketed by a family of that name who had been in the liquor and grocery business in Perth since 1800. A member of the family, Matthew Gloag remained with the company after it joined Highland Distilleries in 1970, and at that time the whisky, by then long known as The Famous Grouse, began to receive wider distribution and advertising support. The advertising has, however, been restrained and traditionalist in style, and has no doubt helped emphasise the integrity and quality of this excellent blend. Beneagles, another Scottish favourite, is

Laden with barrels of whisky, ponies trekking through the mountains to Perth made a spectacle in 1983. This retracing of the smugglers' trail was organised by a customs man, Irvine Butterfield. Interested in the history of whisky, he organised the 140-mile, 12-day trek for research and charitable purposes. Commemorative crocks of whisky were sold to raise money for a hospital for ex-Servicemen.

blended by a wholesale wine and spirit merchant, Peter Thomson, of Perth. The brand-name was created to have both a Scottish and a local allusion, and the company is noted for its ceramic flasks of whisky, including some shaped like eagles and other birds of prey. Cream of the Barley is produced by Stewart and Son, of Dundee, a subsidiary of Allied Breweries. Cream of the Barley is a light, rounded blend, well balanced, with a sweetish finish.

The blending, bottling and distribution of whisky is so much the traditional business of the Midlands, especially Perth, that there are numerous other, smaller labels emanating from this area. There are also a number of distilleries in this part of the country. Although there is no recognised regional style, several of the local singles are notably malty. They are regarded as Highland malts.

The Northernmost distillery, owned by Bell's, is Blair Athol, at Pitlochry, Perth-shire. It's a very old distillery, having been established in 1798. It subsequently closed and was revived in 1825, enlarged in 1860, rebuilt in 1949, and extended in the 1970s. Visitors are welcomed. The whisky is bottled as an eight-year-old single malt under the distillery name. It is a notably clean malt, with some smokiness in the aroma and more in its light but flavourful palate. Blair Atholl (in this instance with a double "l") is a village with a restored 13th-century castle in Scottish baronial style. Pitlochry is a mountain resort noted for its Festival theatre, and the area is rich in historical interest.

Nearby at Balnauld is the smallest distillery in Scotland, usually known as Edradour but sometimes as Glenforres. Believed to have been founded in 1837, it is the last operating "farm" distillery, with some very traditional equipment. The appearance of the place was left unchanged when it was refurbished in 1982. This tiny distillery, with a staff of three producing 1,000 gallons a week, is owned by one of the world's biggest drinks companies, Pernod Ricard. Because output is so small, whisky is not generally released to the trade, but there has been the very occasional merchant's bottling. It is a complex whisky, with an aroma and palate that is fruity and sweet but also smoky, faintly reminiscent of sugared almonds. Its palate is creamy, malty-smooth, but dry. A delightful dram. The Edradour can be enjoyed as the defining whisky in a 12-year-old vatted malt called Glenforres. It is also an important component of two blends, the eight-year-old House of Lords and the 12-year-old King's Ransom. It is claimed that King's Ransom, a smooth, flavourful, de luxe blend, always contains some whisky that has been carried by sea. This practice originates from the time when casks of maturing or marrying whisky were often carried as ballast in ships. There is a similar tradition in respect of akvavit.

High on the Tay is the resort and market town of Aberfeldy, again rich in historical interest, and with a distillery that bears its name. The Aberfeldy distillery was built in 1896, and some of the original buildings remain, despite major reconstruction and expansion during the 1960s and 1970s. It was built by John Dewar and Sons, and is still linked with that subsidiary of D.C.L. The Aberfeldy whisky can be found in merchants' bottlings. It is a very pleasant whisky in a decidedly dry style. It has a fruity nose and palate, a soft body, and a dry finish.

Closer to Perth is the Glenturret distillery and "heritage centre". On the banks of the river Turret near Crieff, this is a small, working distillery with a museum, bar and restaurant. Glenturret presses strongly its claim to be the oldest distillery in Scotland. There are records of a distillery in the neighbourhood at least as early as 1717, and some of the buildings on the present site are said to date from 1775. The distillery itself was dismantled in the 1920s, then revived in 1959 by a noted whisky enthusiast, James

The famous names in blended whisky may reside in Perth, but in the gentle countryside nearby is the tiny malt distillery and "heritage centre" of Glenturret . . . tucked away, but not hiding its light under a bushel.

Fairlie. He continues to run Glenturret, although it is now owned by the French liqueur company Cointreau. As a result of this arrangement, Glenturret whisky is available from some of those outlets in Europe that stock the Cointreau range. The whisky can be tasted at the distillery, and is marketed as a single malt at eight, 12, 15 and 21 years old, at, respectively, 75 and 80 British proof (42.8 and 45.6 per cent alcohol by volume). It is a delicious, malty whisky, with a smoky, almost roasted aroma; a full, chewy body; and a long, smooth finish. Small wonder that it has won several awards.

South of Perth, half way to the old town of Stirling, is the Tullibardine distillery, at Blackford. The wells of Blackford were once famous for the ale they produced. It was on the site of a brewery that the Tullibardine distillery was opened in 1949. In the 1970s, the distillery was taken over by Invergordon and largely rebuilt. Tullibardine is marketed as a bottled single malt under the distillery label at five and ten years old. It is a distinctive whisky, whose soft aroma belies a medium-to-full palate, fruity, with a sweetish finish. Further down the road at Doune is another Invergordon distillery, called Deanston. This distillery produces a light and fruity malt, but it has been silent recently. The handsome, riverside premises were ori-

ginally built as a cotton mill in 1785, and converted as recently as 1966. A vaulted weaving shed is used as a warehouse.

There are yet more distilleries in this area, at Cambus, Alloa and, of course, Cameron Bridge. These all produce grain whisky, though the Carsebridge distillery, in Alloa, has not distilled for some years. The confusingly-named North of Scotland grain whisky, from Cambus, and the better-known Cameron Brig, can both be found as singles, though in that form they are something of a curiosity.

There is much about which to be curious in Scotch whisky, and its enigmatic nature is its joy.

A taste-guide to Scottish Midland whiskies

The biggest names in blended Scotch whisky have their headquarters in the Midlands of Scotland, especially in the city of Perth. The Midlands is less well known for its single malts, yet it has several interesting examples. These are regarded as Highland malts, and a couple come from Scotland's smallest distilleries.

Tullibardine is a single malt with only a soft aroma but quite a full body. It is fruity and medium-sweet, with a well-sustained finish. A pleasant, well-made whisky that is not well known.

The Glenturret is one of the malts that cleaves to the definite article. It is another claimant to being the oldest distillery in Scotland, and it is very visitable, with its own restaurant. Its single malt is delicious, chewy, almost roasty.

Glenforres, vatted relative of Edradour

Blair Athol is a pleasant, pre-dinner single malt. It is notably clean, dry, light-to-medium in body, with plenty of flavour. The distillery is in the Bell's group.

Deanston is a light and fruity single malt, with some sweetness in the finish. Like all the Perthshire "singles", it qualifies as a Highland malt, despite the relatively Southerly location of the distillery.

Edradour comes from Scotland's smallest distillery. It is not the only single malt to have reminded a taster of sugared almonds, but perhaps the first to have inspired this sophisticated comparison.

Aberfeldy is a very pleasant single malt that is available only in merchants' bottlings. Perhaps the typically fresh character of the Dewar's blends owes something to this component malt?

IRELAND

It's always reassuring when people live up to their image. Arguably, this is especially satisfying when the stereotype is to their credit. The Irish are, as they are reputed to be, a gregarious nation. Those among the Irish who like a drink, and they are in the majority, enjoy it with a sociable pleasure which is neither furtive nor compulsive. They like to drink in public places: pubs, more basic bars and "lounges" – sometimes referred to with colloquial accuracy as "shops" – and, in grander moments, hotels.

That is not to say the Irish will be found wanting when they are prevented from procuring a drink by orthodox means. It is perfectly legitimate to buy a drink at 7.0 in the morning in one of the pubs and bars near Dublin's docks and produce markets, before the regular establishments open at 10.30, but in urban areas there remains the dark problem of the one-hour closure each afternoon, between 2.30 and 3.30. This is intended to ensure that bar staff are not exploited to the extent that they miss their lunch. That problem doesn't arise in country districts, where most bars are family-run. Cynics have long held that the real purpose of the one-hour closure is to permit the clergy to enjoy a quiet, discreet drink. It is thus dismissed as "the Holy Hour", notwithstanding plentiful evidence that priests in Ireland feel perfectly relaxed about visiting the pub along with everyone else.

At night, the pubs close at 11.0 in the winter and 11.30 in summer. On Sundays, hours are shorter: 12.30-2.0 and 4.0-10.0. It is the Sabbath, and Ireland is a religious country. In the Six Counties of the North-East, pubs open from 11.0 in the morning until 11.0 in the evening but close on Sundays.

Although it seems fastidious to bring the full weight of the law to a mere 60 minutes of the day, the Holy Hour can on occasion be enforced with punitive zeal by the *gardai* (police), backed by the threat that a publican who transgresses too often may lose his licence. Should a publican absent-mindedly find himself serving drink during the Holy

A pint of stout makes the natural chaser for an Irish whiskey. The spirit was once dispensed from the stone jars which still decorate the window of this bar and grocery store in Abbeyleix, County Laois. Inside, stout and whiskey sit alongside biscuits and sweets.

Hour, he may take the precaution of locking the door. If the *gardai* knock, the customers can crouch below the window-line and drink bent double, in silence until the danger passes. The publican may also crouch in hiding, behind the bar, allowing only his hand to appear, Excalibur-like, to remove the glasses and wipe the counter.

If the *gardai* persist, the publican may then lead his customers, still bent double, upstairs to his living quarters. Once there, they may be treated to drinks legally as friends, so long as no money is proven to have changed hands. Unlikely as such an episode may be, such things happen. Ireland is holy, but pragmatic.

This was also evidenced in the period a

decade or so ago when the pubs closed on, of all days, St Patrick's. Whatever its connotations elsewhere, St Patrick's remains relatively quiet in Ireland, a day to spend with the family, or on which to have an outing or attend a sporting event. In the days when the pubs were shut on St Patrick's, thirsty Dubliners would hie to the annual dog show, where there was a licensed bar. At the mention of St Patrick's, the story is still told of the man who, after a good day's drinking at the dog show, tripped over the lady's prize poodle. "Darned silly place to bring a dog", he is alleged to have complained. The Irish have always been animal-lovers, with an inexhaustible delight in horses and ponies, but the number of dog enthusiasts has declined since the pubs began to open on St Patrick's.

A dog show is, however, by no means an inappropriate place at which to drink in a country where alcohol is served in some very eclectic surroundings. There are true pubs, of the marble and mahogany kind, in some of the cities – Dublin, Cork and at a stretch Limerick, in the Republic; Belfast, but not Derry, in the Six Counties. Far more typically Irish, though, are the pubs that look

Bushmills and Midleton are today the centres of whiskey production, with some blending in Cork, Dublin and Tullamore, the latter providing Irish Mist. Once, almost every town had a distillery, but even important cities like Belfast and Derry have lost theirs. Ireland is, of course, a very small country, but its contribution to the tradition of whiskey distilling remains beyond measure.

from the outside like handsomely-painted shops. In so doing, their frontages often recall the day when they warehoused and blended not only whiskey and perhaps wine but also a wider range of provisions, most likely including tea. Although they no longer blend their own whiskeys, many country bars still serve as provision merchants, grocers, hardware and general stores. This is most typically the case in distant rural counties like Galway and Mayo, Sligo and Donegal. Many a drinker has relaxed too far and knocked over a pile of tea packets which had been artistically arranged on the bar counter, or found himself engaged in earnest conversation with a side of bacon hanging from the ceiling.

Nor do the services offered by bars in Ireland stop with provisions, groceries and hardware. In the main street of a country town, it is possible to find one bar offering coffees and ice-creams, another taking bets on horse-races, and a third willing to organise a funeral. A bar may have bottles of whiskey in one window and vases of funeral flowers in another; handy if you want to arrange a wake. Its shingle might announce: "Bar and Lounge, Funeral Director and Embalmer (Overseas Service), Auctioneer and Valuer, Property Consultant, Estate Agent, Irish Mutual Building Society". Some bars even, dangerously, rent – or sell – cars. There are bars, too, where regulars arrive after dinner, astride farm tractors, and leave in the dark with the chug of their exhausts punctuating the still of the night as they make their way home.

A bar in Ireland can be a place of entertainment, too, and perhaps more deeply grass-rooted than any. There are bars which specialise in music, like O'Donoghue's, the pub in Dublin where the Chieftains were "discovered", but there are countless others where a "shush" will spread from one drinker to another as a customer prepares to sing a ballad of lost love or tragic heroism. Often enough, the song will be unaccompanied, unless there happens to be a fiddle or tin whistle in the house. A song from one customer will likely be followed by another from elsewhere in the bar until the evening becomes a spontaneous recital on the subjects of happiness, sadness and emigration.

Even such informal entertainments are more stagey than anyone requires of the distractions in a bar in Ireland. A place's best recommendation is its anecdote and repartee, colloquially known as its "crack". If an Irishman favours a particular bar for any reason other than its convenience, his loyalty is probably due to the quality of the "crack". His choice is less likely to depend upon the types, brands or quality of drink served, since these are much the same, at least in the more traditional style of pub or bar, all over Ireland.

When an Irishman calls for a "ball of malt", which seems to happen mainly in "B" movies, he could mean any one of four drinks. He could be indicating one of the very ordinary international-style lager beers which find favour with the young in Ireland, fecklessly intent upon turning away from their country's most distinctive traditions; he could, of course, mean no such thing. He could mean one of the characteristically russet-coloured, full-bodied, sweetish ales brewed in Kilkenny and Dundalk, a definitely Irish variation on a larger theme. He could even mean, and that might seem likely, a stout of the dry type which Ireland has generously given to the world. He could, however, mean Ireland's other national drink, equally distinctive – whiskey.

Ireland has a good climate – moist with-

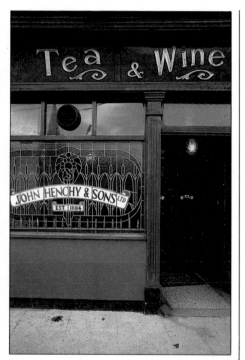

The "shopfront" style of bar, sometimes declaring its origins as a store for the retailing of spirits, wine, tea and perhaps other provisions, is found all over Ireland. It is more common in country towns but there are examples in the cities. The unlikely-sounding William Blake's, and Magee's, are both in Enniskillen, County Fermanagh. Doheny & Nesbitt is a famous Dublin pub. The premises of Fitzgerald, Mahony and McCarthy are all close to the source, in Midleton, County Cork. Henchy's is in the city of Cork itself, at St Luke's Cross.

out being too wet; cool but not cold – for the cultivation of barley. It has a substantial barley-malting industry, which is an important exporter. Since a good malting barley can be the original raw material for either beer or whiskey, both can readily be produced in healthy quantity in Ireland. Since the climate favours drinks which are sustaining, but gently so, stout and whiskey are happy companions. Creamy stouts and sweetish, full-bodied whiskeys have been said to go together like milk and honey, and so they do.

Either could be poetically nicknamed "a ball of malt" but whiskey is. Coincidentally, and perversely, the Irish versions of both stout and whiskey are unusual in that they characteristically contain proportions of unmalted barley. They are, in consequence, unmistakable to the palate, and it should be a sin to drink anything else in a pub or bar in any of the thirty-two counties. For a time, the Six Counties were the most traditional, in that they clung on longer to "plain" porter, the older, lighter-bodied but equally black brother of stout. These days, their tastes are in general more clearly Northern, at least in Protestant areas, but their whiskey is better than ever.

Whiskey is one of Ireland's national drinks on both sides of the border. It is customarily served straight, without ice, though with a small jug of water so that the customer can achieve the dilution he prefers, rarely more than half-and-half. Or a glass of water may be offered as an accompaniment or chaser.

What is sometimes affectionately known simply as "Irish" is one of the world's principal whiskey styles, with a long pedigree, a great deal of character, and shoulders broad enough to shrug with compliant amusement when it is required to perform hot toddies, flirt with coffee, or be married to chocolate in "Irish Cream" liqueurs. None of these activities is central to the life of Irish, but it carries them out well. Likewise each of them has an, albeit lesser, time or place in the pattern of drinking in Ireland.

The whiskeys of Ireland

In a country whose greatest obsession is with horses, it seems apposite that people sometimes talk wistfully about the aroma of saddlery, or new leather, when they seek to define the nose of Irish whiskey. It may be a romantic analogy, and is certainly an evocative one, but it does seem to pinpoint the most emphatic characteristic of Irish.

One evocation leads to another, much as whiskeys do. Is it the aroma of linseed oil, perhaps? Or is that an even more deeply subconscious rationalisation, with the seed of flax and thus of Irish linen? Such comparisons, in efforts to capture aromas and flavours, are not always quite as fanciful as they appear. Natural oils are, indeed, formed in the production of alcoholic drinks, and contribute to their perfumy aroma and to their palate (especially to texture, or what tasters refer to with some accuracy as "mouth feel").

The perfumy character which is typical in Irish whiskey, its faintly oily palate – and a roundness of body – all derive, as they must, from specific aspects of its production process. Each of these aspects represents an important distinction.

In the beginning, and most surprisingly, despite the great deposits of peat which are available to them, Irish maltsters do not generally use it to stoke their kilns. Although no one is quite sure why, perhaps it is because the early size of the malting industry in Ireland, especially when the country was the world's premier whiskey producer, made coal a more manageable or convenient fuel. The absence of peat in the kilning means that there is no smokiness in most Irish whiskeys.

The absence of smokiness has a twofold impact on the aroma and palate of Irish whiskey. On the one hand, while an intentionally imparted smokiness is an important defining note in Scotch, its very absence is one of the features which helps to identify the character of Irish. On the other hand, the absence of smokiness prevents the masking of other palate characteristics in Irish.

The Midleton distillery embraces this lovely old maltings, now disused and perhaps to become part of a museum. County Cork no longer markets a malt whiskey but its barley remains at the heart of Irish . . . as it was when it illustrated an advertising calendar for the year 1917.

These are, in particular, the perfumy note of the barley and the roundness of malt.

The distinction between malt and the barley from which it is made is of special significance in the production of Irish whiskey. This derives from a time, about 150 years ago, when, because of a tax on malt, Irish distillers felt the need to augment this material. In this instance, the Irish were less perverse about their natural resources, and opted simply to use a proportion of unmalted barley, that grain being in such good supply in their country. This blend of malt and "raw" barley was, and still is, distilled in a pot still. The traditional ratio of the two ingredients has been between 40-60 and 20-80. The product of this distillation is known in Ireland simply as pot still whiskey, and that term is used very specifically in the industry and in labelling.

Most Irish contains some pot still whiskey made with unmalted barley, and that is an important flavour component. The greatest Irish distillers held fast throughout the first half of the 20th century to the production of whiskeys containing only malt and pot-still barley, and refused to countenance the use of cheaper, lighter grain spirits. Eventually, they felt that the fullness of their whiskeys was inhibiting their export sales, and started to use a proportion of grain spirit to cater for the timorous tastes of foreigners. Today, the major labels of Irish whiskey in both domestic and export markets have a proportion of grain spirit. It nonetheless remains the case that Irish whiskey may contain a distillate of malt, one made in a pot still with barley, and a third portion comprising grain spirit. Of the three, the barley distillate is central, and it contributes the greatest character to several Irish whiskeys. In the past, a tiny proportion of oats was also used, and rye was occasionally employed. Because the Irish consider the pot still as the "master", they distil their grain spirit close to neutrality; its job is merely to lighten the body of the whiskey. The Scots distil their grains slightly less thoroughly, with a view to their making a definite, if small, flavour contribution.

Perhaps because the Irish use unmalted barley, a robust material, they distil their whiskeys three times. This is not unique to Ireland, but it is unusual in whiskey distillation elsewhere in the world. It is a troublesome way in which to do the job – first to choose *al dente* raw materials, then to process them once more than is normal. It seems especially masochistic to carry this out by using the good, old-fashioned, imperfect pot still rather than the more thorough, but less interesting, column system; again, though, this contributes to the creation of a more distinctive product.

Because Irish whiskey is distilled three times, it leaves the still with a higher alcohol content than does Scotch. Since both – like all spirits – are diluted to a drinkable potency before being bottled, there need be no differences in their strengths in the marketplace.

All Irish whiskeys are marketed at 40-43 per cent (80-86 U.S. proof). The 43 per cent versions, however, are found only in certain export markets, notably duty-free shops. However, the original strength from which a spirit is diluted will influence flavour, and this represents another, albeit lesser, difference between Scotch and Irish.

Another such detail is that pot stills in Ireland have traditionally been much larger than those in Scotland (the North Americans giving more emphasis to the column type). This is probably because large stills came into use when Ireland was the biggest whiskey producer, with its distilleries serving cities – Belfast, Dublin and Cork. Distilling began to be legitimised through various laws in Ireland earlier than it was in Scotland, where much of the industry has remained in its original hiding places in remote hills, glens and islands. Scotland has in consequence retained far more of its distilleries, but many of them are very small.

Although the large pot stills of Ireland were not built on that scale with a view to their influence on the palate of the product, their size does have an effect. This cannot be analysed with any certainty but, as in the production of all alcoholic drinks, the size, shape and surface area of vessels, and the way in which liquids, vapours and gases behave within them, play a part in the character of the final product.

In that the distinctions concern the raw materials, the number of distillations and the size of stills used, the Irish feel that their art of whiskey production has an emphasis different from that in the making of Scotch. The Irish perceive their whiskey as, first and foremost, the product of the distiller; Scotch, they argue, owes as much or more to the blender.

The art of the distiller is well illustrated at the village of Midleton, in County Cork. At the large distillery complex there, a dozen different single whiskeys of one type or another are produced. Each of these is triple distilled through a different permutation of linked stills, pot or column. Each is pro-

The emphasis given to the phrase "pure pot still whiskey" in this early advertisement clearly implies consumer interest in what might seem an esoteric point. Pot stills, unusually large ones, are used especially to distil the unmalted barley in Irish.

duced from a different combination of malt and barley or grain. Each is matured for a different period in a different type of cask. Three years is by law the minimum aging period in Ireland, though exports to the U.S. follow that country's four-year rule. Most of the whiskeys in a typical bottle of Irish are older – five to ten years perhaps. There are also some differences in weight, with whiskeys sold in the British Isles slightly heavier than those marketed elsewhere.

That a dozen different single whiskeys can be produced in one place says much for the skill and sophistication of the distillers, and is unusual. They are, however, the pre-ordained components for most of the whiskeys produced in Ireland, and that is some

indication of the lesser role of blending. In fact, the Irish prefer to call it not blending but vatting.

The emphasis on the vat is significant.In recent years the Irish have done a great deal of work in studying the rates at which whiskey ages. This research has, as its by-product, the whiskey Midleton Very Rare.

The dozen whiskeys of Midleton, and the fine malts from Bushmills, County Antrim, are variously the component parts of all Irish whiskeys. In a country which was once dotted with distilleries, there are now only the Midleton complex and Bushmills, and they are both owned by the one group, called simply Irish Distillers. The group also has vatting warehouses in Cork and Dublin.

Each of the Irish whiskeys distilled or vatted in these various places is a quite different product with its own character. Each has its own loyal following but they are all the products of a distinct, national distilling tradition. So are the older Irish whiskeys that can still occasionally be found. Some long-closed distilleries left considerable stocks of whiskey in maturation. A 30-year-old pot-still whiskey, with a noticeable rye content, produced at the Comber distillery, near Belfast, is still available. This is bottled as Old Comber, by the firm of James McCabe, in Northern Ireland. Another example is a rather woody-tasting whiskey from Locke's Kilbeggan distillery, in County Westmeath. This distillery closed in 1953.

The pedigree of Irish whiskey

Irish may have been the first of all whiskeys and it most certainly has an impeccable pedigree, though this is not always appreciated. The claim to have produced the first whiskey rests on the exploits of Irish monks who travelled in Continental Europe to spread Christian teaching at the end of the Dark Ages. The story is that they acquired the knowledge of distillation in the East, where it was used to make perfumes. A much-loved version even has it that the first to apply the art was St Patrick.

Since Ireland was a refuge of learning and Christianity at that time, and monks did, indeed, further the arts of drink production, the essence of the story may be true. Having learned to distil spirits, the "water of life", *uisge beatha*, *usque baugh*, or whichever version of the Gaelic is preferred, the Irish probably settled quickly upon cereals of one kind or another as a convenient raw material.

The corruption "whiskey" is believed to have been coined by the soldiers of King Henry II of England, who encountered the spirit when they invaded Ireland in the 1100s. By the 1400s and 1500s, the Irish spirit was attracting legislation. Laws introduced in the late 1700s and for a century after that gradually shaped a formal whiskey-distilling industry. Given the scientific advances during that period throughout Europe, it was probably also the time in which whiskey began to assume a character which would have been broadly recognisable to the present-day drinker.

In the late 1800s and early 1900s, Irish whiskey was the dominant spirit not only in its own market but also in England, and enjoyed very considerable sales in the United States. Sad to say, the commendable traditionalism of the major Irish distillers in staying with pure pot still whiskey saw their splendidly full-bodied products superseded by lighter blended Scotches in the English market. This situation was exacerbated by the problems which preceded and followed the establishment of what is now the Republic of Ireland.

The various difficulties encountered by the Irish distillers in the early part of the 20th century came to a head with Prohibition in the United States. When that Act was repealed, the Irish were simply not ready to restore supply and, in the time required to produce new stocks of whiskey, they once again lost their market to the Scots.

Since Irish already had something of a reputation as a big, bruising spirit, it was done no favours by the activities of bootleggers during Prohibition. Anxious to capitalise on the popularity of Irish in the United States, they gave its name to their illicitly-distilled rough spirits.

Traduced and misunderstood, Irish has in the years since been unsure which way to face. It has in some ways sought to make itself more identifiably different yet in others tried to join the crowd. It has strengthened its identity by settling on the spelling whiskey with an "e", originally a Dublin foible but now agreed upon also in Cork. It has recognised that, among the connoisseurs who set trends, the pendulum might be swinging back toward bigger-bodied whiskeys; Old Bushmills Malt is a welcome gesture in this direction, some competition for the fashionable singles from Scotland. On the other hand, across the range, most Irish whiskeys have become lighter in body over the years. If they were to lose their flavour, character and authenticity, that would be not only Ireland's loss but also the world's. Irish should be what it says, and not a bastard cousin of Scotch.

Should the Irish blend their robust pot-still whiskeys with the lighter product of the "patent" continuous still, in the Scottish manner? Or would that be nothing less than a betrayal of the spirit? This Celtic schism was the subject of much Press attention, including cartoons like the one above. The theological fervour seems appropriate. Wasn't whiskey invented by St Patrick? He was, though, presumably using water in The Baptism at Tara, as depicted by John Byam Shaw.

Poteen

The Irish have only themselves to blame if their addiction to romance and whimsical humour has forever associated their legitimate whiskeys with poteen (also spelled potheen or, in the Gaelic, poitín, and pronounced pocheen, with a short "o"). Although every spirit-drinking nation has a tradition of illicit distillation and battles with the authorities, the Irish are better story-tellers than most.

They also have better stories to tell, in that illicit distilling was a widespread rural industry in the 1700s and early 1800s, and was the subject of viciously repressive laws and corruption on the part of the authorities. If anything, illicit distilling in rural areas of Ireland seems to have become more entrenched as a result of the relatively early legitimisation of commercial whiskey production in the cities. What was illegal became more clearly and defiantly so because of the line which had been drawn.

Poteen is still produced and there have been a number of legal versions, if that is not a contradiction in terms. Hardly surprisingly, none has been convincing enough to find a market.

The word is a diminutive of pot (as in a still, rather than in smoking materials), and nothing to do with praties. Potatoes surely have been used on occasion, but a great many vegetables, fruits and cereals are suitable for distillation. Accounts of poteen production usually refer to the use of malt, barley or oats.

Irish neighbourhoods in other countries

The young distillers on the far left and the party of visiting samplers in the centre picture indicate the extent to which the making of poteen permeated family and community. These photographs are believed to have been taken in the 1890s in Connemara. Wherever there have been illegal distillers there have also been police keen to stop them, and proud to have seized their equipment.

as well as the old one have a habit of producing the odd glass of poteen but it is harder to find on demand. A favourite Irish story concerns the police sergeant who led a raid on an illicit still. "You know why we are here, don't you?" he said to the proprietor of the still. "Indeed I do", was the reply. "But I'm terribly sorry I can't oblige you. We are out of stock at the moment."

Poteen is usually colourless, with a strong aroma and taste of alcohol. Although it may be referred to as "the good stuff", and it has an authenticity of its own, poteen is inevitably less well distilled than legitimate whiskey. It is, therefore, more likely to contain the higher alcohols that produce a fiery palate, quickly followed by a burning head. Sometimes, the headache is instant.

Poteen will, nonetheless, do no lasting harm unless someone has been irresponsible enough to produce wood alcohol, the consequences of which have been madness, blindness or death. In his book "Brendan Behan's Island", that robust Irishman was unequivocal, on a subject which he had explored more than once: "Potheen is just murder. It's the end, and you can take it from me, for I have had a wide enough experience of it".

"Thousands of his contemporaries and his ancestors would beg to differ", comments Tony Lord in his "World Guide to Spirits". "Poteen was, and is, part of their life."

Dublin

The most Irish of whiskeys are the pot still products, matured for long periods in sherry casks, from Jameson of Dublin. Jameson has been known in the past to mature whiskeys for more than 20 years, and some of these products were used in blends which may still be found here and there. However, none bears the legend 20 years old, since such a blend would also contain younger whiskeys. In recent times, makers have begun to argue that, at 20 years in the cask, a whiskey begins to lose some of its character and to take on excessively woody tones.

No one, though, would argue with a 15-year-old whiskey. The product known simply as Jameson 15-year-old is the classic example of a pure pot still Irish whiskey, matured in the sherry cask. This revered product is beginning to have rarity value as it is replaced by a 12-year-old version, again an excellent product. In the current theology, a 12-year-old whiskey is thought to have just hit the perfect pitch of maturity. The move to slightly younger whiskeys, and it is only a small shift, is based on the argument that modern distilling methods are more efficient, and need to be followed by a less exhaustive maturation. It is also true, of course, that lengthy maturation of whiskey ties up expensive stocks at considerable capital cost. In any event, these mature, pure pot still whiskeys express more fully than any, and in their particularly mellow way, the intensely perfumy aroma, oily palate and rounded body of the Irish tradition.

There is also a splendidly smooth, mellow Irish which is a blend of very well matured Jameson whiskeys, the youngest being 12 years old, under the Redbreast label. The whiskeys are from Jameson but the brand is bottled and distributed by another respected house, the Irish branch of Gilbey's, which is now part of the Grand Metropolitan group. This product, too, has a certain rarity value.

A much less hefty, but still mellow – enthusiasts say "sophisticated" – blend of pot still whiskeys, again matured in sherry casks, is produced by Jameson under the Crested Ten label.

None of these whiskeys is widely found outside Ireland. The regular Jameson Irish Whiskey, the best known and most widely sold product of the house, also has a pronounced pot still character, although its component distillates are younger and generally lighter. It is matured in charred American oak. This is the favourite whiskey in the Dublin area and the most widely sold in the United States.

As his surname suggests, John Jameson was a Scot – his wife was a member of the Haig whisky family – but he moved to Dublin in the 1770s and quickly won a reputation as a demanding perfectionist in the production of Irish. Another Scottish distilling family, the Steins, had their Dublin distillery taken over by a Jameson as the dynasty established itself in Ireland. Eventually, the Jamesons owned a number of distilleries in Ireland and had two million gallons of whiskey maturing under the streets of Dublin. Members of the family are still involved in the business, though in 1966 Jameson became a part of the newly-formed Irish Distillers Group.

The Jameson headquarters, in dour, grey stone, with Georgian, Victorian and more recent buildings, now house Irish Distillers' offices in Dublin, along with a small but interesting museum called Irish Whiskey Corner and a bar-style tasting room, "The Ball of Malt".

Jameson, in Bow Street, near Smithfield

The Long Hall pub, in South Great George Street, typifies Dublin's blend of flourish and insouciance. It was one of the last pubs in Dublin to sell whiskey from the cask, though it no longer does. With bottling came miniatures... and Power's wry "three swallows".

fruit market and the river Liffey, used to look across at its neighbour and great Dublin rival, the John Power distillery. Then, for a time, production of Jameson shifted to Power's premises before the structuring of Irish Distillers was completed. The handsome John Power building has now been restored and taken over by the National College of Art. Although Jameson and Power whiskeys are still vatted in Dublin, production begins at the group's distilleries elsewhere in Ireland; the old sites in the city had become just too congested.

While Jameson whiskeys are especially popular in Dublin, the sole product of Power's – Gold Label – is the biggest seller in Ireland as a whole. Away from local favourites, it is very much the national whiskey of Ireland, most certainly of the Republic, with big sales in the West, where there are no longer any regional distilleries (Limerick and County Galway lost theirs in the distant past).

Gold Label is arguably less aromatic than its home-town rivals, but its own distinctive pot still component is underpinned by a malty body. It is a big and very well balanced Irish whiskey, with a quiet finish.

It is labelled in some markets as Power's Irish, but it is also sometimes ordered by another, more folksy, name. This name has its origin in the fact that Power's pioneered miniature bottles of Irish whiskey. These miniatures were held to contain three swallows of the stuff. Eventually, this reference became institutionalised to the extent that three swallows – the birds – were designed on to the neck label, even on the larger bottles. As a visual and verbal pun, a whiskey dubbed "Three Swallows" perfectly epitomises the elliptical humour for which Dublin is famous.

Cork

The second city of the Republic is Cork, the southern port, with its Georgian quays and balustraded bridges over the river Lee, undecided whether it is seeking the Irish Sea or the Atlantic. It is a proud city – elegant, if run down – with one or two fine hotels within its environs, and some handsome pubs. The rest of the Irish say Cork people are too businesslike, perhaps even mean, though it is the eloquent city and county of Sean O'Faolain and Frank O'Connor. Elsewhere in Ireland, all the same, they have begun to attach some of the glamour of an "import" to the once-local whiskey of Cork, at least to that named after Paddy O'Flaherty.

Paddy O'Flaherty was the popular star salesman for the Cork Distilleries Company in the 1920s. Customers so often asked for supplies of "Paddy's whiskey" that this eventually became the official name of the company's premium brand. Today, it is labelled Paddy Old Irish Whiskey, but is generally ordered simply by its Christian name.

Paddy is a firm-bodied whiskey, with some maltiness and a crisp finish deriving from the grain. A fruitier whiskey called Hewitt's, a lighter, export product called Murphy's (a popular basic bar brand in the United States) and an even slighter, lighter, crisper blend, Dunphy's, are all produced in the same distillery complex, about a dozen miles from the city, at the village of Midleton.

The names of the lesser brands recall a number of distilleries which existed in the area in the late 1700s and early 1800s. The merger which created the Cork Distilleries Company took place as long ago as 1867, and the area has continued to be an important centre for the production of whiskey ever since. The Cork group became a part of Irish Distillers when it was formed in 1966. Midleton is now Irish Distillers' principal centre of production. Since 1984, Midleton has made an annual "limited edition" bottling of a maximum of 50 of its finest casks. These have on each occasion, yielded between ten and twenty thousand bottles

under the name Midleton Very Rare. The exact yield, and the precise character of the whiskey, has varied from year to year.

Midleton is an attractive, typically Irish, one-street village. At the top of the village is a tiny public park, with two pretty, stone bridges over the fast-flowing, choppy little brook that provides water for the distillery. Next to the brook, behind a stone arch, is a building which was constructed in 1796 as a woollen mill, used as a barracks in the Napoleonic Wars, and in 1825 became the original Midleton distillery.

In the old distillery is the world's biggest pot still, a magnificent copper vessel with a capacity of 31,648 gallons. This still remained in use until 1975, since when there have been moves to build a whiskey museum around it. Another exhibit will undoubtedly

The old distillery at Midleton watches over ranks of former sherry or bourbon casks that have been used three or four times. These are "retired" and will end their lives as plant-pots or firewood. Full casks are usually of greater interest to the excise man (left).

be the distiller's horse-drawn fire-engine, which has been preserved.

Behind the old distillery is the new one, very large, in buildings of geometric simplicity and some ugliness, softened by a wide backdrop of low hills. Its pot stills, in gleaming copper, are also large – at about 16,500 gallons each. There are a battery of them, linked to a system of column stills, together comprising a distilling system of unusual flexibility.

The whiskeys which emanate from Midleton are all the more enjoyable if they are chased down by one of the two local dry stouts that are produced in Cork city. The distilling family of Murphy founded one of the stout breweries, though there are no longer any links between the two. Murphy Stout has a toasted-barley palate; its local rival, Beamish, is slightly less dry, with chocolatey undertones. The two are Ireland's only competitors to Guinness, which is available throughout the country.

An aperitif of Paddy, followed by a glass of Murphy or Beamish, with a plate of oysters, or some crab or lobster from the gastronomic resort of Kinsale or the fishing village of Baltimore, is a Southern delight.

The brook alongside the distillery flows with soft water that has been used in distilling since at least the early 1800s. Its particular character has contributed to the palate of long-established Cork whiskeys like Murphy's, a product which was once served in bars from glass decanters.

111

Tullamore

In the Midlands of Ireland, on the Grand Canal, which links West with East, in boggy, peat-cutting country, the small town of Tullamore, in County Offaly, was an important centre for whiskey production throughout the late 1800s and the first half of the 1900s. A glance around the town, centred on one, broad main street perpendicular to the canal, bears witness to this. A number of the larger buildings recall their past use in malting, distilling and the warehousing of whiskey. It was convenient to bring in barley from the farmlands by canal, and to distribute the subsequent whiskey across the middle of Ireland by the same means.

Once very active, with the canal facilitating distribution of its products, the Tullamore distillery still announces itself in decorative ironwork, though today only the blending of Irish Mist takes place in the town. Neighbour Smyth's contribution is in trompe l'oeil masonry.

The widespread renown of Tullamore whiskey also owes something to an inspired gesture of punning, a form of humour which the Irish clearly enjoy, on the part of the man who ran the town's distillery in its heyday. His name was Daniel E. Williams, and he appended his initials, D.E.W., to the label of his product. It thus became Tullamore Dew, providing just the grass-roots level of poetry with which distillers and drinkers equally like to invest their tipple. He stopped short at calling it Foggy Mountain Dew, but not at devising an advertising slogan of painful memorability: "Give every man his Dew".

Tullamore Dew survives and thrives, though it is today a product of Irish Distillers. It is said always to have been a notably light Irish whiskey and it certainly is today – the lightest of them all. The same type of whiskey is marketed in a crock bottle under the name Uisge Beatha, for devotees of Gaelic romance.

The blending of alcoholic drinks continues in Tullamore, though distilling there stopped in the mid 1950s. The Williams company, still in the same family, produces a whiskey-based liqueur called Irish Mist.

Most regions of traditional drink production have some history of the maceration of plants, flowers or herbs in alcohol, and Ireland's story is of "heather wine". The loss of this product is romantically explained away by a "legend" that the recipe was taken to Continental Europe by the "Wild Geese", the Irish noblemen who were refugees from the Williamite Wars.

This is a convenient legend in the light of more recent events. It is said that in Tullamore, in the heathery heart of Ireland, the enterprising Williams family spend decades trying to recreate such a "wine". The recipe was cracked towards the end of the Second World War with the help of a liqueurist who was a refugee from . . . Continental Europe. The liqueurist, who was from Germany, spent some time working at Tullamore. The outcome of his efforts was the first Irish liqueur, long before some denser confections.

Four pot still and grain whiskeys, aged between five and twelve years, are blended as a base for the liqueur. Some of the whiskey is aged at Tullamore, and the blend rests for a time before the maceration of three or four honeys, including heather and clover, and a number of herbs. This maceration continues for some weeks, and the finished product has a typically sweetish liqueur character but with a surprisingly fruity finish. While it has its own distinctive palate, it is broadly in the category of other translucent, spirity liqueurs such as Drambuie (based on Scotch whisky), Bénédictine or Cointreau.

Like them, Irish Mist is sometimes served as an aperitif, in a shot glass, its palate made drier by a hefty slug of ice. More often, it is presented straight up as an after-dinner drink. That is really the role of these liqueurs; it is one which they perform well, and it is a sound *raison d'être*. However, it is no sin – if an extravagance – to use Irish Mist for more culinary purposes. It can make an interesting variation on Irish coffee, or be used in dessert sauces, on crêpes, in soufflés, even in savoury sauces (where a little fruity sweetening might be required) or, appropriately for an Irish liqueur, as a glaze for ham.

No wonder the Epicurean French speak fondly of a place called *tous l'amour*.

Among the several bars which punctuate Tullamore's main street, that of Thomas J. Lawless offers a range of services which is eclectic even by Irish standards. It is an engaging town in which to stop for a drink.

THOMAS J. LAWLESS
FUNERAL DIRECTOR & EMBALMER
OVERSEAS SERVICE
TELEPHONE   0506-21649

Bushmills

That the Celtic mists should have parted to reveal man's first whiskey in the far North of Ireland, in County Antrim, seems a delightfully credible notion. This is where the whisk(e)y-distilling nations of Ireland and Scotland almost meet. There is just a hint of that in the fine Irish whiskeys made here, especially in their very slight smokiness and their pronounced, faintly sweet, maltiness.

The North is the most Irish part of the island in its depth of Gaelic legend and dramatic history, yet it is also that most subject to Scottish influence, especially in Antrim. It is easy to see how the ancient Irish believed that a giant had built a path of stones across the sea so that he could walk to Scotland; there is still an astonishingly manmade look to the Giant's Causeway, though it was carved by the sea from the basalt rock of the Antrim coast. The basalt, and the peat which overlays it inland, give a particular character to the water used in the distillation of the local whiskeys.

The county of Antrim and the town of Coleraine are important in the story of St Patrick, and this part of the country has strong associations with early missionary monks. Saint Columb gave his name to the stream or "rill" from which water is taken to distil the whiskeys.

St Columb's Rill rises in boggy, peaty land and flows into the river Bush as it approaches the sea. The river Bush was named as one of the "king waters" of Ireland in a Gaelic saga of about 1100, and by 1276 there are references to the availability of *acqua vitae* in the area. There is more evidence of distilling in the late 1400s. By the early 1600s, there were watermills by the river Bush, and the beginnings of a town with a name which would become famous among whiskey-lovers. This was also the period when laws and taxes began to be applied to the production of spirits. The first licence to be given to a distillery anywhere was granted in the king's name to Bushmills in 1608. On the basis of that, Bushmills rests its claim to be the world's oldest whisk(e)y distillery.

In the little town of Bushmills the distillery is the dominant feature. Its oldest buildings were destroyed in a fire in 1885 but its pagoda-style towers, built in the early 1900s to ventilate the then maltings, set the visual tone of the present day premises.

Inside, the distillery is very traditional in style, with a cast-iron mash-tun (the Irish term is a *kieve*) and wooden fermenting vessels (made of uncoated oak). Bushmills is unusual in Ireland in that it uses no unmalted barley. Its pot stills are charged only with malt. Its products are vatted exclusively from a single Bushmills malt, aged for between five and ten years in sherry casks and charred American oak, and from just one grain whiskey. The malt used has a very brief peating in the kiln, to Bushmills' own, unusual specification. The distillery stopped doing its own malting in 1972.

Four whiskeys are produced. The lightest of these, with a substantial grain content, is called Coleraine Whiskey. It has a very local market and does not generally leave the North of Ireland. The principal and best-known product, which is widely exported, is Old Bushmills. This used to be identified as "three stars", but the distillery eventually decided, with justification, that this designation implied a lesser quality than the

The cooper's craft is maintained at Bushmills (above), and at many other distilleries, out of practicality. Casks are expensive and their contents even more valuable. A cask is, inevitably, subjected to considerable handling, and leaks must be quickly spotted and repaired by the cooper. With its malting towers reflected in its dam, the distillery is a handsome landmark (left). It is a significant provider of employment and an extra attraction for tourists in an area with several small seaside resorts. Salmon breeding and farming are the other local occupations. A moist fruit-cake, a tangy marmalade and a sweetly aromatic tobacco (right) all benefit from a kiss of Bushmills whiskey. Each is a happy combination and they are among the more agreeable souvenirs offered by distillers. The products are all made in the North of Ireland.

whiskey manifested. Old Bushmills comprises more than half malt whiskey. The premium brand, Black Bush, is predominantly malt, matured in sherry casks. This product was for many years hard to find, with something of a cult following, but it was introduced to the American export market in 1984. Also in 1984, the distillery began to market, but initially only in Ireland, a single malt. Since there had not been a single malt Irish for many decades, this was a significant development. The product is known simply as Old Bushmills Malt, and is a most distinguished and unusual whiskey, from one of the world's most interesting distilleries.

A taste-guide to Irish whiskeys

Ireland likes to claim that it invented whiskey, which would be contribution enough. It has its own style of whiskey, too, and an enthusiasm that belies the sparsity of its distilleries. Classic "Irish" is distilled in Cork, and there is blending in Dublin and Tullamore. Bushmills is a small town with its own claims and style.

Dublin

Jameson is the premium brand that best exemplifies the character of "Irish". It gently expresses the pleasantly perfumy oiliness and roundness of body that is typical.

Jameson 1780 at 12 years old is the most readily-available "super-premium" Irish. With its classic Jameson character, and its maturity, it is a hearty taste of Dublin's distilling heritage.

Jameson Crested Ten has the family palate, but in a lighter, cleaner manifestation, with a hint of sherry. A purportedly "sophisticated" Irish whiskey for Dublin's ambitious executives and businessmen.

Redbreast 12-year-old comprises Jameson whiskeys vatted and bottled by another company, the Irish branch of Gilbey's. Hard to find, but worth sampling if sighted, as it is full of pot-still Irish character.

Power's Gold Label Irish, sometimes known as "Three Swallows", originally came from Dublin, but is very much a national brand. Arguably less aromatic than its home-town rivals but big, malty and well-balanced.

Cork

Paddy is the classic whiskey of Cork, the second city of the Republic. It is distilled just outside the city, at Midleton. Paddy is firm-bodied, with the crisp finish that is typical of the native Cork whiskeys.

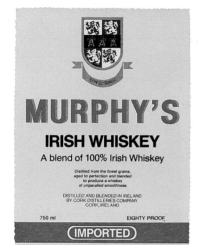

Murphy's is a light-bodied Irish whiskey distilled at Midleton and very widely marketed in the United States as a bar brand. There are distant links between Murphy's whiskey and the stout of the same name.

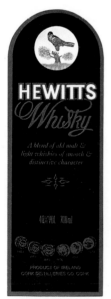

Hewitts is a fruity, fairly light Irish whiskey distilled at Midleton. The original Hewitt's distillery was in the city of Cork. It was founded in 1793, merged in 1867, and ceased to distil grain whiskey in 1975.

Dunphy's, distillery label ("special export")

Dunphy's, distillery label ("imported")

Dunphy's is a very light-bodied Irish whiskey distilled in Midleton. It can be found in Ireland, but describes itself there as a "special export". Once it has reached its destination, it obligingly becomes "imported".

Midleton Very Rare grew from a methodical study of maturation characteristics. It has elements of pot-still "Irish", but is accented toward a sweetish maltiness. It is remarkably smooth, medium-bodied, with hints of Bourbon.

Tullamore

Tullamore Dew is the lightest of Irish whiskeys. It is popular in France, where its name is pronounced *tous l'amour*. The whiskey originates from Tullamore, though it is no longer made there.

Irish Mist is a whiskey-based liqueur. Some of the whiskey used is aged in Tullamore, and the liqueur is blended there. Irish Mist is owned by the family who originally distilled Tullamore Dew.

A taste-guide to Irish whiskeys (*continued*)

Bushmills

Old Bushmills is an Irish whiskey that represents a style of its own. It is a blended whiskey made from just one malt and a single grain. The result is a blend of malty sweetness and perfumy dryness.

Black Bush is a de luxe blend containing an unusually high proportion of malt whiskey. The components are, of course, the same as those in the far-from-ordinary Old Bushmills.

Bushmills Malt also represents a style of its own. It is the only single malt Irish whiskey. It has a warm sweetness in the aroma, a clean, delicious maltiness and a dry, perfumy finish without smokiness.

Coleraine Irish Whiskey is a blend from the Bushmills malt and a single grain. It is a very pleasant blend for a light, clean, "session" whiskey. Coleraine's own distillery closed in the early 1980s.

Comber

Old Comber is the product of an independent distillery noted for its pot-still whiskey. The somewhat woody whiskey is still being marketed, at "at least 30 years old", though the distillery closed in 1953.

Irish whiskey liqueurs

Like all whiskeys (and whiskies), Irish tastes best unadorned, except perhaps by a splash of water. However, since it is a perky tipple, it has suggested itself in all manner of strange arrangements.

The most reasonable of these is, quite simply, the hot toddy. This is best made to the drinker's personal requirements, but the lazy might be encouraged by a bottled version under the label Snug, which is sold in their local market by Irish Distillers. This contains whiskey flavoured with sugar, lemon and cloves, at an alcohol content of 30 per cent by volume. One measure of Snug with two of boiling water makes an easy hot toddy.

A more elaborate flavoured whiskey, with a sweet start and some bitter orange in the finish, at 40 per cent alcohol, under the label Mulligan, is also sold in the local market by Irish Distillers. This might serve as an after-dinner drink or nightcap, though it is really intended to be presented on the rocks, or in cocktails, as an Irish counterpart to Southern Comfort.

The most popular combination could be regarded as a mixed blessing. Irish whiskey might be more readily given its due as a serious drink, but less well known, had it not encountered coffee. The meeting place was the bar at Shannon airport, in the west of Ireland, in 1952, in the days when planes had to stop there to refuel before crossing the Atlantic. It was a cold and damp day, and bar-keeper Joe Sheridan made a warming whiskey-and-coffee drink for a passenger who turned out to be newspaper columnist Stan Delaplane, on his way home to San Francisco. Delaplane, on his arrival home, introduced the idea to the bartender at his then-favourite café, the Buena Vista, by the Hyde Street cable-car terminus at Fisherman's Wharf, San Francisco. It's a crowded tourist spot in summer, and they have been turning out Irish Coffees by the score ever since. The trouble is that a really good Irish coffee probably has to be made individually, with special care. Instead, it has become something of a clichéd drink. Worse still, all sorts of non-Irish spirits have leapt aboard, to produce everything from Scottish to Peruvian Coffee. Perhaps such notions should have been left in the safer hands of people like the Viennese.

Europeans sometimes prefer larger servings, but the Irish-American masters favour a six-ounce glass, two thirds full of coffee. It must be freshly made so that it has plenty of flavour and isn't bitter. Perfectionists might choose a medium roast, nothing too light. The coffee must be very hot, since it is to be diluted. It helps if the glass is gently warmed first, in which case there will be less risk of it cracking. Before any dilution takes place, while the coffee is still piping hot, dissolve the sugar. Use two teaspoons, or perhaps three cubes – demerara is ideal for flavour. Stir well. Then pour in a measure, or perhaps even two, of whiskey. Needless to say, it must be Irish, preferably one of the bigger-bodied examples. Finally, pour on the garnish of fresh cream. Since this has to float on the surface, it must be poured gently. Break its fall by pouring it over the rounded back of a spoon. The gentleness and skill with which this is done – and practice makes perfect – is the crowning art of Irish coffee-making. It is easier, but a slight cheat, to use lightly whipped cream, and it is arguably gilding the lily to sprinkle a few grains of coffee – or even chocolate – on top.

The proper way to cheat is to buy a bottle

Irish whiskey liqueur . . . Bailey's outsells all its imitators. It is, indeed, the biggest-selling liqueur of any type in the world, and it fills cases by the thousand at the headquarters of its makers, in Dublin.

Whiskey liqueurs . . . Snug is meant for a toddy, Mulligan to go on the rocks, Velvet for a short- cut coffee, and Gallwey's after dinner.

Irish coffees are dispensed to the tune of half a million a year at the shrine of the faith, the Buena Vista bar. The use of stemmed glasses, ideally heatproof, is one way in which to avoid burning your fingers. A good half-inch of cream provides just the right balance.

of Irish Velvet, which contains whiskey, coffee and sugar. Add two parts of boiling water, and cream. This product is made by Irish Distillers and sold in their local market. So is a dark, translucent, whiskey-based coffee liqueur called Gallweys, which is intended for after-dinner drinking.

The rich marriage of Irish whiskey with coffee – or chocolate – for years aroused the envy of liqueurists until one devised a way of getting them all into the same bottle. The result has not excited gastronomes, but "Irish Cream" liqueurs have established a new category of alcoholic drink with astonishing success. Bailey's Irish Cream, launched in 1974, had ten years later become the biggest-selling liqueur of any type in the world. The drink took three or four years to develop, and the signature Bailey's was devised simply as an Irish surname which was

relatively universal, easy to pronounce, neutral and yet reasonably memorable. A company called R and A Bailey was set up to market the product. R and A Bailey is a subsidiary of the Irish operation of Gilbey's, which is itself part of the British group Grand Metropolitan.

Bailey's whiskey is provided by Irish Distillers. The company owns its own creamery, in County Cavan, and adds chocolate and other flavourings when the drink is blended at its premises in Dublin. The whiskey stops the cream from turning sour, and Bailey's has succeeded in preventing separation, a problem which had bedevilled early attempts to produce similar products. Bailey's was the first liqueur to use real cream and, after the product was launched, initially in Ireland, there was a gap of four years before anything similar arrived in the mar-

ketplace. Bailey's has retained about 75 per cent of the worldwide market for cream-based liqueurs. A quarter of its sales are in Britain and a half in North America but the product is in about a hundred countries.

Its Irish-produced competitors include Carolan's (again, owned by a British-based international company), Waterford and the lower-priced Ryan's (both from Irish Distillers), O'Darby (produced in Cork by a Bacardi subsidiary), and Emmet's and Royal Tara, from dairy companies. Including drinks based on other spirits, or with different flavours, between 30 and 40 cream liqueurs established themselves in the international market during the late 1970s and early 1980s.

The Irish had hit on a remarkable recipe for success and were, once again, the recipients of flattery in its most sincere form.

A taste-guide to Irish whiskey liqueurs

Whiskey lovers are inclined to prefer their drink without any sweetening, but each of its distilling nations use it as a base for the odd liqueur. The most famous whiskey-based concoction from Ireland is also the biggest-selling liqueur in the world. In such cunning ways does "Irish" reach the unwhiskied.

Bailey's was the first of the "Irish Cream" liqueurs, and it has inspired many imitators, some of them short-lived. Thus is the name of Ireland proclaimed in millions of bars and homes, and perhaps a reminder offered that it is a whiskey-distilling nation, too. The trouble is that the liqueurs are so creamy, and chocolatey sweet, that the whiskey has difficulty in making its presence felt. The similarities between these products are more evident than the differences.

O'Darby, from Bacardi

Emmets, from a Dublin dairy company

Waterford Cream, from Irish Distillers

Ryan's, from Irish Distillers

Carolans, from Allied Breweries

Royal Tara, from a Cork dairy company

CANADA

The world's view of every country embraces contradictions, and its image of Canada more than most: a huge land of wild, snowy open spaces; a small nation of only about twenty or thirty million people, most of them clustered in big cities strung along the border with the U.S. It is at once a wild frontier and a sophisticated urban culture. Populated with people of every nationality, Canada is a land of diversity, embracing the history of many cultures, including those of the original French and English-speaking inhabitants.

Of all the lands that are Canadian, it is the country of mountain streams, icy rivers, peninsulae and archipelagoes that charges the imagination of the drinker elsewhere in the world. Canada's beers, of both the Pilsner and ale types, and its whiskies, are known far beyond its borders, and especially in the bigger nation to the South (for Canadians of Scottish origin, this must be a familiar situation). Within their home country, the choice of drink, and the circumstances in which it is purchased, depends upon the location; in which of the Canadas is the drinking being done? The real Canada is multicultural and eclectic, its 26 million people forming an ethnic jigsaw puzzle.

In the Maritime Provinces, dark rum is popular, no doubt a hangover from a tradition shared with neighbouring New England. In Quebec, where ale is preferred to Pilsner beer, there is a yet older spirit tradition: the Dutch style of gin. The Quebecois identify this variously as *gin, type Hollandais; Genièvre*; and, most often, *Geneva*. In whichever of its many spellings, the *jenever* of The Netherlands derives its name from the French word for juniper. The style of gin first produced in The Netherlands in the mid 1500s was the earliest spirit to gain widespread acceptance in Western Europe. It is still common beyond the present-day borders of The Netherlands, in the geographically and culturally contiguous Flemish regions of Belgium and Northern France.

However eclectic its drinking habits, Canada is known for one spirit in particular. Canadian Whisky is a style of its own. The destination of the train carrying distilled rye through the grain belt is long forgotten. Canadian Mist, on the other hand, most definitely travels in great quantities to the United States.

(Across the English Channel, there is less of the fruitiness of malt and rye, and more flowery, juniper dryness, in the adaptations popularised by London and Plymouth.)

The commercial development of gin is usually dated from the foundation of Bols' distillery, in The Netherlands, in 1575. The popularity of the drink in Europe in the decades that followed might explain why the Frenchmen who settled Quebec in the early 1600s had a taste for it. In the early days, gin is believed to have been shipped from Europe as a profitable ballast on ships that went to fetch lumber from Canada. It seems likely that the Quebecois began to distil their own in the 1700s, but it wasn't until the late 1800s that their domestic production of Dutch-style gin became a serious commercial industry, with the foundation of a company in Canada by Dutch immigrant Jan Melcher.

The traffic between the Old and New Worlds (especially the Caribbean) introduced to Europe spices and fruits that encouraged liqueur-making in port towns from Riga and Danzig, Amsterdam and Rotterdam, to Angers and Bordeaux. This, too, transplanted back to the New World. One of The Netherlands' most famous producers of both gin and liqueurs is De Kuyper, based in the distilling town of Schiedam, near Rotterdam. De Kuyper also has a distillery in Quebec, and is an important drinks company in Canada. As it happens, De Kuyper's output there is predominantly of gin, though liqueurs are very popular in Canada. They,

EST SHIPMENT OF RYE WHISKY

TRAIN, CARRYING A RECORD SHIPMENT OF RYE WHISKY

too, have a regional bias. So long as the Quebecois cling to gin (and brandy), the English-speakers must drink something different, and it is they who most favour liqueurs, which sell especially well in the Northwest Territories and the Yukon. An extreme, Canadian, polarity is at work.

Ontario was probably the birthplace of Canada's whisky-distilling industry. Although the beginnings are not well documented, they seem to have been at the end of the 1700s and in the first few decades of the 1800s, in the area around Kingston, which is between Ontario's two most important cities, Toronto and Ottawa, and on the route to Montreal, Quebec. In his book "Canadian Whisky", William Rannie talks of there being, by the 1840s, 200 distilleries strung along the shores of Lakes Erie and Ontario and the St Lawrence. That line may be the axis for most of Canada's population and business, but it is also very much a whisky-distilling region, from Windsor by way of Waterloo, Toronto and Belleville to Montreal. Today, there are about a dozen companies, some with distilleries in more than one province. Among these companies is Seagram's, the world's biggest distiller. A second Canadian company, Hiram Walker, is also one of the international giants. Through these two companies, Canada is a massive force in the world's whisky industry. Seagram's is based in Waterloo, Ontario, and Montreal, Quebec. Its principal Cana-

dian rival is headquartered in the company town of Walkerville, a district of Windsor, Ontario. All the whisky makers are headquartered in either Ontario or Quebec, except for two small producers in British Columbia: Great West and Potter, both of which are known for their extremely competitive pricing.

Each province has its own laws and customs concerning drinking, and most of them are restrictive. There are ironies in this. Canada had only partial Prohibition when that in the U.S. was meant to be total. Thus Canadian whisky could be produced, and somehow find its way South of the Border. Canada at that time sowed the seeds of a reputation which still flourishes. Ask him about the principal products of Canada, and beer and whisky will most likely be on the lips of an American. The Canadians, through their elected representatives, begrudge themselves the very pleasures for which they are best known.

Taxes on drink are high, and advertising is hedged with restrictions. More drinking is done at home than in public places, though that is changing somewhat. The ease and pleasure with which a drink may be obtained varies greatly from one province or territory to another. Except for Quebec, the provinces and territories largely restrict the sale of alcoholic beverages to a government monopoly (as do several states of the U.S.). For decades, provincial government liquor stores

were intentionally drab, with a view to discouraging the purchase of their grudging offerings. However, they failed to drive drinkers to abstinence, and today some pleasant and forthcoming stores are beginning to emerge. Nor are all drinking places in Canada as dour and male-orientated as they once were. The big cities especially are beginning to blossom with restaurants and pubs. The type of pub that brews its own beer has become quite a feature of the Canadian scene. When that was first permitted, in the mid-1980's, major changes of attitude were clearly in the making.

Once again, every nation has its contradictions. The Canadians might point their fingers across the Detroit river to a nation known for the world's biggest, most powerful cars and some of the most restrictive speed limits. There is, though, in Canada's drinking laws and customs something of a national persona, conservative with a small "c", liberal in a virtuous way. The persona derives, no doubt, from the Protestant ethic of Northern Europe, not least Scotland, though drinking laws there are also much changed.

It is in these cold countries – an arc through Canada, Scotland, Scandinavia, Russia and Poland – that the drinking of spirits can be most intent, and no doubt that is why, over the years, they have been the most girded with constraints. Canada is perhaps ungirding itself.

123

The whiskies of Canada

In its home country and elsewhere, a Canadian whisky is often offered to the drinker who has asked for "a rye". Some Canadian whiskies are even designated as rye on the label. This is an accurate, but confusing, description. Whatever their labels say, all Canadian whiskies are of the same style. The classic method of production is to blend rye, and perhaps other whiskies, with relatively neutral spirit. These are, indeed, rye whiskies – but as blends. They are quite different from the traditional straight rye of the United States. That is the original "rye".

In palate, the best Canadian whiskies have at least some of the spicy, bitter-sweet character of rye, lightened with the blending spirit. In some instances this, too, is distilled from rye but the raw material hardly matters, since it is rectified close to neutrality. More often, the blending spirit is made from corn. A further component of the palate is a dash of the vanilla sweetness to be found in Bourbon. This may result from a proportion of Bourbon-type whisky having been used in the blend, or it may derive from the wood used in aging. Such is the pungency of straight rye and Bourbon that their characteristics are powerfully evident in the palate of a good Canadian whisky, despite its being a very dilute blend. There is as little as three per cent of straight whisky in some Canadians, more often four or five, but not as much as ten. This dash of flavour is counterpointed with the lightness of body provided by the far greater proportion of the neutral spirit.

It's a shame that the Canadians don't market any straight rye, since they have over the years developed numerous refinements in its distillation. One characteristic of many Canadian whiskies is their use of rye that has been malted. This provides a characteristic smoothness and fullness of flavour. Unmalted ryes are also used. Most blends include more than one rye whisky, and for this purpose a single distillery may produce several. The character and weight of these will vary according to the mash bill and distilla-

tion methods. The mash bill for a rye whisky being produced for blending may also include a small proportion of barley malt, and perhaps some corn. The proportion of these ingredients can be varied to produce ryes of differing characters. Canadian distilleries also produce their own Bourbon-type whiskies for blending purposes. They also make corn whiskies, and even distil unmalted barley, again to produce components for their blends.

The biggest producers, Seagram's, have half a dozen distilleries in Canada, using several different yeasts, and making more than 50 different straight whiskies for blending. A large number of these will go into some of the more complex blends, and general Canadian practice is to use perhaps 20 different whiskies. Even the least complex blend will probably contain 15 whiskies, built around six or seven basic types.

Although all Canadian Whisky is column-distilled, different styles and permutations of equipment are used. Canadian distilleries are inclined to have very complicated still-houses. There are American-style column "beer" stills with pot-still doublers; Scottish-type Coffey stills; multi-column rectifiers; and extractive stills using a dilution method.

The changes are also rung in the extent to which the various whiskies for blending are aged. In the case of rye, aging tends not only to smoothen the whisky but also to make it heavier. This effect is more evident if the rye is aged as a straight – and that raises another variable. The extent to which whisky is aged before or after blending is a matter on which there are different, and passionate, schools of thought in Canada. One argument says that whisky off the still manifests its true characteristics; the blender should work with that, then let the constituents enjoy a long marriage. Another view is that the matured whisky is what the drinker tastes, so surely it is better to blend from that. A third element here is the question of "flavourings", like sherry, other grape or fruit wines or juices. These ingredients, notably prune

"wine", are a curious element in some (though by no means all) Canadian whiskies. Perhaps they help explain Canadian whisky's affinity with dry ginger ale (soda water is also a popular dilutant). The choice and proportion of these flavourings (never more than one or two per cent at the very most) can differentiate one whisky from another. So, of course, can the wood used for maturation. Canada uses new wood, Bourbon, sherry and brandy barrels. It is all "small wood" – no butts are used. Aging must be for a minimum of three years. The cheapest whiskies, and some of the bulk export brands, bottled in the U.S., have only three, four or five years' aging. The premiums may have anything from six to eight, and the top-of-the-line whiskies ten, twelve, or more.

Despite all of these variables, the differences between the various Canadian whiskies are subtle. They are also influenced by the buying policies of the provincial government liquor stores and to some extent by a set of price-bands. Super-premium brands are categorized as "A", premiums as "B", and so on, all the way through to "E". A distilling company may have brands in all of these categories. Naturally, the odds are that the more expensive brands will contain a higher percentage of straight whiskies, be more lengthily aged, and have fewer flavourings. Among export labels, the more expensive ones will be bottled in Canada, the cheaper examples shipped in bulk at barrel proof and reduced in the country of destination, notably the United States.

One company that makes even its neutral spirit from rye is Alberta Distillers, with plants in Calgary and Burlington, Ontario. On the label of its super-premium Alberta Springs product, the company also makes a point of "charcoal mellowing". This, however, is a conventional filtration process, not the leaching method used in Tennessee. Alberta Springs is marketed in Canada at 40 per cent alcohol by volume – the national standard – and exported in the bottle at 90 U.S. proof (45 per cent). This company does not have "B" or "C" products in the Canadian market, so its next label is the category "D" Windsor Supreme, a very popular brand on both sides of the border. Its category "E" Alberta Premium is a major brand in Canada, while Windsor Deluxe and the lighter, 35 per cent Autumn Gold are lesser labels. The Alberta range are generally very smooth whiskies. The Company is owned by National Distillers, of the U.S.

Another company with a distillery apiece in Alberta and Ontario is Gilbey Canada. Its distilleries are at Lethbridge and Toronto. Gilbey Canada takes a particular pride in the worldwide sales of its mature-tasting Black Velvet label. This was originally a super-premium brand, but is now sold at a popular price. The super-premium in the U.S. market is Regal Velvet. Red Velvet, on the other hand, is the super-premium brand in the Japanese market, along with Colony House. In Canada, the company has labels in every category, from Triple Crown, through the well-aged Royal Velvet to Number Eight, Red Velvet and Golden Velvet.

Also based in Ontario is McGuinness Distillers, owned by Heublein. This company has distilleries in Toronto and Kelowna, British Columbia. It also owns Central Canadian, in Weyburn, Saskatchewan, and Acadian, in Bridgetown, Nova Scotia. Its super-premium label is Captain's Table, quite a full-bodied blend. It also has the lighter NC Tower, a light-tasting but fairly full-bodied blend called Old Canada, the aromatic Gold Tassel and a couple of Silk Tassels. Of these two Silk Tassels, the Deluxe version has a degree of complexity but the regular label is surprisingly full-bodied. There are also a number of local labels.

The proudest whisky in Ontario may well be Canadian Company, smooth and elegant, with a soft aroma and a hint of Kentucky oak. The clue is in the name; it's an all-Canadian private company, though with a Swiss-German accent. Canadian

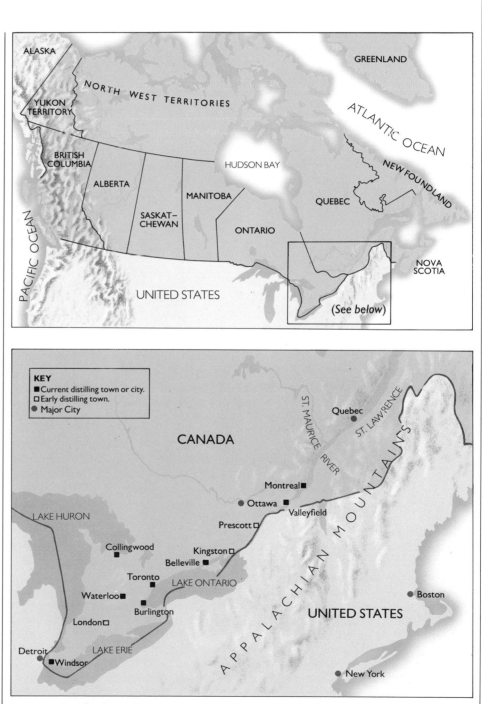

Even in regions that favour liqueurs, gins or rum, there are whisky distilleries, from British Columbia to Nova Scotia, but the heartland is between Windsor, Ontario, and Montreal, Quebec. This is as close as Canada comes to having a defined "Whisky region".

Company is a well-made blend of whiskies bought in from other distillers. The company, Rieder, does have a distillery, at Grimsby, between Toronto and Niagara Falls, but that produces brandies and eaux-de-vie, some of them from local fruit. However. the company is well-connected in the whisky business, as the domestic marketer of Canadian Mist. That very light, clean-tasting Canadian whisky is produced in Collingwood, Ontario, at a very modern distillery owned by Brown Forman, of the U.S. It is a major bulk brand in the American market.

The oldest whisky-distilling companies in Ontario, and therefore Canada, are those that had their roots in farming and grain-milling in the mid 1800s. Millers were often paid in grain, and one way of utilising the surplus was to distil it. Distilling's by-product, spent grain, could then be used as cattle feed. Two such mill-distilleries were the beginnings of entire chapters in the history of whisky. In what is now a district of Windsor, a mill and distillery was founded in 1858 by Hiram Walker. Further East, between London and Toronto, is Waterloo, where a mill established in 1857 later became the original Seagram's distillery.

East again, beyond Toronto, at Belleville, near the point where the Moira river flows into the Bay of Quinte on Lake Ontario, Henry Corby founded a mill in 1857 and a distillery a couple of years later. The distillery was destroyed by fire in 1907, and rebuilt on its present site, with a view through the spruce trees to the rushing river. Across the bay is the island of Prince Edward County.

With several turn-of-the century buildings, Corby's is what passes in Canada for a delightfully old-fashioned distillery, and in this respect is more interesting than some for the lay visitor. It does, indeed, welcome visitors. Although the Corbys were of French Huguenot and Southern English origin, the company went to Ireland to find the rosewood and mahogany bar, from a railway station, that serves visitors in its reception centre.

With a majority stockholding now in the hands of Hiram Walker, Corby produces whiskies under its own name, in addition to having the well-known Wiser's range, which were originally distilled at Prescott, Ontario. It also distils for Meagher's, a company that markets whisky among a larger range of fruit brandies and liqueurs made in Quebec. The Corby's whiskies are generally light in palate, though with a little more intensity in the Park Lane label. The Wiser's products are in the main aged for a little longer ("Wiser and Older" was the classic slogan), some of them also being married in a whisky counterpart to a solera system. The De Luxe version has ten years' maturation, the brand labelled simply "Wiser's Oldest" has 18. This is the oldest Canadian whisky. Another of the company's brands, Burke's, is a very light whisky. The Meagher's product is full-bodied and richly fruity.

Despite Quebec's propensity for producing liqueurs and gins, the province is a major force in whisky. Even the brand named after gin pioneer Jan Melcher was a whisky. This is called Melchers Very Mild, and describes itself very well. It is a light-bodied, youngish whisky. Melchers is owned by Seagram's, and no longer distils its own whisky. Seagram's own first distillery may have been in Ontario, but its Canadian home-base is in Montreal. So is that of Canadian Schenley – now privately owned, by a group of pension funds, and independent of the American company from which it takes its name. The cross-border link had its origins in the distant period when Seagram's of Canada and Schenley of the U.S., after attempting a merger to conquer the North American market, parted as deadly rivals. For a time, the two companies fought for continental supremacy, but U.S. Schenley, which takes its name from a town in Pennsylvania, eventually changed ownership and has reduced its size through divestment.

Canadian Schenley has executive offices in Montreal and just one distillery, at Val-

leyfield, about half way to the American border. It is passionately proud of its products, for which it has won a number of awards. Its range includes not only the Schenley labels but also those of Park and Tilford (a Vancouver distillery, now closed) and Gibson (the exact origins of this brand seem to have been forgotten).

Schenley's first Canadian whisky was introduced in 1948, and thirty-five years later, in 1983, the company decided to mark this by issuing a limited edition that is a collector's item for whisky-buffs. Three hundred crystal decanters were filled with the whisky, called "The Classic by Schenley", one of those ponderous names beloved by marketing men. This blend is made from the oldest whiskies the company had in stock – aged between 17 and 20 years. The Classic has a big bouquet, a full body and a very smooth palate. It is similar in style to the company's super-premium brand, modestly named Order of Merit, which is itself 15 years old.

Schenley is inclined to mature its whiskies thoroughly, and to offer age statements on the label. Its premium brand, Gibson's Finest,

Both the scale and the efficiency of Canada's whisky industry, from the shipping of the grain to the mixing of the blend (right) are evident even at a "small", old distillery like Corby's.

is 12 years old, still full-bodied and smooth, but with less oakiness. A newer premium brand called Schenley Award is ten years old. There can be a fair amount of rye body at lesser ages than that – and a cachet. Hence the elaborate age-warranty label on the eight-year-old Schenley O.F.C. (Old Fine Canadian). This old-established brand greatly outsells other distilleries' counterparts in its category, and they don't all quote their age. A similar product, spiced with some 18-year-old whisky, is marketed under Park and Tilford's Royal Command label, offering a characterful palate for a category "D" blend. In the same category is Gibson's Medallion, a crisper and quite complex whisky. The company also has several brands in the lower price brackets, including its old-established Golden Wedding; "909", "P.M.", Tradition, Five Thirty, Three Feathers, Three Lancers, Bon Vivant and the 35 per cent brand Gibson Extra Dry. American-market brands like MacNaughton and the usually-younger Grande Canadian are usually exported in the bottle, though a small amount is shipped in bulk.

The pedigree of Canadian whisky

The launching of the brand Canadian Club by Hiram Walker himself in 1884 represented the beginnings of a national style of whisky. Because of his distinctive method of production, subsequently adopted by all the country's distillers, Canadian Club managed to combine some of the full flavour of North American whiskies – especially the fruitiness – with a much cleaner and lighter, perhaps crisper, palate than was common at the time. These characteristics have been associated with Canadian whiskies ever since.

The style derived from a wish, which has always been shared by all whisky-producers, to remove some of the harshness imparted by fusel oils, yet to do so without altogether sacrificing flavour. At the time, wheat and rye were the grains most widely and economically available for distillation in Canada. These grains produce whiskies high in fusel oils. The methods being used in North America to remove fusel oils were double-distillation, charcoal leaching, or aging. Walker adopted a different, and two-fold approach. He used an unusually long and intense distillation process to produce a master whisky that was as clean as possible. Then he blended this with neutral spirits. Other distillers were certainly working to improve techniques of rectification and blending at the time, but Walker was a leader in the sciences and arts of fermentation, distillation and blending and in marketing.

Walker, whose descendants were believed to have originated from Norwich, England, and who himself was born in Douglas, Massachusetts in 1816, was an entrepeneur on a grand scale. He had begun his working life behind the counter of a dry-goods store, then started his own business in milling and vinegar-brewing and, in 1858, whisky-distilling. Around his various businesses, he had built a company town – called Walkerville – on the Canadian side of the Detroit river. The distillery was, and still is, at exactly the point where the Americans landed during the Second War of Independence with the intention of "liberating" Canada from the British. What had been frontier country became a vantage point for marketing. By the time Walker launched Canadian Club, there were growing cities to provide a market for such a product. He could see one such city directly across the Detroit river, in the country of his birth.

"Canadian" may have had a cachet even in those days. "Club" certainly did, and that was the idea. This was meant to be a sophisticated whisky for clubmen. It was a whisky for business gentlemen, not for rednecks. At a time when whisky was customarily sold by the barrel, then served from decanters, this one was bottled and labelled, to guarantee its source. Hiram Walker – like one or two famous distillers in other countries – is remembered as a pioneer of branded whiskies.

Canadian Club was such a success in the U.S. market that it was widely imitated. By the time Walker himself died, in 1899, "Canadian" certainly did have a cachet in respect of whisky. There were in the market whiskies claiming to be Canadian that had been produced not only across the Detroit river but in every town from Omaha, Nebraska, to Cincinnati, Ohio. In 1900, more than 40 such fakes were spotted. There was a plethora of "Club" whiskies, too, many with remarkably similar labels. Other whiskies were labelled as having been made by "the Canadian process". The Hiram Walker company used Press advertisements, posters and circulars to proclaim the authenticity of its product and to expose the fakes. Agents were used, with great success, to track down and prosecute the perpetrators.

In their efforts to protect their brand, Walker's also pronounced that there was no such thing as a "Canadian process" that U.S. companies could copy. Surely there was, but perhaps it would have been difficult to patent. The issue became even more heated when the U.S. Pure Food Law of 1906 drew attention to fusel oils in whiskies. The distillers in the U.S. successfully lobbied Washington to make a ruling that fusel oils were, indeed, an essential part of a whisk(e)y, and that rectified spirit had no place in the bottle. This resulted in 6,000 cases of Canadian Club being seized and

Hiram Walker put the whisky of Canada on to the map. One of the world's biggest spirit companies emerged from the success of his Canadian Club brand, launched in 1884. A swindle! Names were named when the Hiram Walker company pursued whisky-fakers. The posters had the vigour of a political campaign. It was well worth the effort.

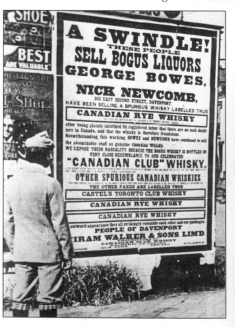

refused admission on to the American market. Then, on the orders of President Taft, hearings were convened, and proceeded for three weeks, to resolve the matter. Industry experts and chemists testified, and the result was a judgment that whisky "includes all potable liquor distilled from grain". A clear ruling, though hardly a satisfactory one – but it allowed Canadian Club, once and for all, into the country. Of such contestations has the history of whisky been made.

Just as the Scots' blended whiskies were licensed to attack the English market by the London judgments of 1905-9, so at the same time did Canada's gain free rein in the United States through a ruling made in Washington. The Scottish example is often cited by Canadians proclaiming the merits of their own national method of whisky-making. Both countries spell whisky the same way, but their methods are not exactly parallel. The Scots generally use a substantially higher proportion of straight whisky (in their case, single malt) than do the Canadians (with their rye). The Scots blend their malt with grain whisky, rather than neutral spirit; the one makes a significant taste contribution, the other barely does. The Scots' tradition of sherry-aging has been augmented by wine-treatment, but they do not use prune wine.

The Canadian style of whisky has, however, its own character and following, and its popularity proved lucrative for Hiram Walker. Five years before his death, he built offices for the company in the Italian renaissance style. It is a magnificent building with working quarters like the hall of a 19th century bank, and reception rooms reminiscent, indeed, of a London gentlemen's club. It sits by its gardens, refusing to be upstaged by the activity all around. Towering next door is the row of cream-painted grain silos, packed together as though they were cartridges in a gunbelt. Across the web of railroad tracks are the 1950s, redbrick buildings that house a highly-mechanised modern distillery. Around is the town of Walkerville. After his death, Hiram Walker's sons

and grandsons ran the business until the Prohibition period. The Hiram Walker company was then reversed into a yet-older firm of distillers, in Toronto, by the splendid name of Gooderham and Worts. That firm was run not by its founders but by a family called Hatch. The family remains a powerful presence in the management of today's public company, which is fully titled Hiram Walker-Gooderham and Worts. One of the Hatches married into the Courvoisier Cognac family, thus bringing a spiritual union to the historic relationship between Canada and France. The company has extensive drinks interests in the U.S. and Scotland, and owns brands as far-flung as Kahlua coffee liqueur, produced in Mexico. A 51 per cent stake of the company is held by Allied Breweries, of Britain.

A hundred years on, Canadian Club remains a classic name in whisky. In palate, it has a dry, rye fruitiness and a crisp, faintly smoky finish, and that might be regarded as the house style of Hiram Walker's Canadian whiskies. A 12-year-old version of this flagship product, called simply Canadian Club Classic, has replaced an earlier super-premium, Carleton Tower. The company also has a younger, lighter whisky called Imperial and the more traditional-tasting Walker's Special Old Rye. There are also a couple of whiskies under the Gooderham's label. Of these, Little Brown Jug has yet more rye character, and Bonded Stock rather less. The flavourful Royal Canadian, the medium-bodied Rich and Rare and the self-describing Northern Light are all Walker brands in the US market.

Canada's population is a tenth of that across the border, so the United States has always presented a huge market. For the liquor business in Canada, the U.S. was an especially tempting market during the overlapping periods of the First World War and Prohibition. This troubled and tangled time was the delinquent adolescence of the whisky business in Canada, a country then still living with its British parents. During the

First World War, the Scots were still allowed to produce whisky, but the Canadian distilleries were required to make industrial alcohol. A lot of the Scotch produced at that time eventually found its way illegally to Canada, where it was blended with more questionable spirits and flavourings and smuggled into the U.S. to mitigate the effects of Prohibition there. When the war ended, English-speaking Canada had what purported to be total Prohibition, but distilleries were allowed to produce whisky for export. Much of this was filtered through French islands in the Gulf of St. Lawrence, or even ostensibly through Havana, Cuba, to defeat a ban on imports of whisky into the U.S. By whatever route, it got there.

In both Scotland and Canada, the Establishment adopted an ambivalent attitude to such activities, glad of the vast income it introduced to their nations' economies, but unable wholly to accept the Runyonesque entrepreneurs who did the work.

During the 1920s, Scotland's distilling giant D.C.L. acquired Seagram's, of Waterloo, Ontario. The Seagram family were British immigrants, from Wiltshire. The first Canadian-born generation, brought up with a background of farming and inn-keeping, moved into grain-milling and distilling, eventually becoming the country's biggest producers of rye whisky, with brands like 83 and V.O. The latter brand's black-and-gold decorative ribbon was derived from the horse-racing colours of the owner, Joseph Emm Seagram, a pompous and flamboyant man – who modelled himself on Edward VII, according to the book "King of the Castle", by Canadian journalist Peter C. Newman. After Seagram's death, control was divided among members of his family.

D.C.L. not only acquired Seagram's but also accepted an invitation to be partners in a company being set up by another Canadian liquor family, the Bronfmans. This family had been successful as liquor distributors in Canada during the period of Prohibition in the U.S., and had now established a distillery at La Salle, a suburb of Montreal.

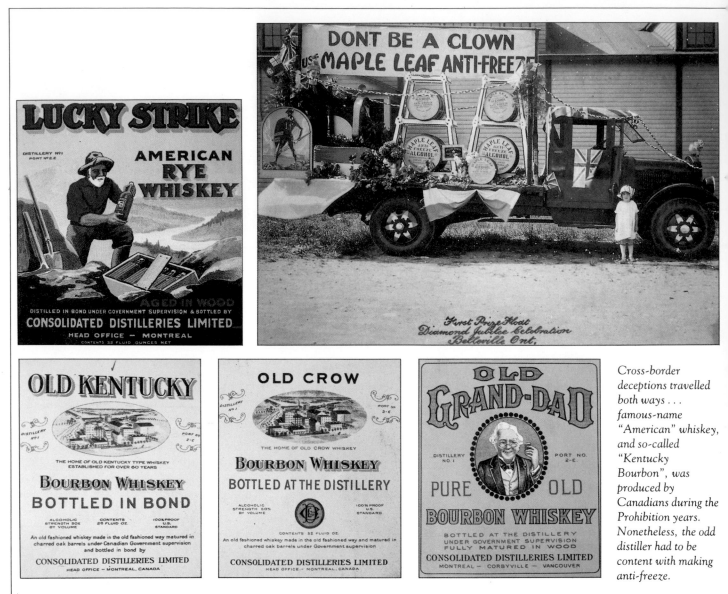

Cross-border deceptions travelled both ways . . . famous-name "American" whiskey, and so-called "Kentucky Bourbon", was produced by Canadians during the Prohibition years. Nonetheless, the odd distiller had to be content with making anti-freeze.

D.C.L.'s bosses at the time felt they could better progress in the North American market by utilising the experience of the Seagrams and Bronfmans but, as the shadow of Prohibition in the U.S. lifted, they changed their minds and decided to go it alone. D.C.L.'s share of Seagrams was sold to the Bronfman family. That was a fateful decision.

It was Seagram's, under the Bronfmans' control, that would prosper most in the U.S. Indeed, Seagram's went on to become the biggest distillers not only in Canada and the U.S. but also worldwide, with substantial interests in Scotland. The company's huge portfolio of products includes Ronrico and Captain Morgan rums, Sir Robert Burnett and Boodles gins, Wolfschmidt vodka and Leroux liqueurs. The Bronfman family also have extensive interests in oil and property.

There are ironies in Seagram's success. Wishing to erase the memories of bootleg liquor, the family's dynastic head, Sam Bronfman, became such a rigid custodian of good distillery practice that his word approached being international law. His greatest preoccupation was with the art of blending, which he saw as the key to the production of whiskies that combined character, cleanness and consistency. In a similar vein, he also preached moderation among drinkers, with Seagram's buying advertising space to dissuade the consumer from excess.

Seagram's Canadian whiskies are in general well-rounded, with a touch of sweetness. They are usually delicate in palate, with a slightly oily body, and with a clean, faintly oaky, finish. No flavourings are used, and the master rye may be blended with whisky made from unmalted barley. A high proportion of charred new oak is used, though the whiskies in any one blend will be drawn from a complex matrix of different cooperage. The super-premium brand is Crown Royal, created to honour King George VI and Queen Elizabeth when they visited Canada in 1939. Sam Bronfman is said to have blended this whisky himself, working his way through 600 samples before he was satisfied. Then comes V.O. (Very Old? Not really, at six years), followed by 83 (named after the date when Joseph Emm Seagram became the sole proprietor of his Waterloo distillery), Great Oaks ("from little acorns" was the title of Sam Bronfman's history of the company), and Five Star (a bar brand that is Seagram's largest selling Canadian whisky in its home country). Crown Royal and V.O. are both soft, rich whiskies, with plenty of aroma and flavour. Seagram's 83 is lighter, with a drier finish. Five Star has more rye character, and a hint of oakiness.

Canadian Lord Calvert, with a full flavour, and quite sweet; the lighter, well-rounded Harwood; and the yet lighter, softer, James Foxe; are all exported in bulk to the U.S. Seagram's also has, as a result of a past takeover, a range of Canadian whiskies under the Adams label. These tend to be drier, with a lively, zesty palate. They include Adams' Antique (12 years old), Private Stock (eight) and Double Distilled (five). Confusingly, Adams' bar brand is known as Four Roses, a label that has also been used on Bourbons and blended whiskies in the U.S., and elsewhere. Seagram's also produces Canadian whiskies for a subsidiary company called Hudson's Bay Distillers. These whiskies are generally light and dry. Yet another range made by Seagram's are the very light-bodied, rounded whiskies owned and marketed by an independent company called Jack Baker.

The creed of whisky-making propounded by Sam Bronfman persists as strongly as ever. At the Montreal headquarters, a Gothic "castle" in the downtown area, the chief blender from Bronfman's time, Art Dawe, amiably roams among the filing drawers full of samples, lifting a nosing glass to ensure that the secrets of Seagram's are being put to work. Out in the suburbs, the handsome, brick-built distillery at La Salle disgorges barrels of whisky to ride a "ski-lift" to the warehouses. At the Waterloo distillery, an impressive whisky museum was opened in 1984. In the United States, the principal distilleries are at Lawrenceburg, Indiana, and Relay, near Baltimore, Maryland, and the 1950s office building by Mies van der Rohe, on Park Avenue, New York City, is a landmark.

The family still have a controlling interest in the company. They were refugees from Tsarist Russia and they became a dynasty comparable with the Rothschilds. With them, Canadian whisky came of age.

Blenders at Seagram's regard their samples as a "library", and keep them on "file". Other companies work in much the same way, but the art of the blender is pursued with a special devotion at Seagram's.

A taste-guide to the principal Canadian whiskies

The national traditions of Canada include its preference for the spelling "whisky" and a style of product that is its own. Canadian whisky is one of the world's classic styles. It is a blended whisky in which the flavour keynote is provided by rye. Canadian whiskies are usually light in body, smooth, but often quite full in flavour.

Crown Royal, from Seagram's

Private Stock, from Seagram's Adams range

Hudson's Bay Special, from Seagram's Hudson's Bay range

Crown Royal, produced by Seagram's, is clean, delicate, well rounded, with a hint of oakiness in the finish. These are house characteristics of the Seagram's range. The Adams blends are drier, those from Hudson's Bay lighter.

Royal Velvet, from Gilbey

Black Velvet, from Gilbey

Royal Velvet is the super-premium brand from Gilbey. That company has a range of mature-tasting whiskies named after various colours of velvet; these include the popular brand Black Velvet.

Canadian Company is a smooth and elegant whisky, with a soft aroma and a hint of Kentucky oak. This label is owned by Rieder, the brandy-producer. Rieder markets the clean tasting Canadian Mist in its home country.

Royal Reserve, from Corby

Burke's Select, from Corby's Burke's range

Wiser's Oldest, from Corby's Wiser's range

Royal Reserve is the biggest-selling of the Corby whiskies, which are generally light in palate. The same distillery produces the very light Burke's and the more mature-tasting Wiser's range.

Canadian Club Classic, from Hiram Walker

Canadian Club, from Hiram Walker

Canadian Club could claim to be the original whisky in its style. Its 12-year-old version, Classic, is thus well-named. These Hiram Walker whiskies have a dry, rye fruitiness and a crisp, faintly smoky finish.

Captain's Table, from McGuinness

Silk Tassel, from McGuinness

Captain's Table is the super-premium brand of McGuinness. It is quite a full-bodied blend. The company's whiskies are in general aromatic, fairly full-bodied and complex. They include the popular Silk Tassel.

Schenley Award, from Schenley

Gibson's Finest, from Schenley's Gibson's range

Three Lancers, from Schenley's Park and Tilford range

Schenley Award is a well-matured whisky at ten years old, with a good rye character. Schenley's premium products also include the smooth Gibson's Finest. As well as Gibson, the company owns Park and Tilford.

Windsor Supreme, from Alberta Distillers

Alberta Springs, from Alberta Distillers

Windsor Supreme is a clean-tasting Canadian whisky with a smooth palate and a hint of rye. It is made by Alberta Distillers, whose other brands include the super premium Alberta Springs.

Meagher's 1878 best typifies the very full fruitiness that is a classic characteristic of some Canadian whiskies. Appropriately enough, the company is better known for fruit brandies and liqueurs.

THE UNITED STATES

In the land of conspicuous consumption, there is a reminder of drink on every other poster or page, yet there remains a peculiar ambivalence about it. The national memory has engaged in a deception as to the spirit, so to speak, in which the country was born. As it happened, when the Pilgrim Fathers sought a place to make their permanent landing in America, they did so, according to their diaries, "our victuals being much spent, especially our beer". They landed in need of a drink and freedom, yet the shadow of their Puritan hats still hangs over the land. In their day, water was frequently unsafe to drink, and the consumption of alcohol bore no opprobrium unless it was taken to excess. Nor would it for a century or so.

Can it be coincidence that the Pilgrims'

points of departure – Leiden, in The Netherlands, and London and Plymouth, in England – are the three towns most associated with the birth of gin? The juniper bush casts a demon shadow, too; more than three centuries later, proposing to restrain the institution of midday sociability, President Carter singled out for his condemnation the "three-Martini lunch".

Gin remains Dutch and English, and in the United States it hides guiltily in the Martini, a difficult trick, since this transparent confection is so often ignorant of vermouth. That a Martini might be made from vodka is an even greater betrayal, and an odd one to emerge in such a Russophobe country. In Russia, the Ukraine and Poland, vodka may be spiced in any one of 20 or 30 ways, with flavours from "bison grass" or dill

to red pepper or ginseng; in the U.S., its most popular version merely undertakes to leave you breathless. It says much for double standards that a drink which may make you drunk is the more acceptable for having little flavour and even less aroma.

No such accusation can be levelled at the world's great spirits, among which at least one is American. That passionate American Bernard De Voto, in his essay "The Hour", was uncompromising: "Let us candidly admit that there are shameful blemishes on the American past, of which by far the worst is rum. Nevertheless we have improved man's lot and enriched his civilization with rye, Bourbon and the Martini cocktail. In all history has any other nation done so much? Not by two-thirds."

"The Hour" refers to the period after work

The White Rabbit Saloon (left) captures the elusive quality of drinking in America. It has plenty of whiskey bottles but no alcohol. It's in the whiskey-distilling town of Lynchburg, Tennessee, but from the drinker's viewpoint the locality is dry. Soda or coffee are served to diners.

The above licence to wholesale liquor was granted at Bethel, Alabama, as long ago as 1872, but state and county laws remain a tiresome tangle more than a century later. 'Package stores' like this one in Louisville, Kentucky, may well be delights of alcoholic archaeology but they hardly mirror the gastronomic pleasures experienced by the eclectic drinker.

and before dinner, during which civilised people in many parts of the world enjoy a drink. The Americans have institutionalised what they call the "Happy Hour", and in 1951 De Voto devoted a book-length essay to the subject. It stands alongside his writings on Mark Twain and his studies of the American West as an exhaustive and trenchant work.

He did, though, fail to explain why he entertained such a dislike of rum, except to imply that it is a crude drink. American rum, which was distilled in New England, was the country's first commercially-produced spirit. It was produced from the 1600s but began to fade in the 1800s as whiskey hit its stride with the help of newly-developed continuous methods of distillation.

In any country, drinks follow their own geographical currents as a part of economic and social history, and this is especially true in a nation as mobile as the United States.

That first thirst was slaked by Colonial beers of the ale type, and that style of brewing has remained a tradition in New England and upstate New York, albeit vestigially. In the mid to late 1970s, the style sud-

denly leapfrogged the entire country, and ales became fashionable among a new generation of brewers in Northern California and the Pacific North-West. Meanwhile, Middle America continued to drink beers brewed in the Germanic lager tradition of the mid 1800s.

Rum followed a different path. New England rum – a source of regret less for its palate than for its role in the slave trade – subsided. Caribbean rum flourished, became popular in mixed drinks in the tropical parts of the United States, and reached its peak in a new generation of long cocktails once again in Northern California, especially San Francisco. These drinks subsequently became less chic and passed into the everyday repertoire of the cocktail hour.

American whiskey had its beginnings in Pennsylvania and Maryland, then headed on South through Virginia to Kentucky and Tennessee. In its more Southerly territories, it remains a part of the local social culture but the emergence of the "Urban Cowboy" mood created a new and fashionable context for it in other parts of the country. Such was the pervasiveness of the mood that it is now largely forgotten that "Urban Cowboy" was

a film, a modern-day Western released in 1981. What it reflected was a renaissance of the pioneer spirit of self-reliance and adventure. At times it might have been a parody and at others a personification of the hedonistic bravado that is the obverse side of the Puritan coin, but it was good for whiskey.

American whiskey was overdue for fashionability, and for something less ephemeral. If macho is one distortion of American social behaviour, faddishness is another, but the popularity of products like Wild Turkey and Jack Daniel's did provide whiskey with an opportunity to reassert itself in distant places where it had always enjoyed a bedrock of support. The most notable among these was, yet again, Northern California. Among metropolitan markets in the United States, the biggest consumer of Bourbon whiskey is the San Francisco Bay area.

There is at first sight a paradox that, either in exotic variety or volume, so many other drinks should flourish in the part of the United States most famous for wines (and even ports and brandies) but the explanation is that one awareness helps the next. In

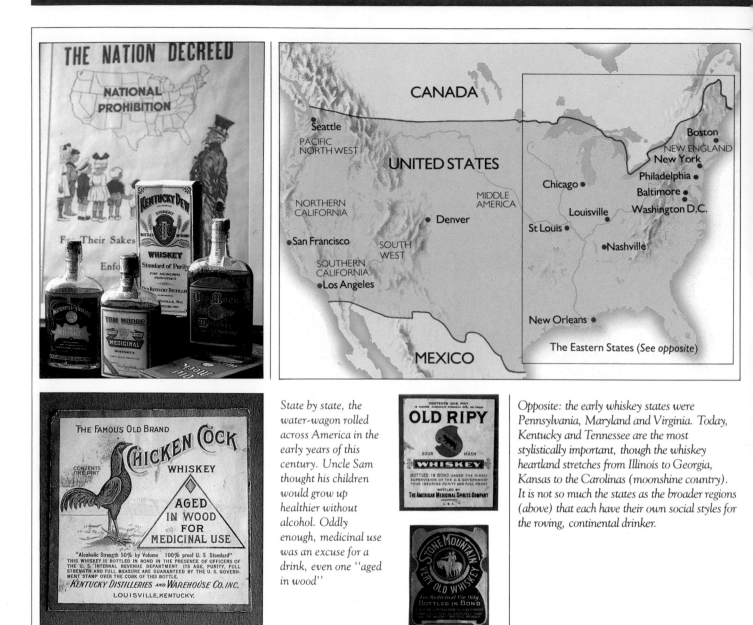

State by state, the water-wagon rolled across America in the early years of this century. Uncle Sam thought his children would grow up healthier without alcohol. Oddly enough, medicinal use was an excuse for a drink, even one "aged in wood"

Opposite: the early whiskey states were Pennsylvania, Maryland and Virginia. Today, Kentucky and Tennessee are the most stylistically important, though the whiskey heartland stretches from Illinois to Georgia, Kansas to the Carolinas (moonshine country). It is not so much the states as the broader regions (above) that each have their own social styles for the roving, continental drinker.

Northern California, wine is important to the economy, and palates are attuned to all types of gastronomic experience.

The loquaciousness of Northern Californians on such matters is just another among the many causes of eyebrow-raising between the West Coast and the East, each convinced that it has the monopoly of sophistication. Back East, tastes are different. When the rest of the country was grappling with Prohibition, cosmopolitan New York contrived to develop a taste for Scotch and Canadian whiskies, and both have endured. The enthusiasm for Canadian whiskies has been fostered, too, by their tantalising proximity: they are within easy reach, and not excessively priced, yet they have the cachet of the import. In those days of Pro-

hibition, it was the East that disguised whiskeys in cocktails like the Manhattan, the Old Fashioned and the Sour.

Like all whiskeys, those of the United States taste best undisguised. Take a small, thimble-shaped "shot" glass, hold two fingers horizontally alongside it, and fill it with whiskey to that level. This is a difficult trick, but worth it. You now have two fingers of whiskey. If that is not sufficient, pour four fingers. Americans always pour large quantities of alcohol. American whiskey has such a big aroma that it should not need the usual drop of water to release the bouquet. If, however, the strength of the alcohol numbs the palate, dilute it with water to an absolute maximum of 50-50. An excessive ratio of two parts water to one

whiskey was suggested by M.F.K. Fisher in her classic "The Art of Eating". She did, however, bravely inveigh against sparkling water or ice, both of which douse the whiskey and shock the palate. It can be difficult to get a drink without ice in the United States. The usual American way is to put generous amounts of ice into a chunky, six-ounce "old fashioned" glass (named after the cocktail), pour on at least two ounces of whiskey, and perhaps top up with water. Or a taller, highball glass, of about eight ounces, might be used. Both of these glasses are cylindrical, plain, without a stem and with a solid glass bottom.

Not only the drinks but also the places in which they are consumed vary from one part of the country to another. In the great old

KEY
- Major City
- Distilling town

cities of the East and Mid West, a handful of taverns survive as they did before Prohibition. These are establishments in which people can meet and informally socialise without being part of a specific "crowd", looking for a pick-up or having a meal. They are not bars like those utilitarian places with long counters, drab decor, high stools, or people drowning their sorrows; nor are they especially for singles, gays, professional people or whomever.

Amenably casual drinking places, sometimes styled "Bar and Grill" also flourish in the Northerly parts of the West Coast – San Francisco and, especially, Seattle. It is said

that people like drinking indoors in Seattle because it constantly rains there. It doesn't, but the Puget Sound climate is neither the driest nor the hottest in the United States.

Much of the West, the South-West and the South are so hot that indoor drinking is rarely comfortable. In some counties – though no longer any entire states – mainly in the South, there is still prohibition. There is even a tangle of local laws about outdoor drinking, whether from a bottle or can, or the camouflage of a brown paper bag.

Outdoor drinking is, though, the definitively American style, from Florida across the Rockies to Southern California:

drinks at the beach, the mountain, the golf club, and at home. In some other parts of the developed world, such as Europe and Japan, life is crowded and people live in houses; Americans, where possible, live in homes. Houses are small, intimate, family dwellings. Homes are expansive purveyors of image, lifestyle and entertainment. Americans like to drink at home, to have cook-outs in the garden. In the summer months they sometimes seem to do little else.

That is a false impression; Americans are among the more modest drinkers of the Western world. What is seen is not excess but the *joie de vivre* under the Puritan hat.

The whiskeys of the United States

Not every country takes a proper pride in its own national drinks. The nation which best understands them, and their contribution to its social culture, is France. A patriotic Frenchman – even a less chauvinistic one, should he exist – would have no hesitation in evincing pride in, for example, the brandies of Cognac and Armagnac. There are spirit drinks of comparable complexity in other parts of the world, but they are accorded insufficient honour in their own countries. This failure to acknowledge a national achievement is by no means exclusive to the United States but it is most evident there. Were that not so, Americans would take a more obvious national pride in their classic styles of whiskey, especially rye (once the preserve of Pennsylvania and Maryland), Kentucky Bourbon, and the sour mash of Tennessee.

One of the three, rye, has been neglected to the point of atrophy. The scandal is compounded by the fact that rye was the first style of whiskey to be born in the United States. Bourbon has suffered largely through being taken for granted, and it began to feel a renewed appreciation with the growing popularity of its more luxurious brands in the early 1980s, though their most notable successes were far from their old Kentucky home, in places like San Francisco, Tokyo and London. The style which has most persuasively communicated the virtues of tradition is Tennessee sour mash, predominantly through the efforts of Jack Daniel's.

Jack Daniel's quiet insistence on its folksy origins has been an act of faith. Even the most patriotic of nations are inclined to worry that their traditions might be old-fashioned, and to complement them with exotic imports. Nothing wrong with that; without imports, there would be no exports. To complement a tradition is to enrich life, but to neglect one is to impoverish. Perhaps a problem for the United States is its fixation with its own youthfulness; like a person on the point of attaining maturity, it sometimes seems unable to accept that it is old enough to have a past. Perhaps in its commendable wish to look forward, it loses sight of its own heritage. In this obsession with what is current, it risks placing more value on the ephemeral than on the durable. Whiskey is durable.

Whiskey has, as well it might, attained maturity. Like one of those movie stars with a lived-in face, it has a rugged attractiveness that speaks of an interesting past. A touch of the Bogart, Bronson or Marvin. Not everyone appreciates that kind of thing, either. Whiskey in America started out as a country boy and spent time in the badlands before becoming streetwise. In the city, it had some roaring days and took up with violent "friends". It has won itself an image which, while undoubtedly romantic, hides the

New oak imparts a characteristic palate to the classic whiskeys of the U.S. The oak is new because each barrel may be used only once – a rule that forestry states like Arkansas are keen to maintain. The decanters below predate bottled whiskey. They were charged from barrels at the bar . . . but did they contain what they advertised?

Fermenting "beer" (left) to be turned into rye whiskey.

depth of its character.

With a background like that, it seems apt that whiskey should be the national spirit of the United States; the two grew up together. This lingers as a personality problem. It is one thing to have a grand-dad or uncle who is a feisty old boy, but do you want to take him to a dinner party? In Kentucky and Tennessee they still do, but perhaps wonder whether they really should. Farther afield, where distance lends perspective, American whiskeys, being a mere couple of centuries old, are finally losing the image of the upstart and gaining the respect due to their rounded, seasoned character.

The most elegant tribute ever paid to American whiskey was probably the description afforded by Bernard De Voto, whose origins were Italian and Utah Mormon: "True rye and true Bourbon wake delight like any great wine with a rich and magical plenitude of overtones and rhymes and resolved dissonances and a contrapuntal succession of fleeting aftertastes. They dignify man as possessing a palate that responds to them and ennoble his soul as shimmering with the response."

H.L. Mencken talked of, "Bourbon whiskey, old, mellow and full of pungent but delicate tangs". He was, as it happens, discussing the Bourbon that was provided by the Mayor of San Francisco to sweeten delegates at the 1920 Democratic convention, the year after the passing of the Volstead Act had implemented Prohibition.

Lyrical descriptions, even melodic ones, evoke the pleasure of the drink without capturing its palate. That is always a difficult trick. All the more difficult in that a palate is a complex relationship of balancing elements. The pivot of the palate is the

strongest flavour within it. On its own, such a flavour might scare off the uninitiated.

Rye grains have a bitter taste. Bitterness sounds unpleasant but can taste appetising. Why else would shrewd New Yorkers insist that their lunchtime sandwich be served "on rye"? Among grains, rye has the image of a peasant, but, like many of the foods of poor people, it is delicious. What the rye grain gives to bread it also imparts to whiskey. Whether it is baked or distilled, the rye character comes through. Rye whiskey has that same hint of bitterness. It is reminiscent of a bittersweet fruit – perhaps a hint of apricot – spicy, a little oily, almost peppermint. The bitterness arouses the appetite, like that of quinine in a patent aperitif, or hops in beer. The peppermint palate, which adds a digestif quality, is especially evident in samples of rye whiskey from the first two or three decades of this century, bottles of which can occasionally be found in bars that care for such delights.

It is difficult to produce a whiskey exclusively from rye. At the fermentation stage, a small proportion of barley malt bears the brunt of the work. In palate, the intensity of the rye is offset by a substantial proportion of corn. These three grains are introduced at the beginning of the production process and cooked and distilled together. They are not distilled into separate spirits and blended later. Nor, under Federal labelling rules, can a whiskey be called rye unless it contains a preponderance of that grain – at least 51 per cent. In order to be labelled *rye whiskey*, the product must be aged in oak barrels, the inside of which have been charred. These barrels may be used only once, so that both the oak and the charring are new. The rules do not set out a minimum period for aging but the product may not be called "straight" rye whiskey unless it has been matured for at least two years, and it must bear an age statement unless it has been in the barrel at least four years.

The other, and more extensively used grain in American whiskey distillation is corn, which has a much sweeter taste. It is, after all, sometimes known as "sweet corn". As a native American grain, it is also sometimes called "Indian" corn. The British term "maize" derives from words originally used in the French or Spanish Caribbean. Again, it would be hard to produce whiskey only from corn, without any barley malt. However, there are American whiskeys made with more than 80 per cent corn. This very simple, unsophisticated corn whiskey is not aged in charred wood. One well-known example, self-mockingly packaged in a Mason jar and wrily named Georgia Moon, bears the legend, "less than 30 days old". Another well-known example is made by the McCormick distillery, at Weston, in the Platte Valley, north of Kansas City, Missouri. This distillery, which traces its history back to 1856, claims to be the oldest in the U.S. Platte Valley Straight Corn Whiskey is marketed in a jug-shaped crock.

Neither a rye nor a corn whiskey, the American classic is *Bourbon*, named after the county in Kentucky where it is meant to have first been made. Bourbon seasons its palate with a small amount of rye, or in some instances wheat: whichever is used, the proportion will be between five and fifteen per cent. A similar proportion of barley malt is used for fermentation purposes. The principal ingredient is once again corn. The more flavourful Bourbons thus have about 70 per cent corn, while the less characterful may approach 90 per cent. It is, however, in the Bourbons that the procedure of charred-barrel aging is most significant. This process imparts the typical vanilla palate, which the distillate extracts from the oak during aging.

Bourbons are produced at a number of different ages, usually not less than four years and rarely more than 10 or 12. If there is no age statement, the whiskey has been aged for at least four years. Bourbons are also produced at a variety of proofs, from 80 to 101 (U.S. proof divided by two equals alcohol by volume). A standard of 100 proof was specified when, in the early days of bottling, a law was introduced to permit distillers to warehouse packaged whiskey without paying tax until it was released for sale. That was in 1894, but the term *bottled in bond* still indicates a 100 proof whiskey. That is about all it indicates, since all whiskey is, in general terms, produced under Government supervision.

Another term that is frequently misunderstood is *sour mash*. This technique is the normal method used in the production of all straight whiskeys and therefore is in no way exceptional. By the time he has labelled his product Kentucky Straight Bourbon Whiskey, a distiller may feel he has said enough. In other states that produce straight whiskeys, the term *sour mash* is often added as an indication of authenticity. The sour mash technique involves the use of the residue from the previous distillation. This is known as "backset" or "setback", and is taken from the base of the still. It may be added to the grain mash in the cooker, the yeast mash, the fermenting vessels or all three. It helps ensure a continuity in fermentation and to guard against the activities of wild yeasts.

The term *straight* applied to rye or Bourbon indicates not only that the whiskey has been aged according to the regulations but also that it has not been "stretched" with neutral spirit. A "straight" may contain more than one distillation of its specified type, perhaps even from more than one location, but it conforms strictly to the designation on the label, whether that is rye or Bourbon. It is permissible to produce a "blended" rye or Bourbon, in which case the indicated product must represent 51 per cent of the total; the rest will, of course, be neutral spirits.

Since whiskey and neutral spirits may be made from the same grain as one another,

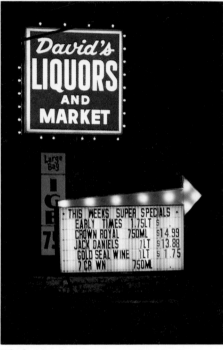

The brasher face of American liquor selling (above) offers a Bourbon, a Canadian and a Tennessee whiskey, plus a blend with a little character missing. Right: the counties of Kentucky. There are no distilleries in Bourbon county.

how are they set apart? The one has "the taste, aroma and characteristics generally attributed to whiskey", say the Federal Labelling and Advertising Regulations. They further seek to ensure this by requiring that whiskey be distilled at less than 190 U.S. proof (95 per cent alcohol by volume) and reduced to not less than 80 proof (40 per cent). Anything distilled to a higher proof may in the process have been rectified to a point where it is too "pure" to be called whiskey. It must be called grain spirit, neutral spirit or simply alcohol.

The most heavily advertised of American whiskeys, certainly within their home market, are not ryes, corn whiskeys or Bourbons. Nor are they blends of any of those

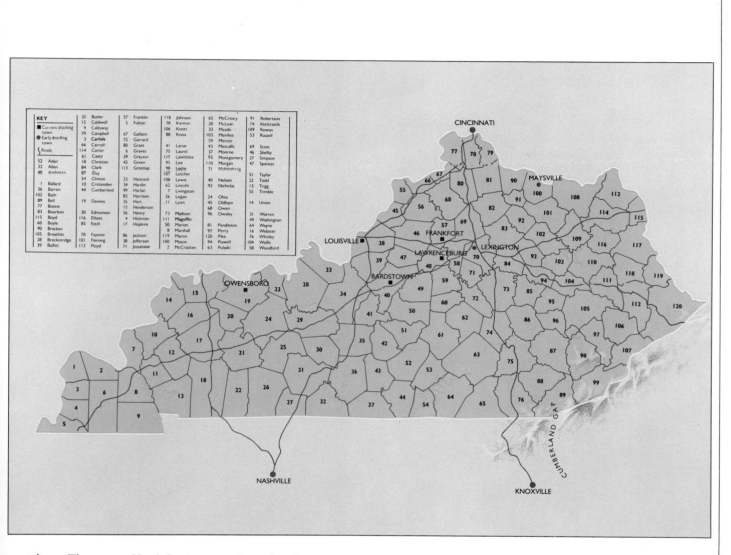

straights. They are *blended American whiskeys* like Seagram's 7 Crown, Kessler, Calvert Extra, Fleischmann's Preferred and Imperial. A single one of these blends may contain as many as seventy-five different whiskeys and neutral spirits. It is permitted to contain only 20 per cent straight whiskeys, and the rest may be neutral spirits.

The merit of blends is that they can be constituted in a way that balances out the idiosyncrasies of their constituents. Their marketers argue this gives them smoothness; critics might say blandness. They are also lighter-bodied than straights, because of their neutral spirit content. Notwithstand-

ing their luxuriant advertising, they are also less expensive to produce. It takes more care, effort and time to make whiskey than it does to turn out neutral spirits.

Despite the extent to which they are advertised, blended American whiskeys began to lose market share at the beginning of the 1970s. One reason was that a product of similar style, with the cachet of being an import, was being marketed agressively from across the Canadian border. What's more, the biggest producers of American blends, Seagram and Hiram Walker, are companies of Canadian origin. No doubt they wish to see both types of whisk(e)y succeed, but

they do not lose if one poaches sales from the other, especially at an "import" price.

Although American blends and Canadian imports are light in style, there have been a number of attempts to create something even more overtly so. This has necessitated the introduction, over the years, of regulations to permit a new category, *light whiskey*, using a high-proof distillation, aging in used barrels, and the addition of flavourings or sweeteners. These products have not been a great success. People who want truly bland, light spirits can find their perverse form of satisfaction in white rums and tequilas, or in vodka.

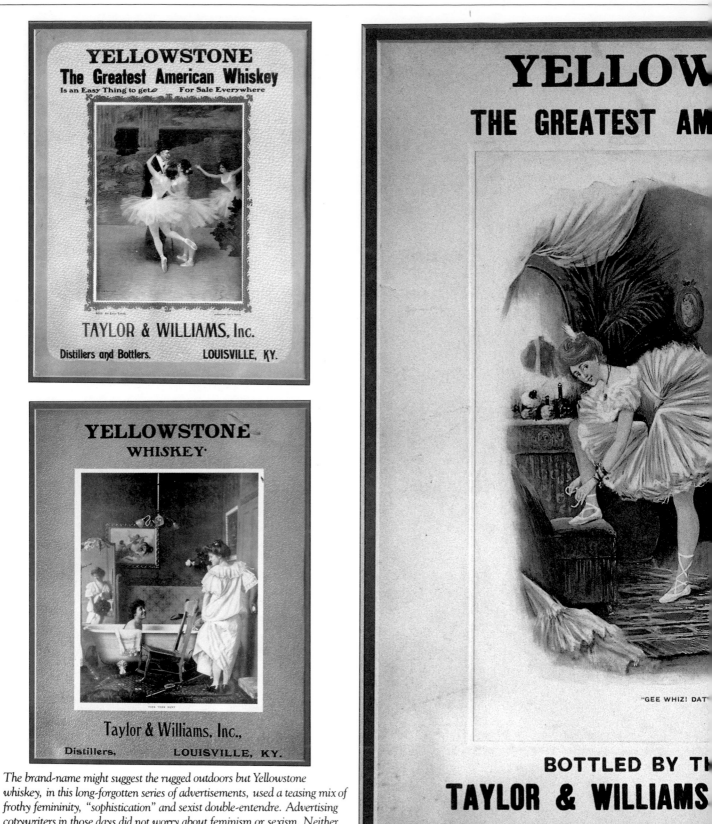

The brand-name might suggest the rugged outdoors but Yellowstone whiskey, in this long-forgotten series of advertisements, used a teasing mix of frothy femininity, "sophistication" and sexist double-entendre. Advertising copywriters in those days did not worry about feminism or sexism. Neither did they feel that the use of women was inappropriate because whiskey was a masculine product. The series offers a look in the rear-view mirror, at social attitudes, whiskey, and advertising art. In comparison, some of today's advertisements seem solemn and equally sexist in their macho approach.

The pedigree of American whiskey

Moonshining is alive and well in the hills of Kentucky. This moonshiner was born with the century, and was photographed in his mid-eighties. He survived the days of fatal shoot-outs (still remembered in Kentucky), though he did serve the odd jail sentence. He is an unrepentant whiskey lover.

Among the people of what is now the United States, the American Indians are the only ones who didn't come from somewhere else, and they didn't make alcoholic drinks, either. They may have smoked but they produced neither fermented nor distilled beverages. It took immigrants, often refugees from religious persecution, to set about such matters, between engaging in their own bouts of repression.

The English Puritans, having settled in Massachusetts and New York, had some difficulty in tolerating the beliefs of subsequent Scottish and Irish immigrants, who thus found themselves sooner or later setting up home in Pennsylvania, Maryland and Virginia (a substantial chunk of which was later chopped off to become the state of Kentucky).

Because it was, at least in part, Anglicanism that had driven them to emigrate, the new settlers of the early 1700s included not only Presbyterians from Scotland and Ulster but also Catholics from the South of Ireland. Even today, Scottish and Irish reels and jigs echo in the Country music of Virginia, Kentucky and points South, notably Tennessee.

The most potent combination were those people sometimes referred to awkwardly as being "Scotch-Irish", from the province of Ulster. Their enduring confusion about nationality could have been compounded in the Americas, but the New World also offered an answer.

The question might be: since he always retains his roots, at what point does an immigrant from Scotland or Ireland (or anywhere else) become an American? It is a question that might be applied not only to the people but also to their adapted culture, including their habits in the matter of producing and consuming spirits. The "Scotch-Irish" had the good fortune to be presented with an opportunity to prove themselves Americans. It was an opportunity they had every historical reason to accept:-

"Historians frequently mention the fact that, while the English settlers in the colonies were often divided in their allegiance at the time of the Revolution, the Scotch-Irish never wavered in their devotion to the cause of liberty and independence. No individuals, no group, endured the hardships and fought more bravely nor with greater distinction in the Revolutionary War than did the Scotch-Irish... they became a distinctive ethnic group, intensely American, with a lasting effect on the American character".

Though they are not mentioned in that tribute, the Catholic Irish fought staunchly, too, to the extent that they were honoured by George Washington through the declaration of St Patrick's Day as the first American holiday. It remains less of an Irish holiday than an American one, belonging as much to the New World as rye, Bourbon and Tennessee whiskey.

The quotation is from "Whiskey – An American Pictorial History", by Oscar Getz. His name is a reminder that German and Jewish settlers promptly contributed their energies to both the production and marketing of American whiskey. As chairman of the board of the Barton distillery company, of Bardstown, Kentucky, Getz was one of the first historians of American whiskey.

It was not only the people who became American but also the materials and techniques that belonged to the New World. Rye was known in Europe, but was not widely used in the production of whiskey. Corn was the principal native grain of North America.

In New England especially, molasses was made into rum; in several parts of the colonies, fruits, especially peaches, were made into brandy; in Virginia, a settler wrote to a friend in 1620 that a drink was being made from corn. This may well have been a fermented beverage, but that was the first step. Though there are many historical references to distillation, and to a variety of spirits, clear allusions to locally-produced whiskey do not appear with any consistency until the 1770s. What took root then would grow into today's distilling industry. Albeit

Gold Seal Whiskey, with no designation of style, came from Missouri, within the limestone shelf. The same limestone provided Old Spring Water, from Bowling Green, a town in the South of Kentucky.

Educated palates should surely have favoured Harvard whiskey. In spite of its name, it didn't come from New England. Nor, as a rye, was it from Pennsylvania or Maryland. It came from Ohio. The states with a whiskey tradition form a contiguous region linking parts of the East and Mid-West with the Central South.

tenuously, Jim Beam traces its beginnings to 1795.

During this period, there is evidence of rye whiskey distillation throughout Virginia and in North Carolina. Whiskey was probably being distilled in the part of Virginia that became Kentucky County in 1776 and the main grain that would have been used there at that time seems likely to have been corn. However, both grains continued to be used, with rye whiskey being the principal distillate. In the course of further subdivisions as the territory was settled, a large part of Kentucky became Bourbon County in 1785. This included all or part of thirty four present counties. The term "Bourbon whiskey" seems to have been used locally in the early 1800s but not to have achieved any widespread esteem until the middle of that century. Sometimes the word "Old" was prefixed to Bourbon, as though to indicate that the reference was to the original, large county rather than its later, truncated version. In the same period, writings for the first time begin to specify certain proportions of rye and corn to be used in whiskey distillation. However, the term Bourbon was not protected by law until a resolution of Congress as recently as 1964, and only since then

has the product been defined. Since the modern, smaller Bourbon County no longer has any distilleries, it cannot claim the whiskey for its own. In law, neither does Kentucky, since the resolution merely insists that Bourbon be produced in the United States. In practice, the term Kentucky Bourbon has ensured its geographical integrity.

It is much less clear at what point the charring of the barrels became the normal practice in the production of Kentucky whiskey. It is mentioned as a means of disinfecting barrels (rather like the use of sulphur candles in wine production) in a work on distilling published in 1818, but does not feature in other descriptions of Bourbon production during that century. In Tennessee, however, an article on Jack Daniel's, published in 1896, lays great emphasis on the use of "heavily charred" barrels to provide the whiskey with its "beautiful red color"

The states historically associated with the classic whiskeys of the U.S. form an arc from the East (Pennsylvania, Maryland, Virginia), Southward to Kentucky and Tennessee. There have been corn whiskeys and blends produced in other places, and a number still are, but all have been in contiguous states. Across the Ohio river, for example,

Indiana, Illinois, Missouri and Kansas have all made their contribution. Further South, so has Georgia, though North Carolina no longer does.

That such a well-defined region should produce all the serious whiskeys of the U.S. is probably a matter, more than anything, of ethnic settlement and economic history. The distillers themselves like to award the credit to a limestone shelf, permeated with springs, which spreads under these states. It can often be seen in outcrops where a highway has been carved through a hill. The limestone and the springs undoubtedly did come in handy. Limestone land produces good corn and, much more important, a good supply of uncontaminated water was at least as valuable in the 1700s and 1800s as it is today. American distillers say their limestone springs produce water free from iron or any other mineral that might discolour the whiskey; that it contributes to the classic texture and sweet taste; and that calcium aids the enzyme activity in fermentation. It might also leave troublesome deposits in the equipment at the distillery, but that can be cleaned. The Scots would argue about that. They prefer granite, but they are producing a different drink.

Maryland and Pennsylvania

Whether they know of Washington Irving in Maryland today is another question. In Baltimore, Maryland's biggest city, they don't make much of a fist of remembering H.L. Mencken. He remembered, though: "Old-time Baltimoreans regarded blends with great suspicion, though many of the widely advertised brands of Maryland rye were of that character. They drank straight whiskey straight, disdaining both diluents and chases". So it might have been in a city with an Irish name and a German community.

H.L. Mencken's home city once had its name on the finest rye whiskeys. "Baltimore rye", "Maryland rye" and, to the immediate North, "Pennsylvania rye" were compounds of provenance and product that sounded unbreakable.

It is not so much hoe-cakes (made of corn) as crab-cakes which are today, as they always were, a Baltimore delight, in the elegant city's downtown waterfront area, much revived in the late 1970s and early 1980s, in trendy Fell's Point and the wonderfully earthy Lexington Market. Crabs from Cheseapeake Bay, mussels, oysters... "the gastronomic metropolis of the Union", it was called by Oliver Wendell Holmes, but they no longer wash down the oysters with "half a tumbler of Maryland rye", as Mencken recalled.

There is still the odd distiller and blender in Maryland, but not a single producer of straight rye whiskey. No brand can be written off, since most of the old names have, in closures and mergers, become the property of someone else, and may occasionally be used on a label. This is a fate better than death.

Even the small towns and suburbs in Maryland once had their own rye whiskeys. There are still people who search hopelessly for Cockeysville Rye. They will more easily find Pikesville Rye, still a lovely, flavourful whiskey, now produced by Heaven Hill in Bardstown, Kentucky. A "Maryland" rye distilled in Kentucky, home of the rival spirit? It wouldn't have pleased Mencken,

"Like their cousins the Virginians, they were great roisters, much given to revel on hoe-cake and bacon, mint-julep and apple-toddy; whence their newly-formed colony had already acquired the name of Merryland; which, with a slight modification, it retains to the present day".
— WASHINGTON IRVING.

———◆———

but that, too, is a fate better than death.

One or two "Pennsylvania" ryes survive, too, as products of Kentucky. The once-famous Rittenhouse Rye is alive and well and living quietly at the Medley Distilling Company, of Owensboro, Kentucky. While both of these whiskeys have a good rye taste, and the requisite 51 per cent of the grain, the most widely recognised product in this category, Old Overholt, has 59 per cent.

The Overholt family emigrated from Germany to Pennsylvania in the 1730s. That was a time of heavy emigration from Germany, especially from the Rhineland Palatinate, to the New World, notably to the tolerant religious climate of Pennsylvania. The first immigrant's grandson, Abraham Overholt, inherited the family's occupation as weavers, and their domestic still, which he ran with great success. He became a full-time distiller in 1810, in Westmoreland County, and the business passed through several members of the family before reaching its peak, still as a producer of rye, in the 1930s. With the subsequent decline in the sales of rye, the company eventually ceased production and Old Overholt passed to the National Distillers company. They still produce Old Overholt as a genuine straight rye at their Old Grand-Dad plant in Frankfort, Kentucky.

Rye having once been the proudest spirit in the land, its decline has been so gradual that it was barely noticed. Why it should have withered is uncertain, though many factors probably contributed.

It might be argued that Maryland has diminished in importance over the years and that Pennsylvania has never since enjoyed the metropolitan regard that it did in the

early days of the country, but it is also true that its first losses were to wild Kentucky. As settlement spread, so people moved on, attracted by incentives to colonise Kentucky and grow corn, from which they made whiskey.

Pennsylvania may simply have suffered the fate of the pioneer in any field, whose efforts are almost inevitably overtaken. There are vague suggestions that some of the first grain distilling in the Americas was carried out in the late 1600s by Swiss-German Mennonites in the area between what is now the Maryland state line and the Blue Mountains of Pennsylvania. There is, more specifically, said to have been a distillery in the 1750s on the Juniata river, somewhere near Carlisle, in Cumberland County, Pennsylvania.

In the counties of Westmoreland and Washington, Allegheny and Fayette, the "Scotch-Irish" farmer-distillers were a tough breed, both during the War of Independence and afterwards. Having fought hard for their freedom, they were furious when their whiskey was heftily taxed to help finance the building of their new nation. There was even a suggestion that Western Pennsylvania should secede from the United States, and a violent "whiskey rebellion" lasted from 1791 to 1794. When, inevitably, they lost their struggle, many "whiskey rebels" left Pennsylvania to make new homes in Kentucky. While the Cumberland Gap had provided the earlier route, the Monongahela river ensured a further flow of distillers to Kentucky. Even in the early 1800s, though, Pennsylvania was producing three times as much whiskey as Kentucky, and rye was clearly the preferred spirit until the latter half of that century. At times, rye was hobbled by having a higher price as a raw material, but its greatest setback was surely Prohibition. During that time, rye-flavoured blends smuggled in from Canada confused the customer as to the true nature of the designation and things have never been the same since.

Rye veterans wistfully say that the last great days of the drink were the 1950s, and that both the name and the palate have been regarded as "old-fashioned" ever since. By the late 1970s, those distillers who still had a rye in their product range were drastically reducing production. This turned out to be a mistake, as tends to happen in such cases. It's true that the complex, bittersweet, fruity, spicy, almost peppermint palate of rye seemed Gothic in the age of Fear-of-Flavour but, faced with demise, this traditional American whiskey began to build a cult following in the early 1980s.

In late 1982, one or two distillers realised that there was actually a shortage of rye whiskey. They began to distil more, though the need for adequate maturation meant that this was not on the market until at least late 1985. In the absence of a substantial distilling industry in either Maryland or Pennsylvania, the rye would once again have to come from Kentucky. The distiller there who saw the trend most clearly, and who had already quietly gained a large share of the albeit-small rye market was Jim Beam, better known as the producer of the world's best-known Bourbon. Jim Beam produces a straight rye (clearly identified as such, and with a yellow label) alongside its various Bourbons (black, white and green labels). At that time, there were still some stocks of genuine Pennsylvania rye on the market in the barrel, though none was being produced.

Here again, the source was Mennonite Country. The Mennonites and their yet stricter neighbours, the Amish, are fundamentalist Christian sects that emigrated to Pennsylvania and Virginia from The Netherlands, Germany and Switzerland in the late 1600s. They are popularly known as the Pennsylvania Dutch (derived from "Deutsch"), and in that state their principal settlements are in Lancaster County, between the town of the same name and Reading. The Pennsylvania Dutch women wear black bonnets and gowns and their menfolk dungarees and rather Hassidic-looking hats. They eschew motorised transport, travelling in enclosed, horse-drawn buggies (incongruously fitted with reflectors to warn other

traffic), and using horse-drawn implements on their farms. They remain farming people, and there are eating places in the Pennsylvania Dutch area that offer the hearty and well-spiced local dishes that are the foundation of so much American cooking. Today, the Pennsylvania Dutch do not drink alcohol, but their influence remains visible on the one distillery in the area, which is almost as much a part of living history as they are. Nor, Pennsylvania Dutch country having become a popular day out for weekend visitors, does the distillery fail to benefit.

A succession of related families with German names owned the Michter's Distillery, of Schaefferstown, Pennsylvania, in its early decades. From 1753, there was a farm distillery on the site, and a commercial plant was built in 1861. Several of the buildings are clap-board structures dating back to the late 19th century, and they are decorated with the hex signs that are a feature of Pennsylvania Dutch country. A hex is more often a good luck sign than the curse of popular myth, and the starburst design on Michter's old still-house simply indicates "welcome".

Michter's Distillery is a National Historic Landmark, and it is unusual in several other respects. Most significant is its continued use of the pot still, in which respect it is unique among American whiskey distilleries. Its claims in this regard have to be qualified: although the company persisted with the pot still long after other distilleries had abandoned it, until the early 1950s, there was an interregnum of twenty-five years. Then, in 1976, without abandoning its column still, the company installed a tiny, one-barrel a day, pot still, as means of restoring its tradition. In 1981 all production ceased, but in 1984 operation of the pot still was resumed. The distillery works only in the summer, from March until September.

Some fine whiskeys have emanated from Michter's over the years. For a period, the distillery produced a much-loved product called Kirk's Rye, named after one of its owners. At another time, it supplied rye to the owners of the Old Overholt label.

Around the beginning of the 1980s, it was supplying rye to Austin Nichols, owners of the Wild Turkey brand. Wild Turkey has a 101 proof rye in addition to its better-known Bourbon whiskeys, which are produced in the company's own distillery at Lawrenceburg, Kentucky.

The only Pennsylvania rye on the market

The sleepy little distillery at Schaefferstown, in Pennsylvania, even displays a sign proclaiming its desire for peace. The place is an item of Americana in its own right . . . and its whiskey is bottled in decanters (top right) that sustain the spirit of folksiness. The Michter's whiskeys are still a distillate of Pennsylvania, while the state's once-famous rye whiskeys are now all made in Kentucky.

in the mid 1980s was whiskey distilled by Michter's and sold to Wild Turkey. Perhaps foolishly, Michter's abandoned rye as "old fashioned" when they resumed distilling in 1984. In the meantime, there had been stocks available of a splendid product called Michter's Original Sour Mash Pot Still Whiskey and this was what the company offered upon resumption of distilling.

In Michter's Sour Mash, the company had created an unusual whiskey – not a rye, but containing a high proportion of that grain (38 per cent rye; 50 corn; 12 malt). The result: a delicious and distinctive whiskey with a full, smooth palate, sweet but clean, and a flavourful, almost gingery, crisp, dry finish. This whiskey has at times been bottled at both 101 and 86 proof. Being capable of producing such a delightful product, it seems odd that Michter's should have decided also to make a novelty whiskey, aged for less than a month in re-used barrels. This product, although it could not by today's law be sold at less than 80 proof, was meant to resemble the rough, white 25 proof "Quarter Whiskey" of Colonial times. It is not the most refined of whiskeys.

At the time of Michter's resumption of production, the company's whiskeys were hard to find even in the surrounding area but they were available seven days a week at the distillery, from the restored "jug house", in bottles, flasks and a wide variety of specially-commissioned ornamental decanters. With the restoration of distilling, this trade was developed, and Michter's was turned into a living museum of early Pennsylvania whiskey production.

Distilling for the tourists might be small whiskey but it is an admirable way of sustaining an element of American heritage.

Virginia

George Washington, the greatest of all Virginians, was – among his several other occupations – a brewer and distiller. Indeed, whiskey seemed forever to be touching on his life in one way or another, though that may merely be testimony to the economic and social importance of the spirit in those times. As a general, Washington emphasised the importance of troops being supplied with spirits to sustain them against tiredness or the extremes of weather. He was also involved in quelling the early 1790s "Whiskey Rebellion" among distillers who refused to pay tax, and on another occasion he spoke out in favour of the regulation of the business.

The production of alcoholic beverages may not be the best remembered of Washington's activities, but it is not especially surprising. In his day, anyone having farming land (he owned an estate) and growing grain would have brewed and distilled just as they would have baked bread. Agriculture was vertically integrated, as we would say today; industrial capitalism was a twinkle in the eye.

What is surprising, in the light of his other commitments, is the apparent extent of George Washington's distilling business. No doubt he appreciated that a President needs the support of a trade or profession, whether it be whiskey-distilling, peanut-farming, the law or movies.

After his military service, he began to carry out work in the family estate and his distillery operations continued throughout his Presidency and for the rest of his life. Perhaps he did little more than supervise but, in the year he became President, his distilling business had sales worth more then $1,000 (hundreds of thousands of dollars at today's prices), according to "Whiskey – An American Pictorial History", by Oscar Getz. "Within a short time, Washington's whiskey had gained considerable fame throughout the Colonies", says Getz, using family letters to support his conclusion. Other histories are less *gung-ho* but the verdict is the same: that Washington eventually produced

whiskey on a large-scale commercial basis.

According to Getz, Washington turned over one of the farms on his estate specifically to be used to grow rye for distillation. He hired as one of his plantation managers a Scotsman with a considerable knowledge of distilling, and at one stage had no fewer than five stills. One of his stills, made in 1787 by a company in Bristol, England, was put on display in Washington, D.C., at the time of bicentennial, in the museum of the Bureau of Alcohol, Tobacco and Firearms.

The Washington family estate at Mount Vernon may well have inspired the continuation of distilling in the area until mod-

ern times. The National Distillers company had two commercial plants in the Mount Vernon area during the post-Prohibition period and these were notable for a whiskey that was widely regarded as the finest of modern ryes. This product was known simply as Mount Vernon Rye, in which form it had a reputation well into the 1950s. Although the two distilleries no longer function, Mount Vernon whiskey still exists. It is no longer a straight whiskey but a rye-leaning blend, still being produced by National Distillers, at their plant in Cincinnati, Ohio.

It is curious and incongruous that the

The trucks suggest serious business, but the distillery is no giant. "When I arrived, I was shocked by the smallness of everything," says distiller Tom Leahy (right) . . . and he himself could pass as one of the Little People.

Washington suburbs of Virginia should to-day accommodate the last working whiskey distillery in the state, at Sunset Hills, near Reston, in Fairfax County. There is no whiskey produced (more to the point, none that is legal) elsewhere in the state. Nor are there any commercial distilleries in the state of West Virginia. It is a long way from the frontier days, when Virginia was in the van-guard of whiskey production.

It is no more than twenty miles from the heart of Washington, D.C., across the city's encircling road, the Beltway, into the Virginia suburbs, past the odd cluster of shops to the backwater that hides the Smith Bow-man Distillery. The backwater itself is a pond, used to cool the condensers. In sum-mer, things get too hot and in May and June the distillery simply closes down, in tradi-tional fashion. There was once a railroad station, and the track ran in front of the distillery, but now the line has been converted into a cycle path, part of a thirty-seven-mile route belonging to the Northern Virginia Regional Park Author-ity. Recreational cyclists pedal between distillery buildings, barely noticing them; neighbours seem as unaware of the place. It hardly looks like whiskey country.

The area is part of the fertile Piedmont Plain. There was once a lot of oak forest in the area, and the distillery had its own stave mill. It was originally on farm land and there are still agricultural buildings dotted around. Guinea fowl wander, and only the grain silos suggest any serious activity.

In its own casual way, the Smith Bowman distillery is a piece of American history to the tips of its fingers. The Bowman family come from the Shenandoah Valley and have roots in both Virginia and Kentucky, and four brothers among them were all officers in the War of Independence. Smith Bowman established the distillery after Pro-hibition and it is still in the family. In more recent times, a Bowman brother-in-law with experience in the advertising industry joined the company to look after marketing. His name is Robert E. Lee IV and he is the great grandson of the Confederate Commander.

Talking to "The Washingtonian" magazine in 1983, the firm's patriarch, DeLong Bowman, then seventy-two, recalled his days of fox-hunting in the immediate area of the distillery. "Bowman is genteel Virginia all the way", commented the magazine. "The first gentleman of Virginia" was a phrase immodestly appropriated by William Byrd II, founder of the town of Richmond. Virginia Gentleman is the brand-name of the company's principal whiskey, now produced at 80 proof though it has in the past been marketed at a number of different strengths. The company has also produced on occasion a 90 proof product called, with almost equal gentility, Fairfax County.

The whiskeys have a big body, a sweetish, magnificently flavourful palate, and a mature, smooth finish. They are Bourbons in style, but a little higher than some in malt and lower in corn. They have been described as "sweet-mash" whiskeys but this is based on some hair-splitting concerning the sterilizing of the fermentation vessels – unusually small, and made of traditional cypress. In fact, although backset is not fed into the cooker, it is added to the fermenters, so the whiskey is in this principal respect made by the sour-mash method.

What might be termed a "special edition" was at one stage bottled, under the name "Gentlemen of the Press". This was for the National Press Club, in Washington, D.C. Whiskey has been produced for a number of clubs and other grand institutions, not to mention state liquor stores in Virginia. More than half of the sales are in Virginia. The rest are largely in the bordering states.

Although the distillery is certainly a serious commercial business, its production is tiny in national terms, but Virginia remains a good market for Bourbon. It was Virginia, after all, that gave birth to Kentucky and to Bourbon County.

The grain silos and the Georgian-style entrance make for an odd juxtaposition, but this is genteel Virginia, no matter how close to downtown D.C.

A taste-guide to Maryland, Pennsylvania and Virginia whiskeys

Is America too young to value its heritage? Where are the straight ryes of Maryland, Pennsylvania and Virginia? They were the beginnings of whiskey-distillation in an American tradition, yet they survive only vestigially, and often in exile. Would France be so careless of its Cognac or Armagnac?

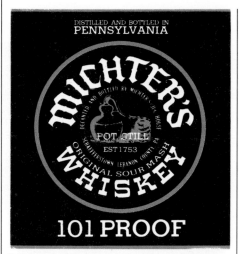

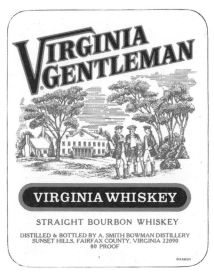

Michter's label is proud to proclaim a product of Pennsylvania, as well it might be. The whiskey has elements of a rye, but is in a style of its own. A delicious, almost gingery, after-dinner whiskey.

Virginia Gentleman is still produced in the state whose name it bears, and which gave birth to Kentucky. This whiskey is in the Bourbon style, with a sweet, malty palate and a big, smooth body.

Mount Vernon Whiskey survives, though no longer as the famous rye that it was. Once, it was produced at Mount Vernon, but now it comes from Ohio. A quite tasty, rye-leaning blend, with a light body.

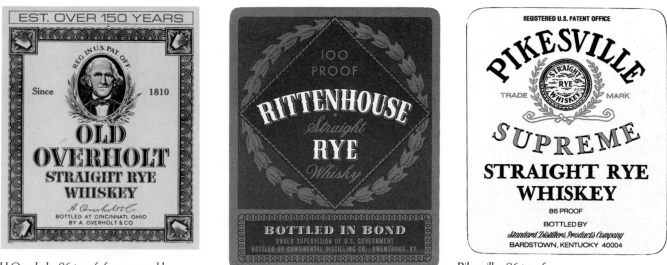

Old Overholt, 86 proof, four years old

Rittenhouse Rye, 100 proof

Pikesville, 86 proof

Old Overholt, by far the best known of the straight rye whiskeys, was originally from Pennsylvania, but is now distilled in Kentucky and bottled in Ohio. Despite the indignity of exile, it retains plenty of the rye character that is its birthright. Indeed, it has slightly more rye than any of its competitors. There is a depth of rye in the palate, a mature flavour, and a medium-to-big body. Rittenhouse is also a great old Pennsylvania name, but this rye, too, is exiled to Kentucky, where it is produced by Medley. It has a big body and a notably clean palate. Pikesville is a renowned Maryland rye, and again an *émigré* in Kentucky, where it is made by Heaven Hill. Pikesville is also big-bodied, and sets a deliciously spicy character against a very smooth palate.

Kentucky

In his play "Who's Afraid of Virginia Woolf?", Edward Albee has one of his principals, George, tell a story about going into a bar as a 16-year-old with a bunch of friends, all trying to be adults. One of his friends ordered a drink: "I'll have a bergin...give me some bergin, please...bergin and water".

They laughed at him until "the colour rose in his neck" but how was he to know? It had always sounded like "bergin" to him. How was he to know it was "Bourbon"? Come to that, exactly what does Bourbon mean?

When familiar things take their names from places, the origin is as often lost and forgotten as it is remembered and honoured. In the instance of Bourbon, the honour is twice removed. Whatever gastronomic delights have come from Hamburg or Frankfurt, Burgundy, Champagne or Oporto, the style of whiskey called Bourbon is purely American.

The French, having at the time their own territories in North America, assisted in the War of Independence against the British. In acknowledgement of this, French names were subsequently used for new settlements or counties. In the Western part of Virginia, the then county of Kentucky was subdivided in 1780s and again in 1786. One of the subdivisions was named Bourbon County, after the French royal house. Kentucky became a state in 1792, and Bourbon one of its counties. Within Bourbon County, on the Ohio river, lay the town of Maysville, then the principal port for a substantial slice of trans-Allegheny territory. Bourbon County thus became associated with the shipping of whiskey, and that seems to be why the name and the spirit eventually became synonymous.

The portability of whiskey is said to have been one reason why the spirit was produced in large quantities in Kentucky from the earliest days of settlement. The Governor of Virginia, Thomas Jefferson, offered pioneers sixty acres of land in Kentucky County if they would build a permanent structure and raise the "native" corn. No family could eat sixty acres' worth of corn in a year, and it was too perishable and bulky to transport for sale; if it were turned into whiskey, both problems evaporated. Moreover, if it had to be stored for some time, or sent on lengthy journeys, the whiskey merely improved in the barrel.

That whiskey (like tobacco and salt) was used as currency in early Kentucky is well documented. One romantic theory has it that whiskey was shipped down the Ohio river and the Mississippi to New Orleans or Natchez on wooden barges and traded for Arab horses, which had been introduced as a result of Spanish colonial influence. The barges were dismantled and sold as wood, and the horses driven back over the trail known as the Natchez Trace to Kentucky; hence the state's subsequent pre-eminence in horse-breeding. The same limestone that provides the spring water for distillation also grows good grass on which to raise horses with strong bones.

Among the surviving evidence of the Kentucky connection is a New Orleans drink based on whiskey with a dash of Peychaud's Bitters and a swirl of an anise-flavoured Francophone aperitif. This evocative encounter is encapsulated in a local patent product, the Sazerac cocktail. The combination of whiskey and peach juice is also said to have been devised way down yonder, in New Orleans, and to have inspired Southern Comfort, which is produced up river in St Louis.

Louisville is the highest navigable point, and it is the largest city of Kentucky. One popular story has Louisville as the scene of the first whiskey production in Kentucky, credited to a distiller with the Welsh name Evan Williams. Another tale has the scene as being near Bardstown and one of the distillers being Wattie Boone, cousin of Daniel. Today, Louisville and the area around Bardstown, along with Frankfort, are the main areas of distillation. Further East, and to the North of Lexington, lies Bourbon County. Despite its importance to the whiskey trade, it was never the dominant distilling centre, and has had no pro-

duction for many years. Furthermore, it is a dry county.

A witty foreign correspondent once wrote that he had been to the Canary Islands and found no canaries; he had been to the Windward Isles and felt no wind; now he was filing from the Virgin Islands. Perhaps his newspaper should have sent him to Bourbon County, too.

In his excellent study "Kentucky Bourbon, The Early Years of Whiskeymaking", Henry G. Crowgey points out that many pioneers would have carried out distillation as a matter of course, and that Kentucky was being settled from 1775. Since pioneer life was largely unrecorded, it would never be possible to say – if it mattered – who was the first distiller in Kentucky. Evan Williams, in 1783, might have been the first in the Louisville area but no one can say for sure. He is especially scathing about claims that the Reverend Elijah Craig, a Baptist minister who founded Georgetown, near Lexington, made the first Bourbon in 1789.

Potent whiskey and lithe, strong-boned racehorses, both nurtured on the limestone soil of Kentucky. The roots are deep, even if these particular brands of whiskey are forgotten. In horse country, the favoured drink is the mint julep, ceremonially served at Churchill Downs, for the Kentucky Derby, in huge quantities. It tastes better when it is mixed individually.

Although boundaries were changing rapidly at the time, Craig never operated in Bourbon County. Nor is there any evidence that he discovered by accident the technique of charring barrels. This is a pleasing legend that is as well substantiated as that of King Alfred and his burnt cakes.

The char makes an essential contribution to the palate of all the straight whiskeys of the United States but it is most significant in the Kentucky classic. Rye whiskeys enjoy the full flavour of that grain; corn whiskeys have the sweetness of maize; Tennessee whiskeys manifest the mellowness of charcoal filtration; in Bourbon, the defining

characteristics are the tones of vanillin and caramel that the whiskey takes from the wood. It is the charring that permits the whiskey ease of entry into the wood.

"The background of Kentucky whiskey is shaded in legend and myth", observes Crowgey, in the introduction to his definitive study, which is published by the University Press of Kentucky. It seems a needlessly qualified way in which to begin such a well-researched work, but Crowgey soon makes his point:-

"There is an undeniable paucity of reliable information. This cannot be attributed solely to backwoods illiteracy or the pressures and preoccupations of pioneer life. It is somewhat likely that some of the records of early distilling have been eradicated by the descendants of the distillers. The temperance movement reached full force in the nineteenth century and its adherents would have viewed such a family background as an opprobrium. It can hardly be mere accident that so many personal reminiscences tend to omit reference to the production or consumption of distilled products, when the facts are known to be otherwise".

Meanwhile, the whiskey industry is one of the principal sources of primary and secondary employment in the Bardstown area especially, in Louisville, and to a lesser extent in Frankfort. In the countryside of central and Western Kentucky, every hollow seems to have a distillery peeping out. A distressing number of these are defunct, and others – like "resting" actors – are still aging but not, at least for the moment, performing. There are, though, about fifteen in production, whether their Bourbon is ultimately bottled in other states, in blends, marketing companies' brands, private labels, or under proud Kentucky names. In some states, more than 100 labels can be found.

Some of the independent Kentucky distillers, like Medley, of Owensboro (Daviess County) and Heaven Hill, of Bardstown (Nelson County) have sheaves of labels. Others, such as Ancient Age, of Frankfort, are less profligate. Austin Nichols' Wild Turkey, in Lawrenceburg, is positively

single-minded. The biggest-selling Bourbon by far is that made at the two Jim Beam distilleries near Bardstown. Despite the slow sale of native U.S. whiskies, Jim Beam has in recent years advanced impressively. The label, owned by the conglomerate American Brands, is one of the biggest-selling spirits of any type in the United States. American Brands also now owns the former National Distilleries plants (Old Grand-Dad, Old Crow and Old Taylor), in Frankfort.

The second biggest-selling Bourbon is Early Times, produced in Louisville by Brown Forman, who also own Jack Daniels, of Tennessee; Southern Comfort of St Louis, Missouri; and Canadian Mist, of Collingwood, Ontario. Schenley has reduced its activities in Kentucky, but still has I. W. Harper, J. W. Dant and Old Charter at its distillery in Louisville. While Kentucky Tavern (Glenmore, of Louisville) still has its roots deep in the local soil, Kentucky Gentleman (Barton Brands, Bardstown) was for a time Scottish-owned, by Argyll, before being bought out by its management. The much loved Old Fitzgerald, of Louisville, was bought by Scotland's D.C.L., before that was acquired by Ireland's Guinness.

The two biggest liquor-producing companies in North America (both of whom have done their share of acquisition in Scotland) are not as conspicuous in Kentucky as they might be. Although Hiram Walker has had some success with its Ten High brand of Bourbon, its only property in Kentucky is the small and somewhat autonomous Maker's Mark distillery, of Loretto, which is run by the local Samuels family. Seagram's has at various times produced Bourbon in four Kentucky distilleries but has had less success than might have been expected with its two premium brands, the well-made Benchmark and the lighter, drier Eagle Rare. The company also has an old-established regular brand of Bourbon called Mattingly & Moore. Another of Seagram's great old favourites, Four Roses, is still a Bourbon in some markets but more often a blend.

Kentucky ~ *Frankfort*

The rocky outcrops revealing the limestone shelf of American whiskey country assert themselves in towering pride as the valley of the Kentucky river winds through the state capital, Frankfort, on its way to meet the Ohio. There is an evocative echo to the word "valley" but this one, wooded with maple and hickory, has an American character that can hardly have reminded settlers of the Oder or Main; the name comes not from Germany but from a pioneer who forded the river here. His family name was Frank. It is as direct, as American, as that.

The whiskey was here with the pioneers, before the state. The distilleries, along the valley, grew to Victorian splendour, then mellowed with age, while the state capital has the neat, clean, well-maintained look that the eye of government servants ensures.

This is one of Kentucky's oldest settlements, and it proclaims its age with every spirit it produces, yet that has been a mixed blessing. Since the days when it was pedantically known as "Old Bourbon", whiskey makers have liked to affect antiquity for both their distilleries and their mature spirit. They did so too earnestly, at times when it may not even have been true, and now they are paying the price. The prefix "Old", marketing men insist, makes a product sound dustily out of style. That is said to have been a problem for the unanimously venerable whiskeys of Frankfort. If that is so, it doesn't say much for the discernment of the consumer.

The oldest settlement in the Frankfort area is Leestown, established between 1773 and 1775 by a group of pioneers who had been following the "buffalo trace" from Big Bone Lick, in Boone County, Kentucky. A clapboard "landmark building" would in later years be used as the office for the distillery supervisor of the Ancient Age company, and still stands there as a reminder of Hancock Lee and his fellow pioneers.

The distillery itself was built in 1869 and has passed through several proprietors. For a time, it was owned by the national company Schenley, and Ancient Age was the biggest

Achieving maturity at Ancient Age (above). There is a beauty to the curve and texture of wooden barrels . . . and to the pavilioned spring house at Old Taylor.

seller among their several Bourbon brands. Then, in a bout of divestment, they sold the plant in 1982 to a company formed by a couple of individuals with backgrounds in the liquor business.

It's a characterful place, with what looks like a huge barrel outside. This turns out to be a thirty-thousand gallon "kettle" still, which has in the past been used for the production of grain spirit but not whiskey.

As if by way of contrast, the distillery also has a one-barrel warehouse (the management's qualifying phrase "the world's only..." seems superfluous). This was built to mark the distillery's two millionth barrel after Prohibition. That was in 1953, and the distillery has since passed five million. From the larger warehouses, barrels can be rolled downhill along tracks that converge at the dumping room as though it were a loco shed.

A Kentucky log cabin built in the 1930s serves as a reception centre for tours. It is an historically interesting distillery, with in one of its offices an application made in 1880 to patent "a new and useful improvement in the process of making whisky". What is described as "our invention" turns out to be the sour mash process. Sadly for Frankfort, the patent was not granted.

Ancient Age whiskey is produced in a four-year-version without an age statement at 86 and 90 proof and, more unusually, at 10 years in 86 proof only. This latter version repeats the word "Ancient". It is labelled as *Ancient* Ancient Age, and known collo-

A taste-guide to Frankfort whiskeys

As well as being the state capital of Kentucky, the town of Frankfort is one of its centres of whiskey-distillation. An early centre, too, whence "old" Kentucky Bourbons seem appropriate. Frankfort has famous names and mature-tasting whiskeys, the appreciation of which requires a certain sophistication.

Ancient Ancient Age, 86 proof, 10 years old

Ancient Age, 86 proof

Ancient Age, Leestown bar brand, 86 proof

Ancient Age whiskeys offer a good example of traditional Bourbon, with just the right amount of restrained oakiness. They are relatively dry, pre-dinner Bourbons. The doubly antique version of

Ancient Age, known to its devotees and their favourite bartenders as "Triple A", is at ten years and 86 proof. This offers a particularly good example of the Ancient Age character. The Leestown version is an

86-proof bar version of Ancient Age, mainly in the Californian market. Leestown was the first settlement in the Frankfort area.

Old Grand-Dad Bourbons are firm and fruity, with some rye character. The ten-year-old, hundred-proof version has a remarkable combination of power and smoothness. A hearty, after-dinner Bourbon.

Old Crow whiskeys are everyday Bourbons, though more flavourful than similar products from other towns. A little fuller in body, perhaps with a dash more maturity, they are satisfying Bourbons for the happy hour.

Old Taylor whiskeys are premium Bourbons, with a fairly light and characteristically soft body, and a sweetish palate. A pleasant mid-afternoon restorative after golf or fishing.

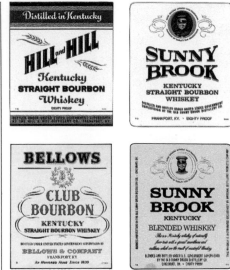

Sunny Brook, Bellows and Hill & Hill are among several regional brands that were produced by National Distillers in Frankfort. Most of them are similar in character to Old Taylor. Sunny Brook is the name of a "straight" and a blend.

Edmund Haynes Taylor built his distillery on a grandiose scale. At Ancient Age (right) the human figure is dwarfed by the size of a fermenting vessel as the yeast is pitched.

quially as triple-A. The unusual combination of a high age with a modest proof provides a welcome opportunity to sample the taste of maturity. Because the age is high, the whiskey has had plenty of chance to get into the wood but the character which it thus assumes is not overwhelmed by a powerful proof. Popular wisdom in the business might argue that triple-A is woody, but lovers of Bourbon might find in it the true taste of the style. The Ancient Age whiskeys do, in general, have a good traditional Bourbon character and a medium to full body. An 86-proof whiskey in much the same style is marketed under the Leestown label as a bar brand in California.

Old Crow, Old Taylor and Old Grand-Dad are also Frankfort distilleries. Each has its own plant; they were owned by National Distillers, but in 1987 were bought by American Brands. The character of the products is, nonetheless, distinctly different. The Old Crow whiskeys are typical Bourbons, with an easy start and an assertive finish, and are marketed as mainline brands. The whiskey is four or five years old, with no age statement, and is available at 80 and 100 proof. The Taylor whiskey is light, soft, with some sweetness, and is marketed as a premium brand. It is a well matured whiskey, as old as 10 or 12 years, though with lesser age statements. It is available at 86 and 100 proof. The Old Grand-Dad whiskeys are firm

and fruity, with some rye character, and represent the top-of-the-line brand.

Though Old Grand-Dad also avoids age statements, its regular whiskey is usually about six years old and is sold at 86 proof. There are further versions at 8 years at 100; and 10 years at 114, which is how it comes out of the barrel. The company is very proud of its "barrel proof" whiskey, which comes from selected batches. It is a very smooth and flavourful after-dinner whiskey. The former National Distilleries also had a number of regional Bourbons and blends, including Hill and Hill, Bellows and Sunny Brook.

Old Crow has nothing to do with birds. The distillery was founded by Scots-born Dr James Crow in 1835. He, too, is credited with having developed the sour mash process, and his claims are still made on the label of the whiskey. That the claim should remain there after all this time suggests that it cannot be challenged, but nothing is certain beyond doubt. With its proud, limestone facade, five storeys high, dotted with windows set around an arched loading hatch, the distillery has the look of a Scottish or Northern English textile mill.

Old Taylor was an entrepreneur in the whiskey business. His polite name was Colonel Edmund Haynes Taylor Jr., and he was the first owner of what is now Ancient Age before building the extraordinary plant that

now bears his name. The Old Taylor building is designed like a castle, with fortified battlements and towers. As if such flourishes might pass unnoticed, Taylor also decorated his spring house, but this time in pillared, Romanesque style, so that it forms a pavilion. Since the buildings were constructed, between 1885 and 1887, the pavilion has been used many times as the scene of receptions and parties and it seems likely that at some time in the future the place will grow into a Frankfort museum of whiskey. It was acquired by National during Prohibition and is still a working distillery, though it has not produced new whiskey for about a decade. Whiskey is still being matured there.

Old Grand-Dad's rambling plant is in appearance the most industrial and least romantic but it is not without heritage. The Old Grand-Dad name dates from 1882, and the company is proud of its apt antiquity, though it had its beginnings elsewhere in Kentucky. The Frankfort distillery was built in 1901, acquired by National in 1940, and is their headquarters in the town. It is proud of its traditions – its insistence on No 1 grain corn and a good proportion of rye, its open cooker, its pre-Prohibition yeast, and its goodly dose of setback in the fermenters – and it produces mature-tasting whiskeys.

It may be a somewhat muscular-looking plant but it is in a pretty location, behind a hill overgrown with hackberry and oaks.

Kentucky – *Lawrenceburg*

The keen-eyed whiskey-spotter might have difficulty with Lawrenceburg. The kind of person who can sit alone, study the light refracted in the drinking glass and inwardly recite the words on the label of the bottle might discover that there are two Lawrenceburgs in the world of whiskey. To the purist, the larger of the two Lawrenceburgs is the lesser one. That is Lawrenceburg, Ind., where both Schenley and Seagram bottle and blend various whiskeys. The serious one is Lawrenceburg, Ky. Who, anyway, would willingly be in Indiana when they could be in Kentucky? There is more than a state line between them.

The confusing thing is that Seagram are in Lawrenceburg, Kentucky, too. It is their main centre of Bourbon distillation, for Benchmark and Eagle Rare. If it weren't for that Eagle, and a few other well-matured Bourbons that have issued from the area, they might settle for re-naming it Wild Turkey Hill.

Twelve miles south of the state capital, Frankfort, and still close to the Kentucky river, the little town of Lawrenceburg (about 5,500 people) is home to the Universal Button Company and a couple of working distilleries. The number of American small towns that have, or have had, button companies was something that struck Jonathan Raban when he surveyed the country for "Old Glory", but this one is different. It puts the buttons on every other pair of jeans in America.

The idea of a town buttoning up America's jeans and supplying the country with its wildest whiskey, the favourite spirit of the intellectual cowboy, seems apposite but that is a hasty verdict. Long ago, in another America, Dwight Eisenhower was said to favour Wild Turkey.

It all started with the firm of Austin Nichols, who were originally grocers and wine and spirit merchants. They grew to have some of the smartest brand-names in the liquor business, to have executive offices in Midtown Manhattan and themselves to be owned for a time by Pernod, and then by

The Wild Turkey is an American symbol, rather than a Kentuckian one, though the bird is to be found in the vicinity of the distillery. The whiskey has cleverly contrived to benefit from the notion of American heritage, without seeming to be old-fashioned or for rustic drinkers.

Heublein, itself subsequently taken over by the British group Grand Metropolitan. Their flagship brand, since the 1950s a favourite in the sophisticated cities of the East Coast, is Wild Turkey.

For many years, Austin Nichols bought in the whiskey to be marketed as Wild Turkey, but in 1971 they took over a very old-established family distillery near Lawrenceburg, Kentucky, so that they could make it

for themselves. Although Wild Turkey had always been more clearly identified by its brand-name than as a Bourbon, its palate had been Kentuckian and assertive. Now it could also be consistently and controllably their own.

Austin Nichols, founded in 1855, must have been pleased to find a distillery of around the same vintage, albeit "modernised" in the 1930s. Far from Midtown

A taste-guide to Lawrenceburg whiskeys

Two Lawrenceburgs feature on whiskey labels. In its volume of whiskey, the one in Indiana is the more important of the two. In the connoisseur's pursuit of "straights", though, Kentucky is the state that counts. Lawrenceburg, Kentucky, produces big, well-rounded Bourbons, and likes to name them after national birds.

Wild Turkey Straight Kentucky Bourbon at 86.8 proof can sell at a more competitive price than the better-known 101 version. In either form, Wild Turkey is a big-bodied, aromatic, well-made, traditional Kentucky Bourbon.

Wild Turkey Straight Kentucky Bourbon is best known as a 101-proof whiskey. Its marketing has concentrated on the brand-name and the proof, but the product is a classic Bourbon. At 101, it has a huge character, balanced by maturity.

Wild Turkey Straight Rye is generally a product known to only serious whiskey lovers. A rye at Wild Turkey's beloved 101 proof is a considerable speciality. This one is big and smooth, with a hint of sweetness.

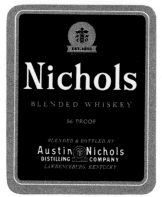

Nichols is a blended whiskey with a dash of Wild Turkey in its character. It is produced by Austin Nichols, makers of Wild Turkey. Such house blends are usually characterful but not a substitute for a "straight".

Wild Turkey Liqueur is based on the Bourbon, with honey and citric flavours. It is one of the few whiskey liqueurs made in the United States. Who would have thought a whiskey with such a macho image would have its sweet side?

Eagle Rare is a Kentucky Bourbon from Seagram's. They, too, have a distillery in Lawrenceburg. Eagle Rare has a medium-to-big body and is lightly aromatic. The distillery also has the smooth Benchmark brand.

Did a moonshiner set up the first still on Wild Turkey Hill? Did his assembly of steaming vessels gradually settle into respectability? There is an impromptu look about some of the classic distilleries of Kentucky whiskey country.

Manhattan, it is as funky a place as ever they could have hoped for, set starkly on a hill that plunges down to the Kentucky river, near the point where it is crossed by a dizzying, 225ft-high girder bridge carrying the railroad to Lexington.

The wood-frame tower-style still-house looks like a mine-shaft inside; the distiller makes his own "sour" lactic yeast mash in malt and rye; the majority of the fermenters are open vessels made of the cypress; the column still's vapour section is made wholly of copper, as is the "doubler" still; the barrels are charred especially heavily; and the open-rick warehouses are not heated. "We think the seasons make a good whiskey", says the distiller.

It's enough of a frontier location for the nearby woodlands to support the odd wild turkey, as promised by the ads since they began to adopt a more overtly Kentucky tone of voice. On a warm, misty spring morning, there is a mellow apple smell from the fermenters, and on the whiskey the rich aroma of charred barrels. It's a full-bodied, traditional Bourbon with an aromatic finish.

For many years, Wild Turkey specialised in a whiskey of 8 years old and 101 proof. The odd notion of 101 proof whiskeys seems to have derived from a wish to be sure not to miss the 100 mark for bottling in bond; to be one-up is to be sure. There are a handful of 101 proof Bourbons on the market, and Wild Turkey considers itself to be the super-premium. The company does, though, also market an 86 proof, which is between 4 and 6 years old. To be precise and sure, this is actually 86.8 proof. There is also a Wild Turkey liqueur, blended at the distillery, based on whiskey and pure honey with two flavouring ingredients. It has a citric character and a proof of 60. Then there is a Nichols blended whiskey, at 86 proof, and the splendid 8-year-old, 101 proof Wild Turkey Rye, bought in, for the moment, from Michter's of Pennsylvania. When Michter's temporarily discontinued production in 1981, there were still adequate stocks for some years' supply of Wild Turkey Rye.

When Austin Nichols acquired its own distillery in Kentucky, it started to issue ceramic decanters in wild turkey designs. At first, there was one a year, from 1971 to 1978. Then came a set of four on wild turkey lore. Then, in 1983, frequency increased to three per year, featuring turkeys with other American animals like the eagle, bobcat and racoon. The first turkey, in 1971, sold for \$20-25; survivors have fetched \$500.

Wild turkey lore, as inscribed on some of the decanters, might be taken at its word in the world of whiskey marketing: "The wild turkey is one of the heaviest birds capable of flight, yet it is unusually fast... predators quickly learn that the wild turkey is an alert, tough opponent".

Kentucky ~ Bardstown

OLD HEAVEN HILL SPRINGS DISTILLERY. INC.
BARDSTOWN-NELSON COUNTY, KY.

My old Kentucky Home", fondly remembered in the song by Stephen Foster, is a substantial Georgian building in its own grounds, the most visited attraction in Bardstown – a community of about seven thousand souls, along the Blue Grass Parkway from Lexington, and South of Louisville. It might be as well to gloss over the fact that Foster, whose 170-odd songs also included "Swanee River" and "Camptown Races", died from alcoholism (at the age of only thirty eight, in 1864). After all, the second and third attractions in Bardstown are the 1785 Talbott's Tavern and the Oscar Getz Museum of Whiskey History. Whiskey is the lifeblood of Bardstown and Nelson County, and this area has perhaps the best claim to be the centre of Kentucky's distilling industry, not only geographically but also historically. Bourbon County never had as much to do with it as Nelson County.

Despite its preoccupation with whiskey,

Kentucky is not famous for its drinking places, and in this context Talbott's tavern is at least of historical importance. It is otherwise unexceptional, but it is a most pleasant place in which to stop for a drink or snack.

The tavern is alongside the rather grand, red-brick courthouse, at the central crossroads of this handsome small town. The courthouse was erected in 1892 on the site of the log building originally put there by William Bard, or Baird, in 1785. The town took its name from Baird and the county from Thomas Nelson, Governor of Virginia, who ordered American guns to fire on his own home after the British had occupied it as their headquarters during the War of Independence.

The museum is nearby, in a former college building called Spalding Hall, on North Fifth Street. It is open all day, Monday through Saturday, and on Sunday afternoons, and is well worth a visit for its

documentary material and early advertising. The collection was made by Oscar Getz as chairman of the board of Bardstown's Barton Distillery, where it was originally exhibited. The museum moved after Barton was taken over by the Scottish company Argyll in 1983. Barton has since been the subject of a management buyout.

Barton and Heaven Hill are a few minutes from the centre of Bardstown; the Willett distillery of Bardstown is no longer producing whiskey; Jim Beam has one plant in Nelson County and another in nearby Bullitt County; Seagram's no longer operates the Henry McKenna plant at Fairfield, Nelson County, or a standby plant not far away at Athertonville; nor is it very far to the Maker's Mark distillery at Loretto, in Marion County. There are also two or three defunct distilleries still standing in the area.

Nelson County once had twenty distilleries, and in the period 1860-1890 some of the most famous commercial names in whis-

Bardstown's Heaven Hill distillery (left) has changed little in half a century. The stepped gables are a typical design feature in American whiskey warehouses. The extra surface helps conduct temperature changes, for natural maturation. The style is sometimes echoed in still-house construction. Heaven Hill is one famous name in Bardstown. Another is Barton, (right).

J. W. Corn Whiskey and North Brook Straight Rye are big-bodied and quite smooth interpretations of their respective styles, from the Heaven Hill distillery. Barton Reserve is a pleasantly aromatic blend.

key established themselves in the area, including several which have since passed to companies in other towns. Several famous whiskey-makers, Jim Beam among them, had their grand houses along one street, popularly known as "Distiller's Row". Today, the whiskeys most strongly identified with Nelson County come from the Barton and Heaven Hill distilleries.

The Barton whiskeys are notably dry and aromatic. The company's main national label is Very Old Barton, which is available at 80 proof in a 6-year-old version and at 86, 90 and 100 in 6 and 8 years old. The 8-year-old versions show the house character to especially good advantage. Very Old Barton is regarded by the company as its premium brand, though it is very competitively priced. Under the Barton label, the company also has blends called Reserve and Premium and a light whiskey known as QT. The company also has a second label, Kentucky Gentleman. This is a Bourbon in the

South (at 4 to 8 years; 80, 86, 90 and 100 proof) and a blend in some other states. Similar Bourbons, both with light counterparts, are marketed under two smaller brands, Colonel Lee and Tom Moore, the latter named after the man who founded the distillery, in 1879. The present plant, largely built in the 1940s, has the redbrick, industrial style of the period. Its best friends would have some difficulty in describing it as good-looking, but it is discreetly hidden in an especially steep hollow. The distillery uses its own yeast, in a sour mash of backset, malt and rye. Despite their flavourful palate, the whiskeys are also very clean, perhaps because the distillate is run twice through the column.

Heaven Hill's whiskeys are unusually malty, with a full Bourbon nose and palate. Those bearing the Heaven Hill label, principally available in the South and East, have a medium to heavy body. Those with the Evan Williams label are decidedly on the

Once a college, Spalding Hall still rewards study . . . it is a museum dealing with the history of whiskey in the United States.

heavy side. Evan Williams, named after the early Kentucky distiller, is the company's nationally-available premium brand. Heaven Hill whiskeys are principally available at 4 years old and 80 proof or 10 years and 100; Evan Williams most commonly at 7 years and 90 proof, though they are increasingly being marketed in greater ages and higher strengths. Evan Williams is a growing brand in the Bourbon market. Both whiskeys, and the scores of private labels issuing from Heaven Hill, are available in many permutations of age and proof.

This is in part because Heaven Hill makes a speciality of selling new whiskey in the barrel to its wholesalers. While there is a cash-flow advantage for Heaven Hill, there is also a greater flexibility for the wholesaler, who can collect the whiskey at whatever age and proof, within the law, that suits market conditions. The company also produces a light whiskey – and the firm, fruity, bittersweet Pikesville Rye, long departed from its native Maryland.

Heaven Hill is one of two or three independent whiskey-distillers in Kentucky, and the one best qualified to describe itself as a small, family business. The company was conceived after the repeal of Prohibition, with production beginning in 1935, and it has been in the same family ever since. In a fortieth-anniversary feature in the "Kentucky Standard", the company was cited as being the largest taxpayer in Nelson County.

The plantation porch of the company's office may be a recent reproduction, but it does echo the heritage of the location. It was William Heavenhill, a member of a pioneer family and subsequently the owner of a farm, if not a plantation, who gave his name to the land upon which the offices and distillery stand. It is alleged to have been a typing error that rendered Heaven Hill as two words, though it certainly makes a romantic name for a Kentucky Bourbon. The Heavenhill family never had anything to do with the company, though descendants of the founder have been employed there.

There is a flourish, too, to the distillery, with floral friezes decorating one of the 1940s redbrick facades. There are two of these frontages, between which stands the traditional, utilitarian ironwork structure of the stillhouse, built a decade earlier. The distillers at Heaven Hill have traditionally been members of the Beam family (practitioners of the art not only at Jim Beam but, over the years, in several unrelated companies). They still use a yeast that has been in the family for six or seven generations. At Heaven Hill, it is propagated in a sweet mash of malt and protected from spoilage by the addition of a small quantity of hops, a traditional method in Kentucky. Backset is then added to the cooker and fermenters to produce a sour mash whiskey. Open fermenters are used, some cypress originals. The whiskey, after being aged, is filtered over charcoal. At this point, a full and relatively oily whiskey has had its way with the barrel and the filtration serves merely to filter out unwanted solids before the whiskey is bottled. This is a not uncommon method, quite different from the Tennessee technique of filtering before aging.

For that sort of thing, you have to go to the other end of Interstate 65.

Kentucky – Loretto

With a little help from one or two enthusiasts in the wine trade, where people are broader-minded than they are credited with being, one Bourbon has achieved cult status among lovers of whiskey. This is Maker's Mark, produced at a tiny, isolated distillery by a rocky creek at Happy Hollow, about four miles from Loretto, a farming community in Marion County, just South of Bardstown. The distillery is the smallest in Kentucky, producing twenty to forty barrels a day. The still house stands on foundations dug in 1805 and the present, tower-style distillery was built in 1889. It is a typical iron construction with an attractive colour scheme of black and red, the distinctive house shade of Maker's Mark. Every window has wooden shutters painted in this red, and the timber floors pick up the theme. The distillery is a National Historic Landmark.

With age, Maker's Mark has become a colourful survivor: a tiny, rural distillery (left and bottom left). The house red shutters stay open, even on a wintry day, and the stylish black anxiously awaits its fresh, springtime coat of paint. Spent grain (bottom right) makes cattle feed for local farms, while new spirit flows through the try-boxes (below).

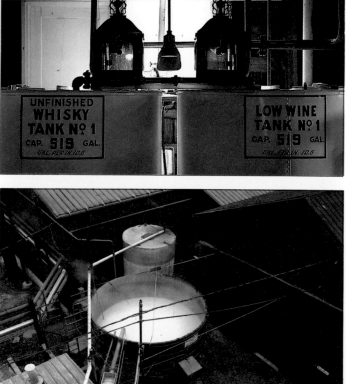

UNFINISHED
WHISKY
TANK Nº 1
CAP. 519 GAL.
GAL. PER IN. 10.5

LOW WINE
TANK Nº 1
CAP. 519 GAL.
GAL. PER IN. 10.5

Generations of Samuels have made whiskey, and proclaimed it proudly. The splendid signpost at T. W. Samuels' stands before a silent still, but the family now runs Maker's Mark. Samuels' Depot is the name of a hamlet where the last armed band of Confederates, among them the James Brothers, are said to have surrendered, 75 days after the end of the Civil War. The surrender took place at the general store. It was still standing – just – 120 years on.

The family who run the place, the Samuels, are Scots-Irish who emigrated to the New World in the early 1700s and headed, by way of Derry, Pennsylvania, to Kentucky later in the same century. A member of the family who was a soldier in the War of Independence set them on the road as distillers. Around the time of the Civil War, another member of the family became by marriage step-father to the James brothers, Jesse and Frank. A tribute from Frank is carved on one of the family's tombstones in a graveyard at Deatsville, near Bardstown. The Samuels used to run a distillery in Deatsville. Nearby is a village called Samuels, where the last armed Confederate band, including the James brothers, surrendered. The James brothers must have had a charmed life with the Samuels, since the family also contributed the odd sheriff. As if to complete their American tapestry, the

Samuels also at one stage employed the father of Abraham Lincoln in one of their distilleries.

To mark four generations of the family who have been commercial distillers, a Roman numeral IV appears on the label of their current whiskey, with an "S" not only for Samuels but also for Star Hill Farm, their property. In the decades after Prohibition, the family gradually slipped out of the distilling business, but then acquired their present plant in 1953, during the period of economic growth after the Korean War. From the time of its acquisition, they consciously sought to capitalise upon its small scale by using it to produce a low-volume, high-quality Bourbon. They were pioneers in this approach, at a time when Bourbon was uncompromisingly a volume business.

In adopting a new, and farsighted approach to the production of Bourbon, the

family knew they would have to present their whiskey in a distinctive and different way. It was from the "maker's mark" on pewter – one of the family was a collector – that the brand-name was derived. The brand was then built into a bottle with a low, elegant line perhaps suggesting a *digestif*. Finally, the top was sealed with red wax. This is still done by hand, as is the labelling.

While the small scale of the distillery, and the style of brand-name and packaging, set the scene for the cult status enjoyed by Maker's Mark, the only justification for its celebrity is the whiskey itself. Maker's Mark is the smoothest of Bourbons. It has the classic Bourbon aroma and palate but with its own definitive smoothness, a medium body and a very clean finish.

Some elements of the quality of Maker's Mark are achieved more easily just because the distillery is so small. For example, while

The distinctive red wax seal contributes to the mystique of Maker's Mark. Every bottle is dipped by hand, by a line of ten or a dozen workers. The plasticized wax comes in tablets like large bars of red chocolate. They are melted to the consistency of sauce. As the bottles are dipped, the wax quickly hardens.

many distilleries have their own water for the still, they often have to supplement their own source by using the town supply; Maker's Mark has a sufficiently low output to use only that in its own spring. In the buying of grain, too, the small scale of Maker's Mark means that it can take a closer interest in the actual source of the corn.

The defining smoothness is achieved, arguably at the expense of some flavour, because Maker's Mark eschews rye in favour of wheat as the grain with which to season the palate. This is an accepted alternative way of producing Bourbon but few distillers pursue it; Old Fitzgerald is a notable example.

There are, too, aspects of production in which Maker's Mark can claim to be "hand made". This is not an uncommon claim among producers of various types of drink but it is not always justified. The pulley

system for the loading and screening of grain may merely be quaint, but the use of a roller (rather than a hammer) mill is kinder to the ingredients of the whiskey. So is the very slow (more than three hours), gentle cooking of the grains, which is not carried out by the common pressure method. Maker's Mark has its own yeast, which it propagates in a sweet mash, using hops. The fermenters are of the traditional cypress type; distillation is run through a lovely old copper "doubler" still; the whiskey is run off and barrelled at relatively low proofs, making for more body and palate. In the warehouses, barrels are rotated so that they do not stay too long in the upper, airy zone. Larger distillers are inclined to deal with this problem simply by blending barrels from different parts of the warehouses.

All Maker's Mark whiskey (the brand-name doesn't use the "e", preferring the

Canadian and Scottish spelling) is aged between five and six years. Most of it is marketed at 90 proof, with a red seal. A 101 proof version has a gold seal. So does a 90 proof version personally labelled for individual customers.

Despite their success in building a reputation for their product, the Samuels had difficulty in attaining sufficient distribution. Today, although the family still runs the business (with another generation as a tireless spokesman both for Maker's Mark in particular and Kentucky Bourbon in general), the company is part of the Hiram Walker group, one of North America's largest liquor companies. With its own international relationships, the group has undoubtedly helped to ensure that Maker's Mark is to be found in some of the grandest hotels and department stores in many different countries around the world.

Kentucky ~ Clermont and Beam

Jim Beam has intentionally, and successfully, promoted itself so strongly as a brand-name that its designation as a Bourbon is amost overshadowed. It is nonetheless, as its label proclaims, a Kentucky Straight Bourbon Whiskey. Even the Beam company's blended whiskey, called Eight Star, contains a high proportion of Bourbon. Jim Beam itself is the biggest-selling Bourbon by a massive margin and, among the top few brands of spirits of all types, it is the only one to have gained volume in the American market in recent years. Perhaps on the grounds of its sales, it claims on its label to be "The World's Finest Bourbon".

Jim Beam is a medium-bodied Bourbon, with a flowery nose, a winey palate and a notably big finish. It has, though, lost a little of the classic Bourbon-barrel character in recent years. The company prefer to say that it is "a little less woody". The principal version is 4 years old, at 80 proof, and has a white label; there is a version called Beam's Choice, with a dark-green label, at 5 years and 80 proof or, more commonly 86; Beam's Black Label has "101" months (a chic, or coy, way of saying not quite eight and a half years) and 90 proof. A version with a pale green label, at 100 proof, can also sometimes be found. It carries no age statement but instead has a homily from, somewhat incongruously, Socrates: "The way to gain a good reputation is to endeavour to be what you appear to be".

It is not widely appreciated, but should be, that Beam also has a rye whiskey, at 6 years (though without an age statement) and 80 proof, with a yellow label. Despite the decline in sales in rye, Beam quietly persisted with its contribution, and now believes it has the largest sale in this, admittedly small, specialist category. That claim is disputed by Old Overholt.

Like most distillers, and especially with its large range and extensive distribution, Jim Beam must respond to local requirements in the ages and proofs of the whiskeys it provides to different markets, and there are a number of further permutations to be found.

Beam also follows the typical practice of cramming its labels with information on the way in which the product is made. The black label emphasises sour mash, the yellow opts for "copper-distilled" and the dark green points out that the whiskey is charcoal filtered – but after aging, in the Kentucky fashion. In fact, all of these processes hold good for all the Jim Beam straight whiskeys.

The company uses its own "sweet" yeast, with hops; plenty of rye in the mash; open cooking, without pressure; backset in the cooker and, in an especially large proportion, in the fermenters; and distils and barrels at notably low proofs, the latter element making the most significant contribution to its taste character. In some ways, it is a traditionally-minded company; in others, it is as "modern" as its volume might suggest.

No one seems to know any more where in Germany the original Mr Böhm came from when he emigrated to Maryland or when the name was Americanised to Beam but the family has, in the years since, supplied proprietors and employees for several of the best-known distilleries in the United States. The Beams' American roots have for two hundred years been in Bardstown, Nelson

Resting in peace . . . the Baptists of Clermont, Kentucky, and the barrels of Jim Beam. With its well-kept graveyard, the tiny Baptist church stands surrounded by huge warehouses. The Bible belt and whiskey country personified.

Beam, Kentucky, perhaps on the ground that nothing happens there but distilling. The Clermont distillery, its estate of pastel-coloured warehouses surrounding the local Baptist church, and the Boston-Beam plant, down a row of cedars and by a stream, are both set in open country. Critics point out, quite rightly, that it is difficult to make an identical whiskey in two distilleries; Beam says it does fine, with a member of the family in each plant.

The two distilleries account for the odd address on the label, printed as Clermont · Beam, Kentucky. Although, as the label says, it still represents the fifth and sixth generation of the family, the James B. Beam Distilling Company is now owned by outsiders. Jim Beam had a partner outside the family, to whom he eventually sold his equity and the company was subsequently acquired, in 1967, by the conglomerate American Brands, whose interests range from Lucky Strike cigarettes to Case knives and Pinkerton's security.

While the family background continues to be emphasised in promotion, the corporate style has undoubtedly changed, with Jim Beam receiving both investment and marketing attention on a grand scale. The Clermont distillery is a major tourist attraction, though the accent is less on production than on a "museum" of ceramic decanters. Jim Beam was not the first distiller to promote ceramics but, since entering the market in 1955, it has undoubtedly been the most aggressive. About ten or a dozen pieces or sets are issued every year, containing various Jim Beam whiskeys, at prices ranging from $30 to $80. Some are made of glass, others a product called Regal china, and some plastic is used, especially in wheeled vehicles. Cars, fire engines and trains of about ten wagons have been made. Ceramics have been made in the shape of famous buildings, objects of Americana, animals, politicians, sportsmen, entertainers, and in a considerable variety of series. There are more than five hundred items, and an independently published catalogue. There are thirty thousand known collectors.

County and the two or three adjoining counties. The first distiller in the family was Jacob Beam, in Washington County in 1795. His great grandson David Beam established a distillery in the mid 1800s at Clear Springs, just up the hollow from the distillery which would bear the name of son Jim, at Clermont, Bullitt County. The Jim Beam distillery at Clermont was established after Prohibition. Jim Beam's grandson Booker,

who still works in the distillery, remembers the old oak-timbered building rocking when the mash tubs were stirred. In the 1970s, it was rebuilt in a structure which is far safer, if lacking in character.

Along the way, the company had also acquired a distillery about nine miles away at Boston, Kentucky. This is in Nelson County. Although the official address is still Boston, the company prefers to refer to it as

A taste-guide to Bardstown area whiskeys

Kentucky whiskey never had that much to do with Bourbon County. Its heartland was, and still is, in the area around Nelson County. The county seat, Bardstown, has two distilleries, and is surrounded by others, whether working or silent. The area has a pride in its Bourbons, which represent a variety of styles.

Bardstown

Heaven Hill, 80 proof

Evan Williams, 90 proof

Heaven Hill, 86 proof

Evan Williams, 100 proof

Heaven Hill whiskeys are unusually malty, with a full Bourbon nose and palate. The distillery's name serves as the brand on a range of medium-to-heavy whiskeys that are primarily marketed in the South and East of the country.

Evan Williams is the brand-name of a range of very full-bodied and smooth Bourbons. These are classic examples of traditional Kentucky Bourbon, full of aroma and taste. They are marketed nationally by Heaven Hill.

Very Old Barton is the principal Bourbon of the distillery whose name it bears. It expresses the dry, aromatic, flavourful yet clean house character very well at eight years old.

W. W. Beam is not produced by Jim Beam. W. W. Beam is a Bourbon made by Heaven Hill. It is similar in style to the Heaven Hill products, with notes of maltiness.

Kentucky Gentleman is a Bourbon in the South and a blend in other parts of the States. As a Bourbon, it has a similar character to Very Old Barton.

Loretto

Maker's Mark (Ninety proof) is a boutique Bourbon. Although its status could be ensured by the small scale of its production, the fact is that this whisky (its preferred spelling) also has the greatest finesse of any bourbon, despite its medium-to-full body.

Maker's Mark (101 proof) retains the smoothness that is characteristic of the marque. This is in part achieved by the use of wheat in the mash. A similar technique is used to produce the much bigger-bodied whiskeys of Old Fitzgerald, from Louisville.

Clermont and Beam

Jim Beam (white label) is the company's principal product: a Kentucky Straight Bourbon at 80 proof and four years old. It has a light-to-medium body, a flowery nose, and a slightly winey palate, developing to quite a big finish.

Beam's Choice "Old Number 8 Family Formula", with the dark green label, is marketed at both 80 and 86 proof, though the latter is more common. It is five years old. A difference of just one year does add character to the whiskey.

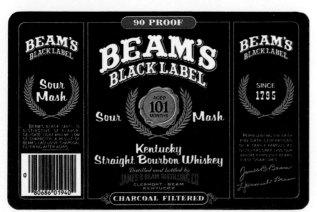

Beam's Black Label emphasises "sour mash" on the label, but the production method of all these versions is similar. The Black Label version has 90 proof and is aged for more than eight years. It is a distinctive Bourbon which best exemplifies the Beam house character.

Jim Beam (yellow label) is not a Bourbon at all, but a rye. It is lighter than some ryes, but with a lot of taste. It has 80 proof, and is aged for six years. Despite its low public profile, it sells very well.

Kentucky ~ *Louisville*

The suburbs of Louisville are stippled with ash trees, which is what you might expect. This is the home of the Louisville Slugger – a classic baseball bat, not a boxer. These days, athletic kids in Louisville are keener on golden gloves, and the city still turns out contenders. The Greatest is honoured in Muhammad Ali Boulevard, a road that runs across the city, through shabby, urban sprawl that saw grander days before the turn of the century, and past a sudden, modern downtown by the riverfront. Louisville is a coal port; in sailboat days, the city made rope from hemp, which grows wild in Kentucky; it grew on the trade in tobacco, not to mention the occasional Kentucky country ham; and down by the riverfront is a plaque honouring Evan Williams, the city's first distiller, in 1783, and perhaps the state's.

On the edge of town, to the South-West, past Churchill Downs and astride Dixie Highway, is the neighbourhood known as "Distillery Row". The distilleries of Louisville are big plants, whose growth continued through the post-war recovery years of the 1950s. At the peak of competition in the Bourbon business there were half a dozen, and there are still four.

The landmark of "Distillery Row", on the skyline, is a huge model of a bottle of Early Times Bourbon. The bottle is sixty-eight feet in height, and cost $9,000 to build in the middle of the Depression. For all its outward splendour, it has the indignity of containing water; it is a water tower.

Early Times was the name of a settlement elsewhere in Kentucky, and the label originated there in 1860 before finding its way to Louisville after Prohibition, but today it is the most determinedly "modern" of Bourbons. It has been aggressively marketed, and achieved large sales, on the platform of what is by Bourbon standards a light palate, with a sweet start and a clean finish. Early Times is marketed at 80 and 86 proof (40 and 43 per cent alcohol) with a four-year age statement, though some of the whiskey used has, in fact, been aged for five years. The company has also experimented with the

marketing of younger variations and with a "Kentucky whiskey" which is not a straight Bourbon. Its premium brand, Old Forester, is also lighter in body than it once was, but has a distinctively fruity palate and a dryish Bourbon finish. It is marketed at 86 and 100 proof, again with a four-year statement, though some of the whiskey has been aged for six years.

Early Times' character derives substantially from the yeast used, the distillery's own new growth. This is employed in relatively large quantities, and at low temperatures, contributing to the rounded palate of the whiskey. A different yeast is used in Old Forester, which has a more intense, aromatic character. There are also different formulations of malt, rye and corn for each product. The yeast is mashed in rye and barley malt, backset is added to the cooker,

The Early Times bottle is the landmark of "Distillery Row" – officially known as Dixie Highway (above). The steam of Early Times blends with that of I. W. Harper in the big picture. Somewhere through the steam are Old Fitzgerald and Yellowstone.

Despite its urban location, in Distillery Row, this Yellowstone whiskey warehouse (left) has the sun-bleached colours of the South. The windows are used to control warehouse temperature. What American whiskey makers call "beer" before it has been distilled is "wine" (above) afterwards.

distillation goes through a doubler, and maturation is in warehouses in which temperature and humidity can be controlled. The company feel this provides the best and most consistent maturation, in shorter times than would otherwise be possible.

Both Early Times and Old Forester belong to Brown Forman, and near the distillery are the company's elegant headquarters, the architectural style of which is modelled on the University of Virginia. They reflect a proud and lengthy dynasty. The Browns were persecuted – to the extent that one was beheaded – as Presbyterians in Scotland.

They were substantial farmers in the Glasgow area and one of their number, James Brown, emigrated to Newcastle, Virginia, some time before 1750. His son William scouted with Daniel Boone, was in skirmishes with Indians, and settled in Kentucky in the 1780s. William's grandson George went into the whiskey business in 1870. His first whiskey was Old Forester, which is variously said to have been named after a favoured customer or in honour of a Confederate General. The company's chief accountant, George Forman, became a minority partner in 1881 but his share was bought back after his death. After Prohibition, the present distillery had its beginnings, though its principal buildings were constructed in the 1950s. During that time, the family began to look for acquisitions, as a result of which Jack Daniel's, of Lynchburg, Tennessee, and Southern Comfort, of St Louis, Missouri, subsequently became part of the Brown Forman group. The company also diversified into crystal, fine china and silverware by buying Lenox Inc. The family still has the controlling interest in Brown Forman, though it is a public company. Its Scottish origins are still remembered, too, in the spelling of the word whisky in the company's brands.

The families and dynasties that built the Bourbon business in Kentucky bought and sold each other's distilleries and brands, helped each other along the way, and were often simultaneously friends and rivals. Their names crop up all over Western Kentucky, and in a good few instances the families themselves are still active in the business. George Brown had a second cousin called James Thompson, from Eglington, County Derry, Ireland, who came to Kentucky in the 1870s. The two were partners for a time, then in 1890, Thompson left to found his own company, with the Scots-Irish name of Glenmore. The Thompson family, personified by grandson "Buddy", a hot-air balloonist and airship enthusiast, still have a controlling interest in Glenmore, which is a public company. With its wood-panelled, picture-hung corporate

A taste-guide to Louisville whiskeys

The largest city in Kentucky is Louisville. Hardly surprisingly, it is also the largest city in the world of Kentucky Bourbon. It has four distilleries, each producing whiskeys of different character. Within their names is a twentieth-century aristocratic house of Bourbon and a folklore of the Republic.

Old Forester seeks to be as flavourful as a "super-premium" Bourbon should be, without being heavy. It is relatively light-bodied, but distinctively aromatic, fruity and dry, with a delicate Bourbon character.

Old Charter is a fairly full-bodied whiskey. It has a medium Bourbon character, faintly accented toward the rye. This provides for a hint of "bitter-fruit" dryness in the middle.

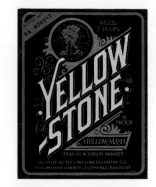

Yellowstone, despite its Western name, is a Kentucky Bourbon. Indeed, it has much the same character as Old Kentucky Tavern, but with a fuller body. Yellowstone has a medium body, and is a tastier whiskey for that.

Early Times is the lightest and cleanest of Bourbons. It has a sweetish start, a light Bourbon character, and a notably clean finish. In some markets, the company has experimented with a blended Kentucky whiskey.

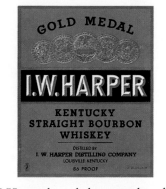

I. W. Harper has a light-to-medium body, and is sweetish, with a warming finish. Like its brother brand, Charter, it is a premium label. Harper is a pleasant, well-made whiskey.

Old Kentucky Tavern is a Bourbon with a light-to-medium body. It has a good, emphatic, Bourbon character, which is sustained through a fresh aroma, a clean palate and a complex finish with both sweet and dry notes.

J. W. Dant has a medium but firm body, a light-to-medium Bourbon character, and hints of maltiness in its palate. It is an easily drinkable everyday Bourbon, with a considerable loyalty in Kentucky.

Old Fitzgerald, 86 proof

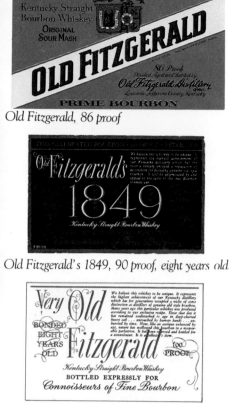

Old Fitzgerald's 1849, 90 proof, eight years old

Very Old Fitzgerald, 100 proof, eight years old

Very Very Old Fitzgerald, 100 proof, 12 years old

Old Fitzgerald whiskeys are clearly the fullest in body of the various Bourbons made in Louisville. They are, indeed, full-bodied by any standards. They are also notably smooth, that characteristic deriving in part from the use of wheat. They have a full Bourbon character, are very well rounded, and have their own distinctive nuttiness. These are elegant, gentlemanly, Southern whiskeys; very fine Bourbons. They are most widely available in Kentucky and the Central South. Similar whiskeys are marketed nationally under variations of the corporate name Stitzel-Weller. This "family" of whiskeys also includes Van Winkle, Nicholson, Cabin Still and Rebel Yell.

Cabin Still is a Bourbon marketed in the rural South. The whiskey-still on the label looks a little too sophisticated for a moonshiner's cabin. The whiskey, too, is very smooth for one affecting humble origins.

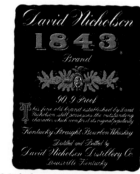

David Nicholson 1843, 90.9 proof

Old Rip Van Winkle, 107 proof, "Ten Summers" old, private label

David Nicholson 1843 is among the range of whiskeys that are also produced as a private label for the Van Winkle family, whose "Pappy" once ran the Old Fitzgerald distillery. The whiskeys are very smooth Bourbons in the Old Fitzgerald style.

Rebel Yell is not intended to be marketed north of the Mason-Dixon line, though there was once such a lapse. It is said to be produced especially for the Deep South, but its palate does not differ greatly from that of the Old Fitzgerald Bourbons. Perhaps a little less smooth in the finish?

W. L. Weller Special Reserve, 86 proof

Old Weller, 107 proof, "seven summers" old

W. L. Weller whiskeys are very similar to the Old Fitzgerald range. W. L. Weller Special Reserve, which has no age statement, is seven years old. Old Weller has an odd strength: 107 proof. That combination, and "seven summers" of aging, is reckoned to produce an especially well-balanced Bourbon.

offices and its down-home distillery, Glenmore is deeply rooted in Louisville. It is undoubtedly proud, too, that its whiskey is used to mix the mint juleps at Churchill Downs at Kentucky Derby time.

Although Old Thompson is the name of a blended whiskey made by the company, and Glenmore appears on some products, the principal Bourbons are Old Kentucky Tavern (80, 86 and 100 proof, four years old) and the higher-priced Yellowstone (80, 86, 90 and 100 proof; 4, 5, 6 and 7 years). Yellowstone may seem a distant reference but the name was bestowed by a previous distilling company in 1872 to honour the creation of the United States' first National Park, in the Rocky Mountain states of the West. As a patriotic gesture, it must have rung a bell, because Yellowstone Bourbon has been a part of Kentucky ever since.

Old Kentucky Tavern (a verbose whiskey: it also variously describes itself as being aristocratic, premium Bourbon and special reserve) has a light-to-medium body with some fruitiness and a dry finish. Yellowstone is a little heavier. The distillery uses "scalding" rather than cooking, and ferments in cypress, but the really distinctive part of its process is the use of an additional chamber on top of the still. This chamber, ten or a dozen feet in height, contains an umbrella-shaped plate to return reflux to the still for a second run. The effect is said to be a mellowing of palate which is not achieved with the conventional use of a doubler. The company barrels its whiskey at a relatively low proof, to enhance extraction from the wood, and does not heat its warehouses. In summer, the 2,250 warehouse windows are opened in the morning and closed in the evening. In making the case for this old-fangled behaviour, the company compares the difference, charmingly, with that between growing fruit in a garden or a hothouse.

Apart from its Louisville distillery, the company owns a plant at Owensboro, Kentucky, but whiskey is no longer produced there. The plant is used for blending and bottling. It also has a grain distillery in Albany, Georgia. These plants are additionally used to produce the huge range of Mr Boston spirits, mixes and liqueurs. Glenmore bought this famous Massachusetts label in 1970. With his sours and schnapps, his fruit brandies, "Old" Mr Boston (he has been coyly phasing out the soubriquet for some years) belongs to Americana. He is the mythical bartender who, among other feats, made a liqueur from rock candy and rye whiskey. His much-thumbed "Bartender's Guide" continues its endless reprints, and he should be happy in Kentucky.

The most elegant Bourbon produced in Louisville – and, indeed, in Kentucky – is Old Fitzgerald. This is a fiercely traditional label, as well it might be. In true American style, it began its life somewhere else. The original John E. Fitzgerald distillery was founded not in Louisville but in Frankfort, Kentucky, in 1870, though its products were always pretty mobile. Upwardly mobile, too. They were made exclusively for railroad companies, steamship lines and private clubs. Fitzgerald was later subsumed in a merger in Louisville. This involved the whiskey houses of Philip and Frederick Stitzel (founded 1872) and William LaRue Weller (1849), which emerged from Prohibition under the guidance of the unlikely-sounding Julian P. "Pappy" Van Winkle, who had begun his career as a salesman in the business but now became president. The names of Fitzgerald, Stitzel-Weller and J.P. Van Winkle all survived on whiskeys produced in a single distillery, and still do, but more has happened in the meantime. Like most distillers, the company forged distribution links with imported drinks, in this case Canada Dry and Johnnie Walker, among others. These led at first to ownership by a distributor and then to a takeover in 1984 by Johnnie Walker's parent, the Distillers Company Limited.

The clubby elegance of Old Fitzgerald is proclaimed by its outward symbols: the gazebo housing the old spring, and the Georgian-style portico on the offices (built in 1949). There is even a certain style to the 1930s distillery building, albeit very industrial-looking, with a sign over the entrance promising: "No chemist on the premises". Inside, a steam donkey-engine still turns the paddles on the mash tubs. Old Fitzgerald and its brother whiskeys are all produced with the style of mash bill that uses wheat instead of rye.

The classic character of Old Fitzgerald and its brother whiskeys is a rich, nutty palate, with a smooth finish. Old Fitzgerald comes in a wide variety of versions: Old Fitzgerald Prime Bourbon comes at 80 and 86 proof, six years old but without an age statement; then, at 90 proof and eight years, it is labelled "1849", in honour of the business's earliest foundation date; beyond which there is Very Old Fitzgerald, at 100 proof and eight years. Finally comes Very, Very Old Fitzgerald, at 100 proof, 12 and 15 years. The eight-year version captures to perfection the Old Fitzgerald character. The yet older versions are fine examples of a

really mature whiskey with lots of Bourbon-barrel character. They make a splendid after-dinner drink. Old Fitzgerald whiskeys are especially popular in Kentucky and the Central South, and the older versions are available only in certain markets, sometimes by special order.

In the rural South, a range of similar whiskeys is marketed under the name Cabin Still, at 80, 86 and 90 proof, 4 years old but with no age statement. A Cabin Still hillbilly in porcelain is claimed by the company to have been the first ceramic decanter when it was introduced in 1954. The company produced some fine ceramics but did not market them aggressively and eventually phased them out.

A more militantly Southern label, again in a similar style, is Rebel Yell. This histrionic product (at 86.8 and 90 proof, with no age statement) is marketed only South of the Mason-Dixon line. Its biggest sales are

There is a swashbuckling traditionalism to the promotion of Rebel Yell (left). A product that is available only in the South defies the canons of modern, nationwide marketing. Such inspired conservatism perfectly fits a distillery powered by a donkey-engine (right).

in Virginia, Kentucky and North Carolina, though it extravagantly promises to have been made especially for the Deep South, and it has become something of a cultural artefact there. A Rebel Yell Brigade, in which six thousand members gather in clubs to foster the life and history of the South, is organised as a promotion for the whiskey. In an isolated lapse, it was once briefly made available north of Dixie, but that was a mistake.

In farther flung parts of the United States, people who enjoy the style of whiskey made by this company will most easily find brands deriving from its corporate name, Stitzel Weller. These include one simply called Stitzel-Weller Bourbon, at 80 proof and four years; W.L. Weller Special Reserve, at 86 and 90 proof, seven years old but with no age statement; and, most unusually, Old Weller 107 Proof, which is "seven summers old". The odd choice of 107 proof is credited to

the original William LaRue Weller, and the company claims, on the back label: "No better balanced whiskey of age and proof has been made in all our generations of distilling".

The Van Winkle family's contribution to the company is also honoured, in a very smooth whiskey at 90 proof (no age statement) and, again 107 proof (but this one is "ten summers old"). These whiskeys are produced in an arrangement with the Van Winkle family, as are a couple of seven-year-olds, at 90.9 and 100 proof, under the David Nicholson label. The family likes to keep a hand in the whiskey business, though it would be difficult not to retain some connection, so dense are such relationships in Kentucky.

Purely by happenstance, "Pappy" Van Winkle's grandson, a forestry graduate, finds himself running the arboretum and nature reserve near Louisville that was established for the people of Kentucky by one of the family's ostensible rival distillers, Isaac Wolfe ("I.W. Harper") Bernheim. Open to the public (it receives half a million visitors a year), Bernheim Forest has 14,000 acres of hills, hiking trails and lakes, with 1,700 varieties of trees and shrubs, and is inhabited by tree toads, salamanders, 289 species of birds, bobcats, coyotes, and raccoons. Occasionally, an old moonshine still will be uncovered in the forest.

"I.W. Harper" Bernheim was, among the many larger-than-life characters who have inhabited the American whiskey world, a considerable man. He was of Swiss-German Jewish origin, and emigrated to the United States in 1867. He first followed a family tradition by being a peddler, with a horse and wagon, selling haberdashery. He began in Pennsylvania and eventually settled in Kentucky, where he worked as a clerk in retail store and as a book-keeper in a liquor company before becoming a whiskey salesman and subsequently building a distillery with his brother, in 1896. No one is sure why Isaac Wolfe Bernheim called his whiskey I.W. Harper, except that he wanted a "good, American name". One theory is that

I. W. Bernheim was a classic case of the immigrant who made his fortune in America, emerging as a patriot and philanthropist. The bronze Bernheim doorway seems to fit a distillery less than a public library. The plaques might today announce a brokerage firm. The grandson of "I.W." was a founder of Drexel, Burnham (anglicized), Lambert.

he took it from Harper's Ferry, Virginia. In his later years, he was a tireless philanthropist, patronising German and Jewish charities but being especially generous to Kentucky, where he had enjoyed his success. He angered some fellow Jews by his liberal views on religion and his rejection of Zionism; he was a devoted American patriot and, for Kentucky, a passionate progressive on racial and social issues.

I.W. Harper, Old Charter and J.W. Dant Bourbons are all still produced at a distillery named in honour of the Bernheims, in Louisville. The Bernheims had actually re-

tired before their name was given to this distillery, and their business passed through a couple of other hands before it was acquired by Schenley in the 1930s. Schenley added "modern" brick-built, temperature-controlled warehouses, which must have been revolutionary at the time.

Harper and Charter are both premium brands. I.W. Harper is a typical Bourbon, light-to-medium in body, sweetish, with a warming finish. Old Charter has a bigger body and a little more of the bitter-fruit rye character. J.W. Dant has a medium body and some maltiness. I.W. Harper is pro-

duced at 86, 100 and 101 proof, at 4, 5 and 10 years old. Old Charter is marketed at 86 and 100, 8 and 10 years. J.W. Dant is the company's basic brand, at 80 and 100 proof, "fully aged". The company also has a pleasantly smooth rye. This is called Cream of Kentucky Rye. Sad to say, the company has in recent years paid little attention to the once famous, and in its day very well matured, whiskey called James E. Pepper. This is claimed to have roots in the late 1700s, when commercial distilling began in Kentucky, and it was once famous for its slogan: "Born With the Republic".

Kentucky ~ *Owensboro*

Bold palates know that one treat they make in Owensboro, Kentucky, is a stew called burgoo. It is cooked with four meats – one of which was customarily opossum – okra, other vegetables and cayenne pepper. Another thing is whiskey, traditionally with a powerful Bourbon character.

In the far West of Kentucky, on the Ohio river, the small town of Owensboro, Daviess County, is the commercial centre for this part of the state, with some tobacco, a small steel industry and a factory making electric motors. It stands on one of the pockets of limestone with which Kentucky is stitched, and it has an abundance of good water for the making of whiskey. It represents the Western point of what might be described as the Kentucky "whiskey diamond".

There were eighteen distilleries in Daviess County at the beginning of this century, of which four or five survive, but only one still making whiskey. National names like Fleischmann and Julius Wile have made whiskey in the town; Glenmore still bottles there; so does the Stanley distillery, one of several such businesses started at different times by the Medley family. However, only the one called the Medley Distilling Company continues to produce whiskey, and it does so with single-minded pride.

John Medley, an English Catholic, emigrated to Maryland in 1635, and the family is believed to have distilled there before moving to Washington County, Kentucky, in about 1800. In Washington County, the family became related by marriage to the Beams. The Medleys moved to Owensboro in 1904 and bought a distillery there. Among the two or three they have since owned, one backs on to the present property. The Medleys first distilled on the present site in 1937, but they had difficulties in the post-Prohibition period and eventually sold out. A Medley, is, however, still involved in the day-to-day running of the distillery, a dozen generations on, more than half of them in Kentucky. The principal stockholding in the company is held by a former senior executive with the Barton distillery.

Medley's whiskeys are full-bodied traditional Bourbons, smooth and notably clean in palate. They are marketed under a wide range of labels, among which the principal brand is Ezra Brooks. This is an old whiskey name in the area, though no one is quite sure of its origin. Ezra Brooks Bourbon is available at 80, 86, 90 and 100 proof in a four-year version; at 90 and 7 years, a combination in which the brand sells especially well; and at 101 and 15 years. The clean, smooth quality of this whiskey is exemplified in the seven-year version, but the 101 is a splendid "sippin' whiskey", and something of a speciality.

There is also the excellent Rittenhouse Rye, available not only at 80 proof but also 100, a version in which it is especially appreciated. The distillery's other products include an allegedly "mellow" straight corn whiskey at 100 proof.

The Medley people affect a "Good Old Boy" demeanour, but this Southern macho is combined with a fastidious concern about cleanliness and tidiness in the distillery. A mock-rustic sign on the main roads leads to a manicured driveway and, in just a gentle dip toward the river, there is the neat, small distillery in 1940s red-brick. Inside, an antique, ball-topped still, now used as a holding tank, is painted in pristine blue along with the beer still and doubler. The distillery lays great emphasis on taking only the "heart of the run", a principle to which all of its contemporaries would in theory subscribe but which some practise more than others. The company uses its own new yeast (which it has had since 1937) in a lactic mash. Setback goes into both the cooker and the fermenters, some cypress, others stainless steel. The brick-built, open-rick warehouses are unheated but do have forced circulation of air. The barrels are well charred and the whiskey is filtered after aging.

The style of warehousing is discussed in a gossipy label. As the label observes, the company is "mighty proud" of its distillery ..."down in Kentucky, where folks know their Bourbon".

The smart still-house at Medley has an admirable simplicity of design. The beer-still, extending through several floors, is typical. Also in the foreground is the doubler. Behind is an antique pot-still, now a holding tank.

A taste-guide to Owensboro whiskeys

A great home of Bourbon production in its day, Owensboro, Kentucky, still thinks of itself as a whiskey town. There is evidence enough of its traditions, and it continues to produce whiskeys with a powerful Bourbon character. On the map, it represents the Western point of the Kentucky whiskey diamond.

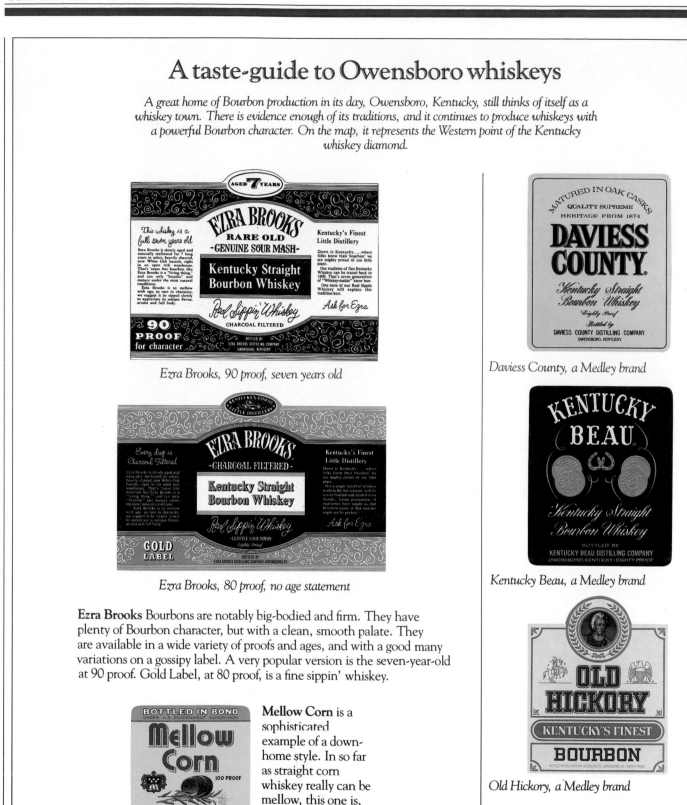

Ezra Brooks, 90 proof, seven years old

Ezra Brooks, 80 proof, no age statement

Daviess County, a Medley brand

Kentucky Beau, a Medley brand

Old Hickory, a Medley brand

Ezra Brooks Bourbons are notably big-bodied and firm. They have plenty of Bourbon character, but with a clean, smooth palate. They are available in a wide variety of proofs and ages, and with a good many variations on a gossipy label. A very popular version is the seven-year-old at 90 proof. Gold Label, at 80 proof, is a fine sippin' whiskey.

Mellow Corn is a sophisticated example of a down-home style. In so far as straight corn whiskey really can be mellow, this one is, and at a hearty 100 proof. A whiskey of some charm, with a label to match.

Daviess County is a Bourbon that clearly proclaims its origins. It is in this county that the town of Owensboro stands. Daviess County, Kentucky Beau and Old Hickory are less characterful Medley brands.

A taste-guide to Tennessee whiskeys

It is not well understood that the whiskeys of Tennessee represent a style of their own. Their home state is ambivalent about this. When people ask for a Bourbon and are offered a Tennessee whiskey, that is good for business. But supposing they asked for a Tennessee whiskey in the first place?

Lynchburg

Jack Daniel's, 86 proof

Lem Motlow's, 90 proof

Jack Daniel's, 90 proof

Jack Daniel's has the intensely dry, aromatic lightness that makes Tennessee whiskeys so different. The regular Jack Daniel's has the familiar black label, but there is also a slightly lower-proof version wearing the green. Lem Motlow's, named after Jack Daniel's nephew, is a less mellow, local brand in Tennessee and Georgia.

Tullahoma

George Dickel Old No. 8 Brand, 86.8 proof

George Dickel Old No. 12 Brand, 90 proof

George Dickel whiskies (their preferred spelling) are very clean, their characteristic Tennessee dryness balanced with a hint of sweetness, and with a crisp finish. They are fractionally lighter than Jack Daniel's whiskies, though the differences between the two marques are, overall, very subtle.

Tennessee

Among those famous whiskeys that are always asked for by name, rather than being identified by their category, Jack Daniel's is a prime example. People order a Jack Daniel's; they do not ask for "a Tennessee whiskey, please". Nonetheless, Tennessee whiskey is a specific style, and that is what Jack Daniel's is. Although it is not quite the only distillery in the state, Jack Daniel's has put Tennessee whiskey on the map, but it has done so without identifying it as a style. If it is considered in that way at all, it is generally thought of as being Tennessee Sour Mash. This does not take account of the fact that all straight whiskeys made in the United States are produced to some extent by a sour mash method. They have not all chosen to proclaim this on their labels, perhaps because they thought that "sour mash" sounded unappetising; Jack Daniel's has the good sense to see that such a traditional term implies integrity. The distinctive feature of Tennessee whiskey comes, though, at a later stage, in the filtration process.

The Tennessee method of filtration is unique in two respects: first that it is done before barrelling, rather than after. Second, that it is such an exhaustive process. It is not unusual elsewhere to use charcoal, but no one employs a filter ten feet deep, nor expects the process to last for ten days. This is not so much a filtration as leaching out of fusel oils. To a considerable extent, these are driven off in normal distillation, but in Tennessee the idea is that the survivors get caught in filtration. Whether some positive flavour characteristics are left behind, too, is a moot point. Jack Daniel's is not an oily-tasting whiskey, but perhaps it loses some texture in this process. Then there is another factor to consider: the charcoal not only takes away but might also add some taste, from that barbecued sugar maple. Some drinkers find in Jack Daniel's a faint but distinctive smokiness. Perhaps because leaching has an unpleasant sound, but also because the process makes a positive contribution, the Tennessee distillers prefer to call it "mellowing".

The significance of this mellowing being done before barrelling is that a cleaner whiskey goes into the wood. It is thus a different character of spirit that makes the extraction of flavours from the barrel, and the end result has its own distinctive balance. Whether these differences are worthwhile – do they enhance, or perhaps even diminish, the product? – is a matter of taste. Do you like the assertiveness of other straight whiskeys, or is that restrained into a greater sophistication and complexity by the Tennessee mellowing method?

If there were a single "best" way in which to make whiskey, they would all taste the same. American consumers are obsessed with knowing which whiskey (or beer, wine, pasta or whatever) is best, but the ultimate logic of this is that only one specification would be produced; variety and choice would cease to exist; uniformity would reign.

Within the Tennessee whiskey category, there are five products, made by two distilleries, Jack Daniel's and George Dickel. In general, the Daniel's products are a little heavier, with a slight, pleasant oiliness of body. The Dickel whiskeys are lighter and very aromatic, with the typical vanilla bouquet of the barrel. Jack Daniel's principal product, with the familiar black label, is marketed at 90 proof. A green label version has 86.4 proof. Both are between four and five years old but carry no age statement. A further product, named after Jack Daniel's nephew, is Lem Motlow's Tennessee Sour Mash. This is a one-year-old whiskey of 90 proof made primarily for the Tennessee and Georgia markets. George Dickel's "black" has 86.8 and an ivory label 90, both at more than four years old, with no age statement.

Both distilleries welcome visitors, and the two are less than ten miles apart. They are very much a part of the tourist route centred on Nashville. The city is the state capital, with handsome government buildings in a small, modern centre, a tiny nightlife district, and the Grand Old Opry, for which tickets have to be booked well in advance. If they cannot be obtained, lovers of country music might content themselves with flipping the dial on the radio, which in Tennessee broadcasts little else. Even the truckers on their CBs offer a greeting to Johnny Cash in case he is listening. To songs of workin', drinkin' and cheatin' on your love, Interstate 24 heads South-East toward Chattanooga and the Alabama and Georgia state lines. Off the highway is the town of Shelbyville (which sounds more like 'Shubville" in the local accent), famous for Tennessee walking horses, with their contorted gait and cricked tail. There are horse ranches, and the odd sign offering bulls for sale. This is the countryside for Tennessee farm sausage with white beans and corn bread. It is also the countryside where the whiskey is made, though travellers may have to settle for Dr Pepper. The small towns are dotted with Primitive Baptist Churches. The First Presbyterian Church, the Church of the Nazarene, the First Church of God. In Eagleville, the city hall is a converted gas station. Every once in a while, a 1950s car or an even older tractor sleeps in decay. As the

"The Hollow", they call it (left). More than one American whiskey is produced in a "hollow", but none as imposing as this. Like an amphitheatre, it presents a spectacle. What looks like matchwood stacked down there is maple, to be sacrificed under the canopy (below). Charcoal-burner Jack Bateman (above) is one of a cast of "down-home" characters who inhabit Lynchburg (pop 361). Nobody hurries in Lynchburg, and the spirit takes ten days to feed, drip by drip, through as many feet of charcoal (below left).

country deepens, buzzards hover, and across the flat landscape is the highland Ridge of the Cumberland plateau.

Beyond Walden Ridge, in the approach to the Smoky Mountains and the state line of the Carolinas, there is a serious moon-shining country, where inquiries may prompt a blast from a shotgun. It was from North Carolina that settlers came to this part of Tennessee in the late 1700s, and by the 1800s there were hundreds of stills in the state. In 1825, the first distillery is said to have been established in the area where Jack Daniel subsequently started his operations. By the 1890s, Tennessee was a major force in commercial distilling, but the shadow of Prohibition was falling. One or two states had already gone dry, and Tennessee followed suit in 1910, ten years before national Prohibition. Distilling was not legal again in Tennessee until 1938, five years "late", and then only to produce whisky for sale in other states. Both of today's distilleries are in dry counties, of which the state still has a great many.

The Public Burning: From a safe distance, tourist visitors may have the opportunity to see the charcoal–burning, and it is an impressive ritual performance, with a cast of four or five seasoned players. The canopy is not a stage but a means of trapping the smoke. There are perhaps 1,500 planks of maple in each performance. They are burned through, but still intact, when the hoses are turned on. The smouldering and steaming persists long afterwards, as the charcoal is shovelled up to be "minced".

Tennessee ~ *Lynchburg*

The name Lynchburg seems incomplete without the parenthetical (pop. 361). That was the town's population when it first featured in the famous series of advertisements for Jack Daniel's, and both parties have agreed that is how it will stay, regardless of births, deaths and, a few years ago, a change of boundaries. Lynchburg and Jack Daniel's have helped make a name for each other. After all this time, they need each other, too. It is an interesting relationship.

Vignettes of life in Lynchburg, simply etched in modest monochrome spaces, have been a running story in glossy American magazines for decades. They have whimsically reminded people of the small-town foundation on which the United States is built, and that has struck a chord. Against the flutters of fashion, Jack Daniel's has found itself on some famous lips, and has loyally stuck with the same provincial ad agency for a quarter of a century. In Lynchburg, they have long forgotten the smart reporter from the business magazine "Fortune" who presumed to "discover" the town and its whiskey in the 1950s, but both were well found.

Lynchburg is little more than a square of shops set around Moore County Courthouse. The layout is that of any small town in the South. The shops date from the 1920s, though some are sun-faded 1940s brick buildings. The courthouse is a stylish little Georgian structure, with a memorial to the Confederate dead.

Three of the shops proclaim that they sell Jack Daniel's souvenirs. A fourth, the Lynchburg Hardware & General Store, is

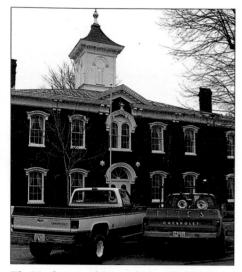

The Hardware and General Store (facing page) sells bottled water from the distillery spring, and the influence of Jack Daniel's is everywhere. Today there are pick-up trucks instead of mules . . . bred as an occupation during Prohibition. The ducks are still around, ready to seize any spilled grain at the distillery. "If it's not to their taste, we don't use it," says the distiller. They make jokes faster than whiskey at Jack Daniel's.

owned by Jack Daniel's. It sells bottled water from the distillery's spring, whittling knives (and the sticks to carve with them), tools, country cooking equipment, Tennessee hams, and a wide range of products, which are also available by mail order. Also owned by Jack Daniel's is the White Rabbit Saloon, which sells coffee and snacks but not alcohol (Moore County being dry). Inside is a poster advertising the saloon in its barely-different earlier days ("Jack Daniel, sole owners") and boasting about its "electrically-powered overhead fans". They still turn, strangely paddle-shaped contrivances suspended vertically on a propellor shaft. On the juke box, Loretta Lynn and Conway Twitty sing Country laments.

There never seem to be fewer than twenty pick-up trucks parked around the square but it is hard to see where their owners have

gone. To the Farmer's Co-op, perhaps? Or are they the people sitting on stoops, men with their arms round girls, or playing checkers with bottle-tops?

Lynchburg stands in open country and on a slight incline, which falls away barely perceptibly to the steep-sided hollow about a quarter of a mile away where the distillery hides. There are high, sweeping hillsides, and in places the hollow is carved out of rock, its buildings softened with age, creepers, and a dense landscaping of evergreen shrubs, parted by brick paths and little iron bridges.

One rockface opens into a cave, about 20ft high and 25ft wide, narrowing quickly until an explorer would have to crawl. It has been explored to 6,000ft, but the water it provides has never been traced to a source. If it were an underground stream, it would

have a big natural basin, perhaps 5,000 acres. Maybe it is: "It takes a darned good spring never to dry, and this one never has", comments one of the distillery workers. If Jack Daniel's people contrive to be relaxed, they do so effortlessly.

The water from the cave is used to make whiskey. A little backset is used in the atmospheric cooker; the yeast, of which Jack Daniel's is proud, is a very vigorous, two-cell strain, which is recovered from each fermentation, kept in jugs on ice and mashed in rye and lactic malt; the fermenters are all open, stainless steel; the original, pre-Prohibition still stands alongside four copper column stills, with doublers. The still-house, a precarious-looking, narrow, red-brick seven-floor building, is covered in ivy.

The old mellowing house is overgrown, too. The wooden mellowing vessels are sunk

into the floor. They are packed with ten feet of charcoal, resting on a wool blanket. Immediately above the top surface of the charcoal is a criss-cross of copper pipes about an inch in diameter. These pipes are perforated, and through the holes the whisky is fed on to the charcoal. It drips, never managing even a dribble, let alone a flow. There are several dozen of these vessels.

The charcoal becomes "tired" after a few weeks, and more has to be made. To maintain an adequate supply, the distillery burns a batch of maple once or twice a week. It is an impressive performance, not stinted.

The maple has first been cut into planks around four feet long, like giant matchsticks. These are neatly stacked to a height of about eight feet. The rick is set ablaze, the flames roar into the canopy above. Twenty feet away, it is almost too hot to stand. The

canopy sucks away the smoke and afterburns it, as a measure against pollution. When the flames are at their height, all the wood burning through in a red glow, the rick is hosed with water. It stubbornly resists extinction, hissing in fury and spitting the smoke of a hundred dragons, before it is extinguished. When they have cooled down, the black, crumbly remains of the planks are milled in a huge "coffee-grinder" to something resembling seacoal. They are then packed into the mellowing vats and given a grudging drink.

The burning ceremony is watched, from the rim of the "amphitheatre", by tour parties, behind them the looming warehouses full of whiskey in its slow progress to maturity. It is a phenomenon: the town, the distillery, the rites, and the shrewd way in which it has all been presented to the consumer.

The Louisville-based distillers Brown Forman own the phenomenon, but cannot be said to have orchestrated it. They still list as proprietor Lem Motlow, nephew of Jack Daniel, and the rural climate of his family and friends prevails.

It was a romantic story from the beginning. It started with Joseph Daniel, an Englishman who worked as a coachman for a wealthy Scots family and fell in love with their fifteen-year-old daughter. In 1772, the couple eloped to America, where Joseph fought against the British in the War of Independence. They settled in North Carolina, then moved to Tennessee. Their grandson Jack Daniel, the youngest of a family of ten, was probably born in 1846. There is some doubt about the date, but 1846 seems more likely than 1850, which is also quoted. Because he wasn't keen on his

The most celebrated name in whiskey? Tennessee's Jack Daniel has distinguished counterparts in Kentucky and Scotland but his memory has perhaps been best kept alive. He was photographed in the late 1880s (right) and, like several whiskey-makers, is captured in a statue at his distillery (left). Nephew Lem Motlow (far right) was photographed in 1947.

stepmother, Jack Daniel boldly left home at the age of six and moved in with an uncle. A year later, he went to live with a family friend, an elder in the Lutheran church, who had a still. The still is said to have employed charcoal leaching even then, and that to have been regarded as a local process, but this is not well documented. When the Lutheran became preoccupied with the demands of his church, Jack Daniel began to take over the running of the still, at the age of thirteen. When he set up his own distillery, on the present site, he seems to have been only nineteen. The distillery was registered with the Federal Government after the Civil War, in 1866.

The Jack Daniel's "No 7" brand-name was introduced in about 1887. There are several stories about its origin but the nearest to an authorised version is that Daniel was inspired by the success of a Jewish merchant whom he met, who had built a chain of seven retail stores. Seven was nothing more than an inspirational number. Daniel also used the designation "Old" for his whiskey. If he aged it, or affected to, that was unusual at the time, and may have helped him develop a cachet. Normally, whiskey was supplied to saloons in the barrel and the aging was their responsibility. From his earliest days in the whiskey business, Daniel had, rather than selling from a store, favoured distribution by horse and wagon, and this undoubtedly helped spread the fame of his products. A big breakthrough came, though, when he was pressed into exhibiting his whiskey in the 1904 World's Fair at St Louis, Missouri. The Gold Medal for the best whiskey in the world went to someone pointed out as "that little guy from Tennes-

see in the stove-pipe hat".

Jack Daniel's normal attire was a broad-brimmed planter's hat and a formal, knee-length frock coat; he was a dandy, but a tiny one, only 5ft 2in. He was the most eligible bachelor in the county but he never married. Towards the end of his life, he became a Primitive Baptist, and he died in 1911, after a tragi-comic incident in which he injured his foot while kicking a jammed safe. After Prohibition, which had lasted twenty-eight years in Tennessee, no one else in the state was interested in re-starting commercial production, but Daniel's nephew Lem Motlow, who was already sixty-nine, went ahead, extending and rebuilding the distillery. He died in 1947, passing the distillery on to his four sons, but none of them had successors, and the family sold the business to Brown Forman in 1956.

Tennessee ~ *Tullahoma*

If the Tennessee whiskey business has an historic centre, it is the town of Tullahoma (population 18,000). This was the home of Alfred Eaton, who is credited with having developed the charcoal-leaching process in 1825. Then, as now, Tullahoma, which is in Coffee County, was the main town for a considerable stretch of countryside, and Eaton's distillery was in the hollow subsequently occupied by Jack Daniel's. The method he used was originally known as the "Lincoln County Process". Before "Lincoln" could become a generic style of whiskey, sub-divisions had taken place to create Moore County. Perhaps it is just as well; Tennessee whiskey seems a simpler designation.

In the small towns that are the foundations of the United States, there are several classic layouts: the town set round the courthouse; the one-street town; and the town where the railroad runs down the middle of the main street. In Tullahoma, the railroad still runs that way, with much shunting and hooting. The railroad made Tullahoma. Not only did it offer people in Coffee and Moore Counties access to Nashville and Chattanooga by chu-chu, it also helped make Tullahoma into a resort. The railway was in itself a curiosity, but all the more so where a town was built round it, as Tullahoma was. There was a double main street, at either side of the track, and it was said in the 1860s to be the widest in the world. The street was flanked with boarding houses, where people sat on the porches and watched the trains. It was a resort town, too, because it was a spa, with limestone water.

Among the people attracted there was George Dickel. He was of German origin, and had been living in Nashville before going to Tullahoma and opening a general store. Dickel decided to put some of that limestone water to better use. Tired of selling other people's products, he thought he would have one of his own, and he called it Cascade Whisky (without the "e").

His distillery was not far from Tullahoma, on Cascade Creek, one or two miles from a hamlet called Normandy. The distillery

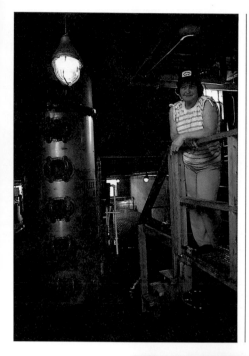

opened in 1870 and continued after Dickel's death in 1894 but closed at the onset of Prohibition. After repeal, the Dickel and Cascade names were acquired in the late 1930s by the national liquor company Schenley. The names' reputation made them worth reviving, and there was the possibility that the distillery itself might be rebuilt at some point.

Tennessee whiskey was recognized as a style in 1941, in a letter from the tax authorities in Washington in reply to an application from Jack Daniel's, who had just restarted the marketing of their product. In 1951, the "Fortune" magazine article on Jack Daniel's appeared, and this account was regarded as being of sufficient interest to reprint in the Congressional Record. Whether either of these developments spurred Schenley into action is a matter for speculation. It was, in any case, the period of post-war recovery and a good time to launch new products.

The Geo. A. Dickel distillery was rebuilt, about threequarters of a mile from the original site in 1958. Even Dickel's general store was rebuilt, and stocked with a collection of products which were pre-war, if not pre-Prohibition. The store still has packets of Cameo Starch, Octagon Soap Powder and Dr Thacher's Senna Laxative.

Standing alone in a long, winding valley fringed with trees, the silence broken only by birdsong and the fast-flowing creek, the distillery and its restored buildings are a pretty place to visit. Dickel use atmospheric cooking; their own original yeast culture, in granulated form; a mix of stainless steel and cypress fermenters; and poplar mellowing vessels. Outside the distillery is piled the hard sugar maple from which the charcoal is produced. Being a smaller distillery than its famous neighbour, Dickel has bonfires with a lesser frequency, but the charcoal is used in the same way by both companies. Back in Tullahoma, Alfred Eaton would be pleased.

This flask of Dickel's Cascade proudly styles itself Tennessee Whisky, though the designation had not been recognized when it was bottled, around the turn of the century. Unless the drawing on the label took artist's licence, the whisky was produced in a pot-still. Today's waterside site hardly cascades, but a crisp, aromatic whisky is produced nonetheless. Above: at the beer-still . . . operator Mary Gordon.

JAPAN

The Japanese can indulge themselves in a wry smile at their reputation as a people powered by the silicon chip. Like most nations, they generally wish to have the approval of others, but they also enjoy a good laugh. Humour and conviviality are, at least among friends and business associates, a very important and evident part of Japanese life. The caution – and the metabolism – of the Orient may not make for the three-Martini lunch but no such inhibition affects the longer hours of the evening. In the daytime, there might be decorous behaviour, but a garrulous indiscretion over a drink in the evening is readily forgiven and forgotten.

In modern Japan, the drink might still be *sake*, fermented from rice. Or it might be sake's distilled counterpart, which is rendered variously as *shochu*, *shyochu*, or *jochu*, depending upon the transliteration preferred. Shochu may be distilled from rice, buckwheat or other grains, or from plants like the sweet potato, and several versions can be available in a single bar or restaurant. Like sake, its distilled big brother is usually clear in colour, with a fruity palate. Just as sake may be served at room temperature or warmed to "body heat", so shochu may be taken straight or diluted with warm water. It is also served with mixers like soda or fruit juices, often plum. Light shochus intended for mixing have become a major factor in the Japanese drinks industry. In this role they echo Western "Vodka".

Then again, the evening's drink might be beer, usually of the Pilsner type, though occasionally an amber Märzenbier, or a "black" lager of the old Bavarian style, or even a dry stout. Beer-brewing was introduced to Japan in the second half of the 1800's, through Dutch and Bavarian (and, it would seem, eventually Irish) influence, after the celebrated visit of the American Navy under Commodore Perry, in 1853, and the subsequent treaty of Friendship and Trade. Japan's entry into the international arena during the rule of the Emperor Meiji, from 1867 to 1912, is now dusty history, as is the increasing interest in European, and especially British, life that was evident at the beginning of the 1920's. That the Japanese have been able to conserve so much of their social culture while also becoming internationally-minded is perhaps surprising. That they have long entertained cosmopolitan tastes isn't, however much it seems to astonish some Westerners.

Nor, of course, does John Barleycorn manifest himself only in the fermented form of beer. Imported Scotch was already a smart drink in Japan when the country first started to distil its own whisky, in the 1920s. Only after the interruptions of two world wars did the Japanese whisky industry begin to find its feet. Today, Japan regards its own whiskies as being in its own national style, though their heritage is respectfully agreed to be Scottish.

Japan also has its own wine industry, which began around the turn of the century. Since the indigenous vines yield dessert grapes, the first wines produced were sweet – of the port type. Ever since, the Japanese have been breeding hybrids, and growing classic European grapes. Some of their most successful hybrids are based on the native Koshu, a pink-skinned, late-harvesting white grape, which has been crossbred with Riesling and Cabernet Sauvignon. Both of those grapes, along with Pinot Noir, Chardonnay, Aligoté, Sauvignon Blanc and Semillon, are widely cultivated in the main growing area, the Yamanashi basin, which lies about two hours to the West of Tokyo. Japanese wines generally have a fresh, fruity character and tend to be light but firm-bodied. In recent years, the vines have turned full circle to sweetness, albeit in a quite different incarnation, by producing some outstanding "noble rot" wines. As a wine-growing country, Japan also produces grape brandies. These are generally similar in style to those produced in Cognac, with a crisp, clean, dry palate.

A country that, in addition to traditional beverages like sake and shochu, also produces beer and whisky, wine and brandy, might be expected to make the other spirit drinks, and so it does. There are, in particular, some well-made gins, in the London Dry style, and Japan has in recent years become well-known for exotic liqueurs like the melon-flavoured Midori.

Japan has one of the lowest rates of alcohol consumption in the developed world, but its drinkers' concentration on sake and shochu, beer and whisky, provides those products with some impressive sales figures. Consumption of whisky per head is higher in Japan than in Britain or The United States.

For the Japanese, the drink of the evening may be determined by the choice of watering hole.

The most basic is the stand-up bar, often to be found around the big, commuter, railway termini. Some of these bars are outdoors, in the arches under the railway tracks; others are in the walkways of the station complex. The drinker simply ducks behind a shoulder-length half-curtain, and leans up against the bar. The half-curtain is intended to offer privacy, though it makes the drinker look as though he is wearing the *kepi* of a Foreign Legionnaire. Some of these basic bars also have sit-down areas, furnished with bare benches. They usually serve sake, shochu or beer, with bar snacks such as tempura or kebabs. When factories and offices decant for the day, these bars are busy, crowded places, though their stock-in-trade is value and convenience rather than comfort. In the unlikely event that a Japanese male needs an excuse for an after-work drink, it is that he missed his train and had to wait for the next one. If he intends to miss several trains, he may decide that the basic bar is insufficiently comfortable, and perhaps just too picaresque in mid-evening clientele. There are a good many other types of place in which to drink.

Like several other social cultures, Japan generally regards a public drinking place as a male preserve. Until recently, this discrimination has been solid. It is now crumbling at the edges, if slowly. If she is accompanied

Brand-names from Japan illuminate every modern metropolis . . . and their own home towns. In the West, Suntory remains best-known for golf tournaments, and for its Midori melon liqueur. In the big cities of Japan, especially in the nightlife quarters, neon signs advertising Suntory Whisky enjoy a dominant position . . . a blossoming of barley.

by a man, a woman may feel comfortable enough in some drinking places, and especially in the "cafe bars" that began to sprout in the 1980s. These establishments, favoured by the bright young things of the metropolitan cities, are an affectionate tribute to the American soda fountain of the James Dean era. Their decor heavily features chrome, mirrors and high stools, and their drinks-list may include some of the more distinctive speciality beers as well as whiskies, especially American imports.

When a "bright young thing" moves into the junior executive bracket, he might prefer a beer garden or cellar. Although these establishments have their origins in the German-inspired growth of beer-drinking in Japan during the late 19th century, they remain as prosperous, busy and smart as ever. In the densely built-up cities, a roof garden may well serve this purpose. A good example is the beer-garden on the roof of the Tokyo offices of Suntory, the brewers, distillers and producers of liqueurs. That is conveniently placed between office and luxury hotel areas, on the edge of the Akasaka nightlife quarter. Elsewhere in Tokyo, the Sapporo brewery has a long-established beer cellar in the Ginza shopping area. The best-known of all the beer-gardens and cellars is a combination of the two, owned by the same company, as its principal brewery in the city of Sapporo, on the Northern island of Hokkaido. These establishments serve beer by the litre, or in divisions or multiples of that generous measure, and their round tables often accommodate a gas ring for the preparation of snacks. Dishes like fried chicken and noodles offer an inspired combination of the Oktoberfest and Orient. Diners wear bibs, and it is hardly surprising that the hearty atmosphere is thought suitable for office parties, or simply thank-God-it's-Friday get-togethers.

The beer cellars and roof gardens may offer the downstairs and upstairs of drinking, but there is no difference whatever in their status. In the West, it has been argued that bars work best if they are below street level –

酒 蔔蒲 養滋 和美

ントワイーホ王赤

Women of Japan . . . the young woman on the left manages to be both demure and daring in a classic 1920s advertisement for Suntory wine. The poster startled Japan but won an international award for designer Mokuda Inoue. The use of colour in the glass could be taken as a visual allusion to the name of the product: Rising Sun. Now that the sun has risen on the drinks industry in Japan, there are plenty of workaday roles, too, for women (right) . . .

the "dive" has a Stygian allure – and that a nightspot is doomed to failure if the customer has to go upstairs to reach it. In Japan, this counts for nothing. Once again, the simple factor of population density means that drinking has to be vertically structured. Nonetheless, the Westerner finds it strange that so often the signposted entrance to a bar merely reveals an elevator. In the Akasaka and Ginza quarters of Tokyo, and the city's younger nightlife areas like Roppongi and Shinjuku, and in similar neighbourhoods in other metropolitan cities, there are tall buildings with bars and nightspots on every floor and corridor. It seems curious to take an elevator, and walk along corridors, to reach a "pub". Even curiouser, it is possible to engage in an extensive pub-crawl without leaving the building.

National influences are eclectic. Like so many other countries, Japan has mock-English pubs, but the characteristics of that institution have also been adapted and subsumed into establishments that are less overtly British in style. Although these

places may have vaguely English-sounding names, serve the odd beer from the British Isles, and have a good range of Scotches, they might best be described as Japanese pubs. They are usually small, quiet, chatty, with plenty of wood panelling and leather upholstery. There are even some similar establishments where, although Scotches are as evident as local whiskies, the decor is in the traditional Japanese style, with no advertising material to disturb the calm of the wood-and-paper screens. This sort of "Japanese bar" is most likely to be found in the older towns, like Kyoto.

That the pubs of England and the whiskies of Scotland should spend such happy hours together in Japan is a situation that inevitably had to lead to the birth of offspring. Creativity flows from the confluence of two currents, and in this instance the offspring was the whisky bar, born in Japan. It's a pubby place but it sells only whisky, predominantly Japanese. It was taken up by distillers, notably Suntory, in the post-war period as a means of establishing domestic

whisky. It has worked so well that its job is now done, and whisky bars are becoming fewer in Japan.

One of their distinguishing features, though it is not exclusive to them, is the custom of "bottle-keeping". This is the principle of each customer buying a bottle of whisky, which is then kept for him in a locker. Whenever he calls in, he has whisky from his own bottle, until it has to be replenished. The purpose of this is not to provide a positive cash-flow for the bar (though that must be attractive to proprietors), or to ensure a captive customer (though it does that, too). Ostensibly, at any rate, its purpose is to facilitate the Japanese custom of the host pouring drinks for his guests. This is an important courtesy in Japan, and over drinks or dinner a great deal of pouring goes on as friends eagerly serve each other. It has been argued that the desire to pour drinks for guests has encouraged the popularity of whisky and brandy as opposed to those spirits normally served with mixers or in cocktails – such as gin, vodka or rum.

Not that the Japanese usually drink their whisky straight, but the custom is simply to dilute it with water and ice. The dilution is considerable: 30ml of whisky, which is just over an American ounce, is served in a full-sized tumbler (a highball, or even a Collins glass), generously topped up with water and ice. The dilution might be two parts of water to one of whisky, but it may be as much as four-to-one, or even more, depending upon the mood of the drinker. This, in turn, might be determined by the time of the evening, or the situation. It is not unusual for an after-work drink to extend until late evening, with a meal along the way. The drinker might stick to whisky even through the meal, but it will be heavily diluted at that point (purists might be horrified, but Scots do like to refer to it as "the wine of the country").

Dilution may blunt the palate of the whisky, but it also tames its potency. The word *mizuwari* (pronounced rather like Missouri, and meaning "diluted with water") almost always refers to an after-work whisky. The mizuwari is meant to be a leisurely drink, accompanied by conversation. Only in its later stages is it likely to lead to a *karaoke* bar, where customers are encouraged to sing to a pre-recorded accompaniment; that's another Japanese creation that has spread to other countries.

The night-clubbish style of bar will often also provide hostesses to pour the drinks, chat and conduct themselves in a mildly flirtatious way. It is usually the understanding of both parties that this coquettish behaviour will lead to nothing more exciting. The bar-girl is simply a modern expression of the elegant lady who serves sake from a crock in a screened, private room of *tatami* matting.

Has nothing changed? Or has everything? Like any deeply-rooted social culture, Japan's can bear a great deal of accretion. This can be seen in its drinking habits and in the diversity of its kitchen. Those European-style beers beautifully quench the thirst left by the ubiquitous *miso* soup (though not as well as tea). Whisky, with its oily texture and peatiness (albeit, in Japan, slight), makes a splendid appetiser with the smoked eel, bonito or salmon's eggs of the sushi bar. There is, surely, room for more beverages in a culinary repertoire that extends through sashimi, shabu-shabu, tempura, tonkatsu, teppan-yaki, yakitori, nabeyaki, sukiyaki, soba, kabayaki . . . with all that it has adopted and adapted, and especially in its most Japanese incarnations, it is one of the world's greatest cuisines: delicate, certainly, but by no means as light as is suggested; complex, inventive and exquisite in its presentation. No doubt there will be yet more alcoholic accompaniments as the producers of wine encourage its consumption with food, as drinking becomes less of a male matter and as Japan becomes a more leisurely society.

The whiskies of Japan

There is no doubt, either in fact or palate, as to the Scottish ancestry of the principal Japanese whiskies. Scotch inspired Japanese whisky. Scottish academic institutions trained the first whisky-makers of Japan. The distillates of Scotland have always been held in great respect by the whisky-producers of Japan, and still are. In the international family of whiskies, the Scottish and Japanese styles are brothers – closely related but each with a slightly different character.

Like the Scots, the Japanese begin by making a mash of pure barley malt, usually peated, and double-distilling it in pot stills to produce a single whisky that is then aged in sherry or Bourbon wood or new, charred oak. Like the Scots, they bottle a small proportion of this to be marketed in the form of single malt but use the far greater share as the basis for blends with column-distilled grain whisky.

The most obvious distinction between Scottish and Japanese whiskies is the extent of their peatiness. The classic whiskies of Scotland all have a definite peatiness, though its extent varies from one to another. In Japan, too, peatiness is usually present, but in a very subtle manifestation. Because of its subtle peating, Japanese whisky has only a light nose. Faint fragrances are favoured by the Japanese in cosmetics and perfumes, and this seems to follow in whisky and other drinks. It has been argued that the Japanese are simply not very interested in aromas and the anthropologist Kinji Imanishi believes this might be because, as an ethnic group, they have virtually no body odour. It is probably the case that no language has a vocabulary sufficient to describe the aromas of the great alcoholic drinks, but Japanese is conspicuously deficient in this respect. With its varied and inventive cuisine, however, Japan cannot be held to lack interest in flavour – or in visual presentation.

The way in which these preferences have led to a stylistic distinction between Scottish and Japanese whiskies does offer its own irony. The notion that a good whisky could be produced outside Scotland was regarded as absurd by the Japanese consumer when the country's first domestic product was put on the market in the 1920s. Yet it was only when the Scottish-style peatiness in the Japanese product was toned down that it began to sell. Since then, there has been a gradual toning down of the peatiness in most Japanese whiskies. Whether this trend will continue is open to question. Japan may cherish its traditions but it is also a dynamic country, and tastes are broadening.

While it was Scottish influence that led the Japanese to use peated barley malt, it is also true that this raw material is locally available. There is peat in Japan, especially on the Northern island of Hokkaido, though it is of a distinctively turfy, less carbonic, character. Japan does grow malting barley, too, though these days it cannot cultivate anything like enough to meet demand. Although Japanese peat has been used in the malting of barley for whisky production, it is not generally thought to be ideal. Peat is, however, imported from Scotland for use in Japanese maltings. Scottish-peated malt is also imported. Although Scottish peating is specified the malt or barley may come from elsewhere. Both malt and barley are imported from a wide range of countries in Australasia, Europe and North America. Among the ingredients of whisky, the water is an element of which Japan is especially proud. Its water, like that of the Scottish Highlands, is crystal-clean, usually rising in granite and sometimes flowing over peat, too. Such waters can make for the subtlest hint of peat in a whisky, and they are a wonderfully sympathetic dilutant. The subtlety of their peating leaves the Japanese whiskies with a pronounced and clean maltiness. That is their defining characteristic. The clean, malty style also has something to do with the number of distilleries and their age.

In Scotland, many distilleries are a century and a half old, and there are more than 100 of them. Each has its own, inured eccentricities, which it is careful to maintain because its particular resonances are known to the whisky blenders. If its character were to change, it might no longer fulfil the role expected of it by the blenders. In Scotland, a blender can pick his malts from any of those distilleries. If his blending company also owns some of the distilleries, he will favour those, but he may nonetheless employ 30 or 40 whiskies in all to arrive at his final product. Whiskies bought from Scottish distilleries are also used by Japanese blenders. Overall, they represent between 12 and 15 per cent of the malt content of Japanese blended whiskies. However, the object is to produce not Scottish but Japanese whiskies. The Scottish malts add variety, rather than volume, and they are used because Japan has relatively few distilleries. Even with the Scottish component, a Japanese blender usually has only about a dozen whiskies from which to work. Although a couple of the Japanese distilleries are small and eccentric, the majority are large, efficient and modern. It is their clean, rich whiskies that establish the character of the Japanese blends. The Scottish blender is orchestrating Beethoven; the Japanese is performing a Vivaldi string quartet.

The distiller with the most resources in Japan is Suntory, which produces more than 71 per cent of the nation's whisky, and has a 67 per cent share of the total market, taking into account imports. No Japanese distillery sells a great deal abroad, but Suntory's two or three per cent export sale – mainly in the Pacific region – is as big as any. The company also has a tiny whisky distillery in Mexico. At home, Suntory extends its blending possibilities by producing more than one single malt in each of its distilleries. This technique is not unique to Suntory, but the company is one of the world's leaders in the techniques of mashing, fermentation and distilling. Different malts and yeasts, and varying cut-off points in distillation, are used to produce a range of whiskies for blending. The company's original distillery at Yamazaki, near Kyoto, produces several whiskies in two distilling lines. Its second distillery, at Hakushu, in Yamanashi prefecture, has two lines from mashing all the way through to distillation. There is also a third complete distillery on the Hakushu site. In addition to these, the company decided in 1984 to build a further distillery at Noheji, in Aomori prefecture. All of these are malt distilleries. The company also owns a grain distillery and has a partnership in another. Each of the grain distilleries produces two principal whiskies but can make half a dozen.

Each of Suntory's malt distilleries has its own warehouses. Although there is nothing in the least subterranean about these, the company likes to call them aging cellars. In addition to each distillery's aging cellars, there are two free-standing maturation complexes, one near Hakushu, and the other at Ohmi, in Shiga prefecture. There are also large cooperage plants at Hakushu and Ohmi. In addition to orchestrating its whiskies, Suntory goes to great pains to do the same with its barrels. The company uses a blend of sherry, Bourbon and plain oak. Some of its sherry wood is imported from Spain and some is wine-treated. Some of the wine-treating is done in Spain, some in Japan. Some of the oak is Japanese, some American. Suntory is vertically-integrated, right from its own maltings, at Kantobaku-ga, in Tochigi prefecture, but the company's skills in mashing, fermentation and distillation are what shape the clean character of its whisky, with the aging merely providing the finishing touch.

The second-largest Japanese whisky company, Nikka, has a characterful little malt distillery at Yoichi, on Hokkaido, as well as its larger one at Sendai and its grain distillery, but the company lays its emphasis on its blending skills, and especially on its adherence to a "marriage" period. Nikka has more than 16 per cent of Japanese whisky production and 15 per cent of the total market. The third company in market share, Sanraku Ocean (4.1; 3.9) has two distilleries, one malt and the other grain. Its emphasis is on

Left: the waterfront at Chita, near Nagoya. With shipyards and grain silos, it could be a new Clydeside. The cranes have long snouts to suck up the grain (top right). Ships of 80,000 tons bring U.S. corn to Sungrain's distillery, blessed by a Shinto shrine (bottom right).

the smallness of its operation, with the implication of hand-crafting, though it also markets its products at very competitive prices. The fourth company in the market, Kirin Seagram (3.9; 3.6) has only one plant, with malt and grain distilleries under the same roof. It has access to the famous malt distilleries owned by Seagram in Scotland, and to the Canadian company's skills in grain-distillation and blending, and all of these elements are evident in its whiskies.

A little more than four per cent of the Japanese whisky market is held by no fewer than 20 companies with predominantly-local distribution. In the main, these are companies that produce a variety of drinks based on column-distilled grain spirit. Their whiskies are made by the blending of this grain spirit with malt distillate bought in bulk in Scotland. They are often rather sharp.

In Japan, the malt content of a whisky influences its tax bracket. Some super-premium brands contain more than 40 per cent malt; the biggest sellers, the premiums, usually have between 40 and 35 per cent. Anything over 30 per cent is in the *Special* bracket, and this is indicated on the label. Then comes the *First* category embracing

principally the take-home, supermarket products; this goes down to 20 per cent. The *Second* category, comprising either very inexpensive or extremely light whiskies, goes down to 10 per cent. Principal brands have 43 per cent alcohol by volume but some of the lighter, or minor, products have 40. The minimum age of Japanese whiskies is three years, though some spirit is matured for a dozen, 15 or even 20 years. Most brands do not, however, carry an age statement.

In the 1980s, Japanese distillers began to broaden their portfolios by adding new styles of whisky. These reflected their belief that, as in other countries, there was something of a polarisation of tastes. On the one hand, very light whiskies were introduced, aimed at the youth market. Despite their extreme lightness, these products still have the characteristic Scottish-Japanese whisky palate, albeit very delicate indeed. Their low malt content is blended with especially light grain whiskies. There has been a proliferation of new brand-names in this category. The young were further seen as a market for whiskies produced in Japan but broadly of the American style. This new style of whisky was, again, low in malt, emphasising a

corn-sweet grain character, with obvious Bourbon aging. The suspicion was that a young man might order the light type of whisky if he went out with his girlfriend but the "Japanese-American" style if he were with other males.

At the opposite extreme, Japanese distillers also introduced in the 1980s their first single-malt whiskies. These were seen as appealing to the mature drinker. They remain of the clean, malty style, but they are a category that could be expanded to accommodate more individualistic whiskies if the market appears to be available. Where Suntory and Sanraku Ocean lead, their rivals seem set to follow.

The pedigree of Japanese whisky

The first whisky distillery in Japan was built in 1923. If that is taken as its birth-date, Japanese whisky came of age in 1944, not the easiest of times for the world. In practice, the 1960s was probably the period when the character, quality and variety of Japanese whisky began to assert itself, with a growing number of high-quality blends.

In the first half of the 1970s, production of Japanese whisky doubled. The level reached in the mid 1970s increased by around 50 per cent in the decade that followed, exceeding 375 million litres a year. Scotland, with a much smaller home market (only five million people within its own borders and 50m in Britain as a whole) lies behind Japan (pop 100m) in its volume of whisky production, though the United States (pop 200m) has a larger output. In terms of individual distilleries, Suntory's plant at Hakushu has the largest malt whisky output in the world, producing 55 million litres at barrel proof each year.

The Japanese sell most of their whisky in their own country, and engage in only modest export efforts. In general, they have so far regarded international markets as the preserve of the original whisky-producing nations.

Whether in the matter of whisky, cameras or cars, Japan has, though, surely earned the right to shrug off the mantle of the copyist. Even in ancient times, no nation was an island (did not, for example, distilling itself originate in the East and only slowly seep to the West, being adapted from the making of perfumes and medicines to the production of alcoholic drinks?). The Japanese laugh at themselves over their enthusiasm for taking up the habits of others but add, on reflection, that they are really in the business of adaptation.

Japanese sake is a refinement of a cruder, ancient rice wine of China. The Japanese *hiragana* and *katakana* alphabets are adapted from the *kanji* characters of China. Japan has its own form of Buddhism, adapted from the version that spread through Asia

Aging cellars and what appear to be sacks of barley at the Yamazaki distillery in its early days. Such big marrying vessels are unusual, though some distillers still have them. Barley still comes in sacks, emptied by hand, at some modern maltings in Japan, Kanto-Bakuga being an example.

from India. Japan's tea ceremony was modified from Chinese tradition, and its porcelain was adapted from the Korean style.

Like some other nations that are, geographically, islands, Japan has at times been insular and in other eras been positively porous. In its receptive mood, it has taken to whisky with what the Japanese call an *akogare* (loosely translated as a "yearning" by George Fields in his book *From Bonsai to Levis*). It is a romantic yearning but one that is made credible by Japan's feeling of affinity with another extremely mountainous, often snowy, island nation . . . a country of fisher-

men, marine engineers, builders of bridges and railways . . . a land that, at its leisure, can seem obsessed with golf. With its Old Town, its hills, its endless schools and colleges, Kyoto could be Edinburgh; with a huge grain whisky distillery, shipbuilding and steel industries, Nagoya could be Glasgow. Kyoto's traditions are, of course, at least as old as those of Edinburgh; it was the capital of Japan for 1,000 years, and was famous for its pagodas long before the country had a whisky industry. Nagoya's preoccupations are a little more recent. It makes a rather young and ambitious Glasgow.

Suntory

There are other producers, but the name of Suntory is synonymous with Japanese whisky. Suntory was the first Japanese whisky-distiller; it is by far the biggest, with its 71 per cent market share; and, as its sales suggest, its products are the most adapted to the local taste.

In Japan, and in the international drinks business (where it ranks in size with giants like Seagram, Hiram Walker and D.C.L.), Suntory is a household name but it is, in fact, a compound of two words. The first syllable is a reference to the Japanese national emblem the rising sun. The second is a slight contraction of Torii, the family name of the founder. The company is still family-controlled, and is run by the son of the founder. That the word *Torii* in Japanese means the gateway to a shrine can hardly harm the company.

The headquarters of Suntory is in Osaka, the second city of Japan and the country's traditional centre of business. The company also has substantial offices in Tokyo. In neither city does Suntory carry out any distilling, but its buildings do have wine-cellars, restaurants and beer-gardens. They also maintain an information desk for anyone seeking education in the matter of drinks and, for visitors in abstemious mood, the Tokyo building also has a museum of art. The company is heavily involved in the sponsorship of fine art and music, and takes an interest in a number of cultural, social and environmental issues, including the protection of bird life. It also sponsors sport, especially golf, though that serves a more obviously promotional purpose.

It was in Osaka that the company's founder, Shinjiro Torii, started the business in 1899. He was very much a child of the outward-looking Meiji restoration, and he was only 21 – an adventurous young entrepreneur. He started out as a wine merchant, selling imports from Spain. Then, in 1907, he started producing a domestic sweet wine, in the port style, from Japanese grapes. As a pioneer of the Japanese wine industry, Torii developed skills that would lead to his becoming known as "the Nose of Osaka". He also earned good profits from the business.

These profits he re-invested, amid much scepticism, in an effort to introduce a second new product: Japanese whisky. Torii built his distillery in 1923, in the Yamazaki valley, near Kyoto, and his whisky was introduced to the market in 1929. It was not an immediate success, and only after the passing of a couple of decades did whisky, in the 1950s, begin to show substantial profits.

This time the profits were re-invested in beer-brewing. In 1963, Suntory entered the beer market, in which three large, established companies were already active. Coming into the market in fourth place, Suntory quickly established a position for itself in what are now the Big Four brewing companies, the other three being, in ascending order of size Asahi, Sapporo and Kirin. Once again, a new business was generating profits for further investment.

With wine, whisky and beer under its belt, Suntory in the late 1970s made a substantial investment in the development and marketing of liqueurs. This came to fruition just in time for the renewed fashionability of liqueurs, a tidal change that somewhat surprised the international drinks industry in the early 1980s. Suntory's innovative, melon-flavoured liqueur Midori has been a considerable success, especially in the United States.

Suntory has also diversified into high-quality restaurants, fast-food chains, soft drinks, confectionery, convenience grocery products and pharmaceuticals. Through its activities in restaurants, bars and pubs, it has become interested in other leisure activities, with diversifications into magazine and book-publishing, and mail-order.

What began in Suntory's early distilling days as a research department concerning itself with alcoholic beverages and fermentation technology grew first into a fully-fledged institute and eventually a campus. It now embraces separate institutes for bio-organic and bio-medical research. Suntory is very active in the highly-competitive field of bio-technology, and is developing techniques of DNA recombination and synthesis.

The company's annual sales exceed

800,000 million yen, or more than three billion U.S. dollars. Its worldwide interests include vineyards in France and the United States (where it has a share in the respected Firestone winery), and several subsidiaries in Latin America. It is a major importer of food and drink brands into Japan, and its own products number between three and four hundred. Of these, fewer than 20 are whis-

The very first Suntory whisky, "White Label", had a Scottish flavour in both palate and packaging. When that proved not to be popular, it was toned down in palate and, as "Extra White", it still retains a loyal following. Within this same group of older, relatively inexpensive, Suntory whiskies are, in ascending order of price-bracket: Red Extra (a popular brand for home-consumption), Gold and Extra Gold, and Kaku (meaning "Square Bottle"). This last product was the one that established in its home market the Japanese style of whisky. It was also Suntory's first premium brand.

Today's principal premium brand, and by far the biggest seller, is Suntory Old. It has Suntory's typical, lightly-peated maltiness, with an almost chewy body and faint hints of bitter fruitiness in the finish. Then, in ascending order of luxury, come Suntory Reserve, a slightly fruitier whisky, popular among young executives; the drier, elegant Royal; the clean, malty Excellence; the flavourful Imperial, a whisky known in some export markets as Signature; the sherryish "1899", named to mark the year the company was founded, and with something of a Scottish character; and the definitively-named Suntory "The Whisky", containing some notably well-aged spirit, and with a lot of maturity in the finish. In addition to all of these products, which are blends, Suntory also has its Yamazaki Pure Malt Whisky. This is fairly light-bodied for a single, with a crisp start and a malty finish.

In the youth market, Suntory has two light whiskies, in sanserif-labelled green bottles that look as though they might contain something to be used in a photographic darkroom. These are whiskies for a visually-oriented generation; even their names are oddly unverbal. The more modestly-priced of the two is called simply "Q" and the more expensive "21". The company also has an American-style whisky called Rawhide, again aimed at the youth market.

Despite such indulgences, Suntory has a special pride in the part it has played in developing what it feels to be Japan's own whisky-distilling tradition.

Above: the world's biggest malt whisky still-house, a gleaming temple, offers vapours enough to intoxicate Bacchus. In Suntory's research centre (left) the skyline can be changed to suggest a different ambience as new products are reviewed. In the presentation (far left) and advertising of drinks products in Japan, image is vital.

kies, but they seem to remain the products closest to the company's heart.

It might, for that matter, seem profligate to have almost 20 brands in a single product category: whisky. As has happened with major distillers elsewhere in the world, the range has simply grown over a period of time. Early brands that established loyal customers have been retained after newer ones have

been launched; it is a process of accretion.

Some of the earliest brands have, after beginning to show their age, gained a second wind as lower-priced products popular in the student market. An example is Tory's (not dedicated to a political party but named, in a variation on the Suntory theme, after the founder). This brand is now the most competitively-priced of Suntory's whiskies.

Suntory – *Yamazaki*

Since Suntory's founder had begun his entrepreneurial career as a wine merchant in the large business city of Osaka, it was logical that he should look in that part of Japan – but in the countryside – for somewhere to build his whisky distillery. Away from the city, to the North, running between two mountainous chunks of land, watered by three rivers and forested with red and black pines and luxuriant groves of bamboo, is the Yamazaki Valley, on the route to the pagodas of Kyoto, Japan's ancient capital and still its religious and cultural centre. Between these two important cities, which are about 50 miles apart, the Southern segment of the main island of Japan is almost sealed off by the Inland Sea and the enormous Lake Biwa. Japan's first whisky distillery, built there in 1923, is just inside the prefecture of Osaka, but is actually slightly closer to Kyoto.

In placing his distillery in this mountainous, pine-covered, river-flowing scene, Shinjiro Torii perhaps felt – as other distillers elsewhere in Japan have done since – that he had found an Oriental counterpart to Scotland. The physical resemblances between the two countries are striking and, if anything, Japan is the more densely mountainous. Inland, there are mountains or hills almost everywhere; it is almost all Highlands, with scarcely any Lowlands. The hills are, though, different in texture and shape: the dark green lushness of vegetation softens the line of Japan's hills though their bulk, too, is more rounded, so that they form mound shapes. They can be sudden, and precipitously steep mounds, reaching a crown rather than a peak. This crown may be still covered in trees, like an ornamental crest to hide the impetuousness of volcanic youth. Scotland's mountains look like angular old men by comparison. There is the same contrast in the villages and small towns of the two countries: Japan's bustling, pavement-less, with ephemeral wooden houses, pastel rooftops or curling, overhanging terra-cotta pantiling; Scotland's pensive, with sturdy stone, pebbledash and slate.

In its steep, hillside setting, half-hidden among the trees, the Yamazaki distillery created a precedent for the forested locations and landscaped buildings that Suntory has favoured elsewhere for its second distillery, its maturation warehouses and its research campus. Down in the valley, Yamazaki is one of those little, pantiled towns.

A mist almost always hangs over the mountains of Japan, providing in the Yamazaki Valley a perfect atmosphere for the legends and poems from a time when the warlords fought decisive battles there. An important temple once stood on the hillside, and there is still a shrine on the site of the distillery. Within the shrine, as an offering to the gods, are two barrels of whisky. Beneath the forest and the earth, the hills give rise to springs and streams flowing down into the valley, where the rivers Katsura, Uji and Kizu meet. Through the *torii* gateway of the shrine, and the bamboo groves, the view down into the valley reveals the "bullet train" on its ceaseless trajectory back and forth between Osaka, Kyoto and Tokyo, more than 300 miles, and less than three hours, distant. Such juxtapositions are everywhere in Japan. From the roof of the distillery, the confluence of the rivers can be seen, a broad corridor, with its slow waters and fast trains.

The steep roadway from the shrine runs by one of the original buildings of the distillery. The cream-rendered building, with a rather ecclesiastical-looking gable, brown-shuttered windows and a brickwork dado, is hedged with plane trees. It is now used as a guest-house. Every house in Japan, even in the most densely built-up areas, is softened with shrubs or trees: magnolias, flowering cherries, box and ginkgo trees. In their terra-cotta brickwork, the modern, main buildings of today's large distillery, are fringed with shrubberies, each tree neatly labelled. The original building had maltings, with twin pagodas linked by a walkway. Although malting was discontinued ten or a dozen years ago, it still has pagodas, but of an unusual, more modern design reminiscent of the loudspeakers on a 1950s radio.

There is a similar sense of modernistic

Above: the little town of Yamazaki, scarcely more than a village. However, Yamazaki is distinguished by a single malt whisky. In a country where a pagoda might be expected to look like one, Yamazaki's (right) resemble hi-fi equipment.

design about the huge, cylindrical, red-painted malt silos, topped by black boxes to hide their workings. Lightly-peated malts are used, though to more than one specification, embracing both Japanese and imported barleys. There is a single mash-house and tun room (the Japanese use the Scottish term for the fermentation facility), but the still-

house operation is divided into two lines.

Like all of the Suntory distilleries, Yamazaki makes whisky in the traditional way but with the most up-to-date equipment. Traditionalists might be reassured by the Porteous malt mills, and the nameplate "New Mill Engineering, Elgin, Scotland" on the large, stainless steel, semi-lauter mash tuns. The water for mashing comes from a well under the distillery. The fermentation vessels are made of iron, jacketed in stainless steel. Two yeasts are used, but each with the intention of producing a different whisky. With its two yeasts and two distilling lines, Yamazaki can

obviously produce two quite distinct whiskies; in fact, it produces more. Its row of 12 large pot-stills face each other, wash on one side, spirit on the other. They are of conventional enough shape, but it was scrupulously replicated when they were doubled in size.

Despite Suntory's having a separate maturation complex, warehouses are still maintained at Yamazaki. Some are traditional, Scottish-style warehouses, with the barrels stacked four high, and others are concrete-floored, in the American open-rick style, but without heating or fans. Much of the cooperage used at Yamazaki is lightly-

charred new oak, but rebuilt Bourbon barrels are also employed. As a general rule, sherry is not. Apart from the capacity its warehouses offer Yamazaki also has, with those mountain mists, a humidity that favours the maturation of whisky. Its bottled single malt is the pride of Suntory.

The company is proud, too, that this was Japan's first whisky distillery. Visitors are reminded of this by a small exhibit . . . and by two monuments outside. One is a sculpture of the founder. The other is one of the original stills, mounted as a reminder of Suntory's humble beginnings.

Suntory ~ *Hakushu*

The enthusiast for interesting drink has, as it happens, two excuses to set out from Tokyo on a Westward journey of about 75 miles, skirting the Kanto mountains and heading past the town of Koshu, capital of the Yamanashi prefecture, deep into the basin of the Japanese Alps. This countryside is Japan's most important viticultural region, with the Suntory winery affording to visitors a comprehensive view of the industry; and, as the hillsides rise into the Alpine region, there is to be found at Hakushu the world's biggest malt distillery, with its own whisky museum. For those whose interests embrace a broader selection of aesthetic pleasures, the distillery and museum are surrounded by a bird sanctuary, and the mountain country behind, a magnet for hikers and climbers, includes Mount Fuji (12,388ft), Japan's highest and most famous landmark.

It's a journey that at first does not seem promising, simply because the urban sprawl of Tokyo is so reluctant to end: its ceaseless apartment blocks brandishing on their rooftops little gantries holding white, spherical water-tanks, as though they were golf-balls on tees; sometimes the flat rooftops do, indeed, accommodate driving ranges where penthouse golfers can snatch a little practice. Further from the metropolis, the driving ranges find space at ground level, jostling with baseball diamonds – ubiquitous evidence of Japan's favourite spectator sport – then, suddenly, the forests of telegraph poles give way to the cedar trees of Yamanashi prefecture.

Now, the land itself rises and falls and, down in the valleys – sometimes ravines – the white, spherical shapes are of sun-bleached pebbles in the broad, shallow rivers. There are domestic rice-paddies, worked by women in broad-rimmed straw hats; fields of aubergines, the small type grown for pickling; pear and peach orchards; mulberry bushes for the silk industry . . . and grapevines terraced on the hillsides. Suntory's winery is set among 400 acres of vineyards, with views of Mount Fuji. The winery has a tasting room, shop and small museum. It also has its own brandy distillery. The whisky distillery is some miles away, closer to the mountains.

The Yamanashi prefecture is part of the mountainous Chubu district, the central chunk of the main island of Japan. Mount Fuji is due South. To the North-West, in a series of massive ridges running parallel, one behind the other, are the Akaishi, Kiso and Hida ranges of mountains. These three ranges are popularly known as the Japanese Alps. The Akaishi foothills are of granite, and from them rises water that is pure even by the standards of Japan. The spectacular location, the Pastoral environment – and the water – persuaded Suntory that this was the perfect site for its second distillery.

So great is the spread of the hills, and so dense the covering of pines, that they curtain and cushion this huge distillery, their own scale for a moment making it seem inconsequentially small. In an affectionate tribute to the first Suntory distillery, this one has re-created the unusual design of pagodas linked by a bridging walkway, and this structure stands as both a barbican and a badge of Hakushu. This distillery never made its own malt, and stores its supply in the red-and-black silos that seem to have become another characteristic Suntory design feature. The red is, in fact, an anti-corrosive paint on the structure of iron-and-copper alloy. The more conventionally-shaped buildings are tile-hung in an unobtrusive grey.

Hakushu is operated as a complex of three distilleries, each producing one or more distinct whiskies. One of the distilleries is a self-contained unit; the other two have separate mashing, fermenting and distilling lines but are integrated into a single building.

The rivers that flow down the hills here are so clean that fish cannot live in them, the whisky-makers at Hakushu wrily observe. Certainly the water from Hakushu's well has a remarkably clean palate that is carried through in the whiskies made there. Again, lightly-peated malts are used. Both copper and stainless steel semi-lauter mash-tuns are

Enveloped in the pines, only the traditional pagodas reveal the huge Hakushu distillery. Inside the towers is the excellent Museum of Whisky. There is deciduous woodland, too, in the bird sanctuary.

barrels, which are reassembled in a cooperage plant at the distillery. This plant assembles no fewer than 600 barrels a day.

The building of a second distillery complex, and such a large one, gave Suntory pause for thought as to its great progress over half a century, and the company came to feel that at Hakushu it should do something to mark its pride at being in the whisky business. Eventually, the decision was reached to establish a museum of whisky. The idea of the museum would be to tell the story of whisky from its beginnings in Ireland and Scotland, as well as documenting its first 50 years in Japan.

Considerable research was mounted in Europe and North America as well as Japan, and the resultant museum begins its story with items from the 1400s and embraces documents, early dictionary definitions, paintings, artefacts, equipment, bottles and packages used over the years, and advertising and promotional items. It is a thoughtfully compiled study, beautifully presented in half a dozen thematic rooms set into the malting-towers building. There are stills that were used in the Edo period (1603-1867) for the production of medicines; a corner devoted to the company's founder, with the desk he used when he wished to chant from the Sutra (he was a religious man); a 1922 Ford truck that once delivered Suntory's products; and an English pub interior, with a Victorian back-bar, snob screens, and beer handpumps. There is even a room that is, light-heartedly, intended to replicate the feeling of having drunk too much.

Hakushu offers not only distillery tours, the museum, a tasting room and a gift shop, but also walks through a public stretch of the bird sanctuary. There is a summer-house, an ornamental pond with carp, and discreet illustrated signs showing the 60 species of bird that have been seen in the area. Beyond this public stretch is a great swath of hillside owned by Suntory and donated to the birds, their peace disturbed by nothing more than the strut of the bamboo pheasant, the song of the bulbul and gossip of the cicada.

used, made by Suntory's favourite supplier in Elgin, Scotland. In fermentation, several yeast strains are used. The fermentation vessels are of stainless steel, with a distinctive matt finish.

The most striking sight, though, is the principal still-house. An electronically-operated shutter slides open to reveal a long, narrow hall of 24 stills, wash and spirit facing each other in two lines, set into a handsome floor of redbrick tiling.

Although Suntory was careful to replicate the shape of its stills when they were renewed at Yamazaki, it opted for a slightly different design at Hakushu. The principal stills here have a more waisted shape, with the intention that they should produce spirit of a different character. Of the two plants, Hakushu has the smaller stills but, oddly enough, they produce lighter spirits.

While its water and the shape of its stills make a notable contribution to the character of its whiskies, so undoubtedly, does the high, hazy location. Hakushu has a couple of dozen open-rick warehouses, set apart from each other among dense growth of pines. Although all of the principal types of wood are used, there is an emphasis on Bourbon

Nikka

Two people have claims upon the sobriquet "the Father of Japanese Whisky". One was Masataka Taketsuru, who went to Scotland in the second decade of this century to study applied chemistry at Glasgow University. While in Scotland, he became fascinated by whisky, and eventually sought a position as a trainee in a distillery. At that time, about 1918, an application by a Japanese for a position at a Scottish whisky distillery must have been viewed from under well-raised eyebrows. "Overcoming countless obstacles, he visited one distillery after another", the Japanese recall, "until, through sheer perserverance, he finally won admittance to a distillery in Rothes". If the distillery was, indeed, in Rothes, perhaps it was Glen Grant. The doubt arises because the Japanese today recall his training having been at The Glenlivet, which is now under the same ownership but not in Rothes. Today, it is not at all unusual for Japanese to study in Scotland as part of their preparation to work in their domestic industry.

So wholehearted was Taketsuru's love of Scotland that he also married a local girl, whom he took back to Japan in 1921. There, he was recruited by the wine-producer Shinjiro Torii to help establish Japan's first whisky distillery, which ran its first spirit in 1923 (although nothing was marketed for six years). Torii, founder of what became Suntory, thus had his own claim to be the Father of Japanese Whisky. One contributed the first-hand knowledge; the other the entrepreneurial vision and the capital.

Not surprisingly, Taketsuru had a fancy for starting a distillery of his own, and in 1934 took his first steps toward doing so. Just as Torii first made wine, then ploughed his profits into whisky, so Taketsuru initially established a fruit-juice company to raise the capital for his distillery. He produced an apple-juice called Kaju. It was from the corporate name Nippon Kaju that the whisky brand Nikka was compounded. Just as Suntory became Japan's biggest whisky-producer, so Nikka became, and remains, the second largest. Just as Torii's son remains in Suntory (as chief executive), so Taketsuru's is still involved in the management of Nikka, though he does not head the company, which is now owned by Asahi, the brewers. Neither of the fathers of Japanese whisky is still alive, though both are well remembered in the industry.

For his first distillery, Torii had sought a site within reach of his company's headquarters in Osaka, albeit in a mountain valley with excellent conditions for the production of whisky; Taketsuru looked farther afield, to the Northern island of Hokkaido.

In the British Isles, Scotland is (historically and culturally if not, quite, geographically) a separate, Northern land; in Japan, Hokkaido is something of a counterpart. Most of Japan is mountainous but Hokkaido also has peat – and the total separation of being an island. Being so truly isolated, it was barely settled by the Japanese before the Meiji Restoration. Its inhabitants then were a bear-hunting native people called the Ainu, and in that respect it might more closely be compared with Canada or, better still, Alaska, whose pioneer spirit it shares. There are still wild bears – and, more edibly, deer – on Hokkaido, though there are few full-blooded Ainu (a sallow-skinned, round-eyed, full-bearded people, of uncertain origin) except in a couple of model villages and a national park.

Some Scots, of course, would lay claim to Canada as one of their colonies, in which case they might recognise something of Toronto in Sapporo, the capital city of Hokkaido. Sapporo is a large, lively, modern city, developed with the help of an American town-planner during the "opening" of Japan in the 1870s. It is built on an American-style grid layout, with more recent shopping arcades, its famous brewery and beer-garden, renowned sushi bars and busy nightlife, and it is strangely at odds with the rest of the island. The smaller towns and villages have much more of the random, utilitarian, look of frontier country, again offering a parallel with Alaska. From Sapporo, it is an hour's train journey (or more by the winding, steep road) in a Westerly direction, toward the Ishikari Bay, on the Japan Sea, past the substantial port of Otaru, to Yoichi, the little town that is the headquarters of Nikka. Yoichi is a modest holiday town, with a beach and a small fleet of fishing boats.

Both the railway line and the road from Sapporo to Otaru and Yoichi cling to the side of mountains, and occasionally tunnel through the rock, which extends its shoulders almost to the sea-shore. Peaks of four to six thousand feet dominate this craggy corner of the island. Down on the bay, Otaru imports, among other essentials, barley malt for the distillery. Closer to Yoichi are deposits of peat used in the days when the

pany's heritage. The surrounding land is peaty and that character is imparted to the water used. It's a snowy area, too. Snow probably provides much of the water that finds its way into the distillery's wells. Barley malt is imported from a number of countries, to more than one specification. The mash tun is an elderly vessel of the traditional Scottish style, made from cast-iron, with a stainless-steel dome, set into mosaic tiling. A four-water mash is used. Less traditional are the horizontal, cylindrical tanks used for fermentation. There are no switches on the tanks, and the company's house yeast produces a quiet fermentation. Nikka uses only this one yeast, which carries through a lot of fruitiness into the palate and aroma of the whiskies.

The most striking, and traditionalist, aspect is the continued use of coal-fired stills. They are stoked with a soft, powdery coal mined on Hokkaido and similar to British anthracite. There are four low-wine stills and two for spirit. The low-wines stills are pear-shaped and the spirit ones a little more sculpted. Both the still-house and the warehouses are decorated with the white paper tassels, called *gohei* or *nusa* that are a shinto talisman. *Gohei* derive from offerings of cloth to the gods. The warehouses, some with earth floors, have barrels stacked on planks in the traditional Scottish way. Lightly-charred domestic oak and Bourbon barrels are used, but no sherry.

Nikka describes Yoichi as the "core" of its whisky production, but it has since 1969 had a far larger malt distillery at Sendai, in the North of the main island. The red rooftops of Yoichi, and the chunky buildings, are alluded to in the colour of the brickwork and shapes of the structures at Sendai; for its size and recent vintage, it is an attractive distillery. From Tokyo, it is about 200 miles to Sendai, a sizable city that is the cultural centre for the wooded, rugged and relatively thinly-populated Tohoku region of Japan, stretching all the way to the northern tip of the main island. The company likes to regard the Yoichi malt as its "Highland" type and the Sendai distillate as a "Lowland"

company did its own malting.

Yoichi is a town of 27,000 people. It is strung on a long, straggly, main street, behind which, and through a castellated stone arch, can be seen the distinctive, and attractive, dark pink rooftops of the Nikka distillery buildings. These rooftops, the originals in tiling and the newer ones in pristine painted metalwork, are almost an emblem of a distillery that is pretty to the point of being fussy. There are rows of chunky, little buildings in yellow-grey stone, with broad, arched, white-painted doors, small, latticed windows, with pink roofs and pyramid-shaped vents, as the offices, the former maltings, the mash-house, the still-house,

Japanese distillers are given to emblematic architecture . . . the red rooftops of Yoichi far exceed the original requirement for malting towers, and the chunky stone seems to hark back to happy days in Scotland. The Yoichi distillery was founded by a Caledonophile.

◆

the fermentation rooms, a couple of dozen warehouses and a visitors' reception centre set themselves round ornamental lawns with summer-houses, a lake gliding with swans, grass verges with small Japanese yews, and shrubberies with apple trees and azaleas.

Although the maltings has not been used for 15 years, a small stack of Hokkaido peat is still kept there as a reminder of the com-

Both mechanical means and a little hand work go into the stoking of the coal-fired stills at Yoichi. Japan has moments of surprising fidelity to such old-fashioned touches, even down to the besom.

whisky. Geographically, this is stretching a point: with its mountains and fishing villages, Hokkaido may resemble the Scottish Highlands, but Tohoku is pretty hilly, too, albeit there is a wooded, lushly fertile backdrop to the distillery there. In the palates of the two whiskies, the comparison is less fanciful: Yoichi, with its small, pear-shaped stills, produces a richly aromatic, chewy, tangy whisky; Sendai has larger, taller stills, with a "cummerbund" design, and has a softer, more mellow, lighter product.

The characteristic softness of the Nikka whiskies is also, in part, bestowed by the use of traditional Coffey stills in the production of the grain spirit, which is carried out at Nishinomiya, near Osaka. Nikka introduced to Japan this step backward from the more modern variety of continuous still. In addition to its malt and grain distilleries, Nikka has a separate maturation complex at Tochigi, North of Tokyo.

Nikka lays great stress on the importance of aging and blending, with a subsequent "marriage" of six to twelve months, in the achievement of the character it seeks to impart to its products. Long-standing devotees feel that the company's brands have lost some peatiness over the years but Nikka's whiskies still have a characteristic depth of flavour. This derives in part from the bitter-sweet fruitiness produced by the house yeast, from the softness of the Coffey-still grain whisky, and from the house approach to aging and blending. In some of the medium and light-bodied brands, Bourbon aging is noticeable.

The company has been slow in introducing a single malt. However, there is a high degree of firm maltiness in its Memorial 50 (produced to commemorate the foundation of the company) and its expensive, top-of-line Specialage (this brand-name might read more easily if it were rendered as two words but that, of course, would be less distinctive). Both of these are full-bodied whiskies. Nikka has a wide and confusing range of labels, especially in its medium-bodied brands, with Black Nikka (and a similar square-bottled product labelled simply Nikka Whisky), Gold & Gold, and a white-bottled product called The Nikka Whisky. A brand called Super is medium-to-light in body. Fortune 80, Black 50 and Kingsland are all light-bodied. Northland is extra-light, and Hi is one of the new "young people's" brands.

Sanraku Ocean

When the power-brokers of Tokyo, the financiers and political leaders, want a second home or a retirement retreat, they venture deeply into the apex of the Kanto and Mikuni ranges, to the resort of Karuizawa, whence the trails reach toward the smoky peak of Mount Asama, at 8,340ft. It is mountain country for sure but it is more reminiscent of Aspen, Colorado, than Tomintoul, Glenlivet. Nonetheless, it is a whisky-distilling town, with the customary Scottish inspiration.

Prime Ministers past and present – Sato, Tanaka, Nakasone – have a modest, two-hour train journey ahead as they set out for their respective retreats. The flattish land around Tokyo eases into a perceptible, broad valley after the train has passed the city of Takasaki, then the rail line quickly steepens into mountain country, with persistent tunnels and views of winding roads before, at Yokokawa, a second locomotive is added so the last climb can be tackled.

By the time the main line from Tokyo had, in 1893, linked with the little mountain railway between Yokowaka and Karuizawa, the resort had already welcomed its first renowned guest. He must have felt at home. Karuizawa may have a Coloradan atmosphere but its most evident trees are not aspens; they are larches, as plentiful here as they are in some parts of Scotland. The renowned guest was a British clergyman, of Scottish origin – Archdeacon Alexander Croft Shaw. He stopped at Karuizawa in 1886, during a missionary tour. Perhaps he was just passing through – the town had long been a staging post on the route across the mountains to the holy city of Nagano – but he took a particular liking to Karuizawa.

At his encouragement, British diplomats newly based in Japan since the "opening" of the country started to use Karuizawa as an island resort for relaxation during the summer. Other foreigners, and Japanese, took up their example. There were already natural attractions like waterfalls and lakes; in time, golf-courses and tennis-courts were added. Across the square from the railway station is a hotel in the eclectic style of Japanese architecture that was inspired by a wish to imitate Victorian Britain. It is reminiscent of "West Victorian" buildings in Colorado. Signs advertise cycles for rent. Along with golfing financiers and tennis-playing politicians, Karuizawa attracts student cyclists and hikers.

Verges of manicured yews mark out cycle paths – and a grove of white beeches leads through a plot of land planted with acacia blossoms, marigolds and sage (and its own tennis-court) to the clapperboard building that serves as the office of the town's Sanraku Ocean whisky distillery. It is a tiny distillery, almost hidden among the trees, shrubs and flowers, with its low buildings – some of them made with volcanic rock from Mount Asama – overgrown with ivy.

Sanraku is a poetic allusion to joy; the ocean is far away, but it was a word with romantic overtones in the days when Japan was opening its mind to the world across the seas. Although one branch of the company can trace its roots back to the earliest days of the Japanese wine industry, in the 1870s, the Sanraku name did not appear until 1937, and then as the brand-name for a sake. Serious production of whisky did not begin until the 1960s. Wine is produced under the well-respected Mercian label; Sanraku is still a major brand of sake, and shochu; and Ocean is the whisky marque.

The company's corporate name is Sanraku Ocean, and its product portfolio extends through canned foods, animal feeds and agricultural and medical chemicals, the latter deriving in part from its knowledge of fermentation technology and microbiology. Sanraku Ocean is controlled by a family called Suzuki, though it has no connection with the automotive company of the same name. Its corporate headquarters are in Tokyo, and the company has existed in its present form since the 1930s. The older buildings at Karuizawa date from the same period, and the distillery there produces only whisky. It is the company's only malt distillery. Karuizawa is comparable in size with the smallest of the Scottish malt distilleries,

In early summer, the lushness of Karuizawa sings out the Japanese love of trees and shrubs. Hiding among the foliage are barrels refurbished at the cooper's shop on the site. It's an overgrown, peaceful place, in a mountain resort of the wealthy, far from the Ocean of the label.

Coopers at the Sanraku Ocean distillery . . . barrels are repaired and packed with reeds in the traditional manner. Some of the barrels see considerable use, but the company is proud of the care it affords them. Sanraku Ocean argues that in this and every aspect of caring for its whiskies, its small scale permits great attention to detail.

but it is kept busy 24 hours a day, on a three-shift system. The company also has a grain distillery, at Kawasaki.

Spring water from Mount Asama is piped to the distillery at Karuizawa. It is a water with some content of calcium carbonate and magnesium, and is therefore a little harder than that generally preferred by producers of the Scottish and Japanese types of whisky. Sanraku Ocean argue that this harder water helps control the behaviour of the yeast in fermentation, and it may well contribute to the clean, crisp palate of their whiskies. The distillery's malt, which is lightly peated, is imported from, among other countries, Scotland.

The tiny, domed, cast-iron tun for the three-water mash; the closed fermentation tanks, upright cylinders painted in eau-de-nil, and standing on legs as though they were old-fashioned washtubs; the line of four stills, set in brick, heated by steam, conical to the waistline, with straight chimneys and with lyne arms ducking through the rafters; are all packed tightly into a building that could be a stables or a rather grand barn. The

nine warehouses have earth floors, and wooden galleries like those in hispanic, frontier churches in the American West. The warehouses made from the pumice stone of Mount Asama are said to breathe especially well.

The whisky is aged first in new wood – charred white oak, though it has never seen Bourbon – and then transferred either to wine-treated barrels or sherry butts. Wood that has already tasted sherry on behalf of Macallan in Scotland stands alongside butts bearing the imprint of Duff Gordon.

A single malt from Karuizawa is available in the bottle. The package looks less like a bottle of whisky, in fact, than an elegant, feminine, flask of perfume. The whisky is called simply Ocean Karuizawa Single Malt, and it is a well-made, pleasing dram. In the Japanese style, it has a clean maltiness; in body, it is on the light side, with a slight, malty sweetness and a crisp, dry finish; in the aroma, and more especially the finish, it has an emphatic sherry-wood perfume. No age statement is provided, but the oldest whiskies at Karuizawa have been sleeping for 18

years, and there is certainly some mature spirit in the single malt.

The sweetness emerges more strongly when there is slightly less sherry-aged whisky, as in the company's super-premium blended whisky, Asama. The company's blends are Status, again with a malty character, and the drier Gloria. There are also two premium-quality blends that have achieved high sales on the basis of very competitive pricing: SP (Special Old) and Route, the latter being a Japanese interpretation of the style of whisky originated by Cutty Sark and J&B. Competitive pricing has been a salient feature of Sanraku Ocean's policy in establishing itself in the Japanese domestic whisky market. Most of the company's brands are bottled at 43 per cent alcohol, but at the cheaper end of the market it has a 42 per cent product called Victory and one at 39 per cent, known as Bright and aimed at the youth market.

If Karuizawa Single Malt is aimed at Prime Ministers (or their wives?), Bright is presumably intended as a restorative for those student hikers.

Kirin Seagram

Japan's biggest whisky-distillers, Suntory, had the impertinence to enter the beer-brewing business in 1963; a decade later, the country's largest brewers, Kirin, began to make whisky. Rather than starting from scratch, Kirin began whisky production in a joint venture with the world's biggest distillers, Seagram. They thus benefit from the experience Seagram has as a distiller, blender and marketer of its whiskies in its native Canada, in its huge U.S. market, and in Scotland where it owns famous brands like Chivas and distilleries as renowned as The Glenlivet and Glen Grant. In Japan, Kirin Seagram have just one distillery, albeit large and with room for expansion, but are as yet fourth in the market for domestic whiskies, with a share of 3.9 per cent.

Kirin takes its name from a mythical creature, half horse, half dragon, which is said to have visited the mother of Confucius before his birth. The story is similar to that of the Angel Gabriel, and the Kirin subsequently came to be regarded as the harbinger of happy and festive events in Chinese and Japanese lore. Such events may, of course, call for a celebratory drink. As brewers, Kirin have their origins in an American venture started in Yokohama in 1869. This subsequently passed to Japanese ownership and took the name Kirin in 1888. Today, Kirin has a dozen breweries spread through Japan and, largely on the strength of its domestic market, is the world's third biggest producer of beer (after Miller and Anheuser-Busch, both of the U.S.).

Like Suntory's Hakushu distillery, Kirin Seagram's sole whisky-producing plant is not far from Mount Fuji. While Hakushu is North of the mountain, Kirin Seagram's distillery is to the South, and a little closer. It is in Shizuoka prefecture, near the town of Gotemba, one of the principal tourist bases for visitors to the mountain. Gotemba is just over an hour's drive from Tokyo.

◆

South of Mount Fuji, Kirin Seagram's sole plant is the result of an alliance between brewers and distillers.

Hollows, hills and rocky mountain streams are the backdrop of every whisky distiller's romance but none could be more potent than Fuji, the most dramatic manifestation of the country's natural beauty, a symbol of national pride, sacred in Shinto, and having held a mystic grip on the hearts and minds of the Japanese people from the beginning of their history. Small wonder that, in their publicity, Kirin Seagram like to use a photograph of their distillery set alone against the vastness of snow-capped Fuji. On the days when the mountain mists permit, it is a dramatic view.

Tokyo's stockbroker belt is drawn toward the plantations of green tea, fragrant olives and mandarin oranges that garland Mount Fuji. The towns closest to the mountain have a touristy, commercial feel but on the far side of Gotemba there is a landscaping of cedars, rhododendrons and azaleas to enwrap the distillery. The company has counted 20,000 trees, shrubs and plants, and made it a rule that at least 50 per cent of the site be kept green. Even the reserve of water for fire-fighting is kept in a man-made lake full of goldfish. Visitors are welcomed and, with typical Japanese hospitality, are protected by a cache of umbrellas should it rain during their march through the wide, open spaces of the distillery.

The white-painted buildings are dominated by square, concrete towers, but of a soft, bevelled line and sympathetic scale that owes more to the 1950s than to the seventies, when they were constructed. Despite their having windows, and being a part of the architectural whole, they are occupied not by people but by barley malt and grain – they are silos. Kirin has still-houses on the site to produce both malt and grain whiskies. Indeed, the distillery produces several of each, though the company still finds it necessary to import for blending purposes a number of whiskies from Scotland.

Malted barley is imported mainly from Britain, to varying degrees of peating. Each Kirin Seagram brand has a different malt specification. In most of the malt imported, the peating is light-to-medium but in some it

Behind the smart, landscaped distillery of Kirin Seagram (above) are warehouses of space-age efficiency (left). The loading platform is on a monorail buggy, able to track back and forth from the entrance to the depths of the dark, cavernous warehouse. The monorail buggy also supports a vertical axis, up which the loading platform and its illuminated control cabin can climb. By operating both axes, the driver inside the cabin can track diagonally through the warehouse if he wishes, to find a particular barrel that is needed. The rows are 40 barrels long, and the warehouse is 21 storeys high. Within it are 35,000 barrels. A similar system is used by Suntory.

is heavy. The distilling water, which is very soft and extremely clean, comes from three wells on Mount Fuji. The large, modern stainless steel mash-tun, and the cookers for the grain whisky, sit together in an airy, white-painted, quarry-tiled complex. There are a dozen stainless steel fermenters, of conventional shape, divided down the middle into rows producing malt wash and grain beer respectively. The two large pot-stills for low wines have a cummerbund shape, while their partner spirit stills are of a waisted style. These malt stills are part of the main complex, while the column stills for grain are in a separate hall. Grain whiskies are produced in various permutations of a beer-still, four conventional column stills and kettle-shaped doublers.

Whiskies are aged in six large warehouses of pre-cast concrete, each containing 35,000 barrels. Some charred new-oak barrels are used but most maturation is in Bourbon casks. Only a small quantity of sherry casks is used.

Kirin Seagram are anxious that their whiskies be perceived as being Japanese in style, which they are. Nonetheless, they are the driest of Japanese whiskies, and this must in part be because the company persists with the use of some heavily-peated malt. Again, the predominance of Bourbon casks in maturation imparts a definite "Scottish-American" character to the aroma and palate. Finally, the use in blending of some

classic Speyside whiskies makes for a distinctively firm and smooth body.

The company does not as yet bottle a single malt. Its super-premium brand, Crescent, is a well-balanced whisky, notably smooth, full-bodied, and with a hint of smokiness. Its premium label, Emblem, is similar in style, with some sweetness in the nose and a crisp, dry finish. For a less expensive whisky, the brand called Robert Brown has plenty of body, again a sweetish start and a dry, assertive finish. Among the conventional whiskies, the lowest-priced brand is Dunbar, sweet in palate and lighter in body. All of these brands have 43 per cent alcohol. The company also has 40 per cent brand called News, light-bodied and with a distinct Bourbon aroma. This product, labelled almost as though it were ink, is aimed at the trend-conscious youth market. It is very similar to other youth-orientated whiskies in the Japanese market, but its pronounced Bourbon aroma also accents it in the American direction.

That *Fuji-San*, the sacred symbol of Japanese nationhood, should oversee such a confluence of waters-of-life is piquant. A Japanese-Canadian company using American and Scottish techniques to produce a cosmopolitan status-symbol for emergent youth, and under the name of News? Marshall McLuhan would have understood perfectly. Whether this is the spirit of the global village, time might care to ponder.

A taste-guide to the principal Japanese whiskies

Among many blenders, four malt-distillers represent serious whisky-making in Japan. In volume, Japan is an important whisky-producing nation. In style, its whiskies are closely related to those of Scotland. The quality of the major Japanese products is outstanding. If any criticism is to be made, it is that they lack complexity.

Suntory

Suntory "Yamazaki" Pure Malt Whisky

Suntory Old

Royal

Suntory Reserve

Imperial

Excellence

Suntory Whisky ("White Label")

Nikka

Memorial 50

Nikka Whisky

Black Nikka

Gold & Gold

Suntory produce a "Yamazaki" Pure Malt Whisky, a pioneering product that has encouraged other Japanese distillers to think about bottling "singles". It is a fairly light-bodied malt, with a crisp, dry start and a long, soft, warming, malty finish. The house character of the company's blends is typified by Suntory Old, the principal premium label, with its lightly-peated maltiness, almost chewy body and hints of fruitiness in the finish. There are several "super-premium" brands: Suntory Reserve is somewhat fruitier; the elegant Royal drier; and Imperial (or Signature) fuller in flavour. The clean, malty Excellence does not have a label – it carries its name on a metal "necklace". Neither does the mature, top-of-the-line blend called Suntory "The Whisky" – it is presented in an enamelled bottle. "White Label", as White is known, was the first Suntory whisky, and was originally in a decidedly Scottish style. Its smokiness was subsequently toned down and it is now a typically Japanese whisky.

Super

Black 50

Kingsland

Northland

Nikka produce whiskies which tend to have a soft palate and body, but with a characteristic depth of flavour. This has notes of peatiness, fruitiness and sometimes Bourbon. The company lays great stress on its techniques of aging. It has been slow to introduce a "single", but its malty Memorial 50 is a full-bodied blend. Nikka Whisky, Black Nikka and Gold & Gold are all medium-bodied blends. Super, Black 50 and Kingsland are all light-bodied. Northland is extra-light.

Kirin Seagram

Crescent

Emblem

Robert Brown

News

Kirin Seagram produce the driest whiskies made in Japan. Although they are definitely Japanese whiskies, they have the strongest Scots accent. The house character is relatively peaty, with a firm and smooth body, and often Bourbon notes. The "super-premium" blend Crescent is notably smooth, full-bodied, with a hint of smokiness. The premium Emblem has a sweetish nose and a crisp, dry finish. For a less expensive whisky, Robert Brown has plenty of body and character. News, with its light body and Bourbon aroma, is one of the newer, "youth" blends.

Sanraku Ocean

Karuizawa

Asama

Status

Special Old

Route

Sanraku Ocean produce a single malt, Karuizawa, identified by a porcelain pendant round its neck. It is on the light side, clean, with a malty sweetness and a crisp finish. In the aroma and the finish there are notes of sherry wood. The malty sweetness is something of a house characteristic. The company's super-premium blend, Asama, is also identified by a pendant. Status is a malty blend, and Special Old somewhat lighter. Route is a Japanese interpretation of the style originated by Cutty Sark and J&B Rare.

Index

Asterisk indicates reference in picture caption.

Acknowledgments

Whisk(e)y-distilling companies throughout Scotland, Ireland, North America and Japan helped in the production of this book. My special thanks to Suntory, whose help in Japan ensured not only that their products, but also those of their rivals, were properly covered in this book. Many individuals in the whisk(e)y industry were helpful far beyond the interest of their own companies. In this respect, my special thanks to Ron Ralph, of Early Times, and to Bill Samuels, Jr., of Maker's Mark, and his colleague in the Kentucky Distillers' Association, Frank Dailey. Also to Dixie Hibbs, of the Oscar Getz Museum of Whiskey History, and to the Bunch family for their advice on the social culture of Kentucky. I have had assistance from organisations representing the whisky industry and trade in all the countries reviewed, and from a number of merchants. Again, my special thanks to Wallace Milroy, of Milroy's Soho Wine Market, in London (for his endless advice and assistance) and to Ian Urquhart, of Gordon and MacPhail, in Elgin, Scotland (for his patience and kindness). The whiskies and whiskeys described in this book were sampled at distilleries, at the typewriter and with the assistance of the following: Daniel Beck, at Keens, New York City; Jumping Joe Danno ("the Jazz Philosopher"), at the Bucket of Suds, Chicago; the management and staff of Cutter's, Santa Monica; Cyril Boyce, at the Washington Square Bar and Grill, San Francisco; and Mick McHugh, of F.X. McRory's and Jake O'Shaughnessy's, Seattle. For their friendship and encouragement, I would like to thank the author Derek Cooper and the television journalist Andrew Jennings. For their advice and assistance, my special thanks to Alan Dikty and Mark Gruber. For their hospitality and patience, my immense gratitude to Larry Popelka and Pat Kelley. – MJ

Editorial
Research: Gina Jennings (British Isles); Nancy Anthony (North America); and Junko Suzuki (Japan). Research co-ordinated by Peter Murray. Editorial Assistant: Jane Hogg. Text Editor: Paula Turnbull.

Photography
ORIGINAL PHOTOGRAPHY BY IAN HOWES.
Additional material by: Tetsuya Fukui (Suntory); Katsuhiro Yokomura (Nikka and Sanraku Ocean); and Akira Hoshiyama (Kirin Seagram). Library photography researched by Judith Harries.

Design
Presentation by Millions Design. Art Director: Nigel Soper. Designer: David Micklewright. Design Production: Karen Byrne and Allan Mole.

Maps by Paul Cooper

At Dorling Kindersley
Editorial: James Allen
Design: Derek Coombes

Picture Credits
Much of the historical material in this book was photographed in distillery archives and museums by Ian Howes or Tetsuya Fukui. Additional material was provided by courtesy of The Glenlivet (pp 25, 80); the Royal Commission on the Ancient and Historical Monuments of Scotland (p37); D.C.L. (49, 89, 90, 91); Tomatin (67); Gordon and MacPhail (68, 69); I. Butterfield (94, 95); Glenturret (96); the Mansell collection (105); the National Museum, Dublin; the Ulster Museum (106, 107); and Karen Sweetland, of Bohn and Bland (119).

Further Reading
While this book was in preparation, my friend and counsellor Wallace Milroy produced his own taster's guide, the pocket-sized Malt Whisky Almanac (Lochar Publishing, Moffat, Scotland). Among the many books to which I referred in my research, I have found the following notably helpful: The Making of Scotch Whisky, by Moss and Hume (James and James), a very thorough economic history, with details on every distillery; the Schweppes Guide to Scotch, by Philip Morrice (Alphabooks), especially useful in relating brands and labels to owning companies and distilleries. The Scotch Whisky Industry Review, by Alan Gray (Campbell Neill, stockbrokers, Glasgow and London), an annual publication containing many useful statistics; the Century Companion to Whiskies, by Derek Cooper, one of his several excellent books on the character and geographical background of Scottish single malts. Scotch whisky has been the subject of many books, while there are fewer studies of other countries' spirits. I have found especially useful 1,000 Years of Irish Whiskey, by Malachy Magee (O'Brien Press); Kentucky Bourbon, by Henry G. Crowgey (University Press of Kentucky) and Canadian Whisky, written and published by William Rannie, P.O. Box 700, Lincoln, Ontario.